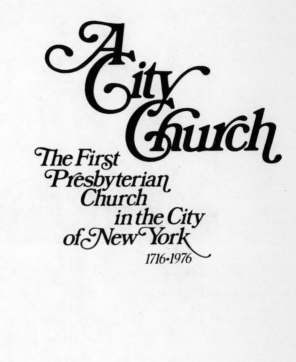

A City Church

The First
Presbyterian
Church
in the City
of New York
1716·1976

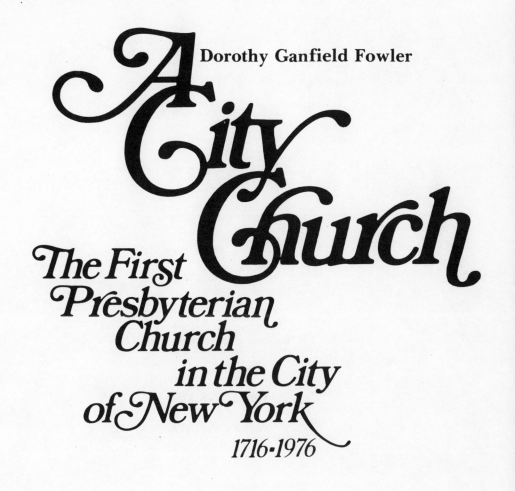

Dorothy Ganfield Fowler

A City Church

The First Presbyterian Church in the City of New York 1716-1976

The First Presbyterian Church in the City of New York

Frontice: The First Presbyterian Church on Wall Street.

Contents

Foreword

The church of Christ is an inherent and even commonplace part
of the American social landscape. As such, it arouses little curios-
ity about its past. It exists and is expected to continue to exist
without any unusual effort on the part of those who comprise its
membership. An exploration of the history of any particular
congregation, however, makes it clear that it abides largely
because of earlier pilgrims of the Way who preserved it with their
faith and devotion. When a past as venerable as that of the First
Presbyterian Church in the City of New York is unfolded, this
awareness of spiritual forebears is stimulated. Behind the present
congregants is what the writer of the epistle to the Hebrews called,
"a cloud of witnesses." In truth, those of us who compose the
current worshipping community sense that we are somewhat like
the nomadic Hebrews who came from their wanderings in the
desert wastes to the settled land of the Canaanites, a move to:

> . . . great and goodly cities, which you did not build, . . . houses full of
> good things, which you did not fill, . . . cisterns hewn out, which
> you did not hew, and vineyards and olive trees, which you did not
> plant . . .

We who are latter-day nomads stand on ground hallowed by the
steadfastness of those sojourners of former times. We are debtors
to people whose names are largely unknown or without meaning
to us. But what they believed and stood for as disciples of Jesus the
Christ endures in their legacy to the present. We come to this
heritage hopefully mindful so to husband what we have found
that those who come after us will find the hallowed place intact,
even as we did. We ask to be faithful to their trust, realizing, of

course, that the church remains and continues only as its people are ". . . strong in the Lord and in the strength of his might."

Professor Dorothy Ganfield Fowler, a Presbyterian ruling elder and the descendant of strong Presbyterian families, has supplied her high competence and professional skill as a scholar for this needed study of the history of one of the nation's oldest Christian congregations. Upon her retirement from Hunter College, where she had ably served as professor and head of the department of history, she agreed to add First Church's story to her other scholarly writings. Fortunately, many documents and records of the past had survived—some by intent, others by indifference. She declined the offer of a small grant to assist in the research, preferring to do her own firsthand exploration. Her only stipulation in offering her services was to be allowed to make the study a sufficient one and in accordance with the best standards of the professional historian. This was beyond what proposers of the project could have asked.

Many of the concerns that appear in this exploration of more than two and a half centuries of one congregation's existence will strike contemporary Presbyterian Christians as curious, perhaps even baffling. A preoccupation with the intricacies of theological doctrine and an adamant insistence on subscription to them in previous years, for example, will seem disproportionate to current disciples. In an era more open to ecumenical efforts among the various communions of Christendom, the sometimes fanatical devotion to denominational creedal differences of former times seems unreal. It was not. In the same vein, a seeming indifference (at least insofar as the records indicate) to some of the major social and political crises of the past will also seem puzzling: e.g. human slavery. In other instances concerns of the past survive in the present but clothed in different garb, as for instance the problem of intemperance, or alcoholism. In earlier centuries the church leaders sought to remedy this with moral judgement and censure that barred offenders from the church's sacramental rites. At the present time the response is to make church facilities available for meetings of Alcoholics Anonymous and to give support and encouragement to those victimized and seeking recovery from the disease. The concern most easily recognized as constant in each century is one for the needy of several descriptions in the society. Again, the forms of this ministry of concern differ but the recognition remains constant that the church is always called to be the servant of a Servant Lord.

Since this history is primarily one of a particular segment of a major social institution, the impression of self-preoccupation, even self-service, looms large. Undoubtedly, there were times when this was primary, even coming close to being exclusive. Whether this preoccupation was as pervasive in fact as the records indicate is not easy to determine. There is no way of knowing the impact of the church's worship, teaching and service efforts on the lives of individual members. This must remain a mystery. Some measure of impact, however, can be surmised from the knowledge of what those Presbyterian Christians did in response to the persistent changes in the life of the nation's largest city. Few of them could be classified as social reformers, but most of them took seriously a need to respond in the name of Christ to the hardship and suffering that was inflicted on those forced to live under harsh conditions that came in a rapidly changing, growing urban center. The need for education, medical service, cultural enhancement, relief from the squalor of crowded tenement housing and the despair of poverty, claimed the church's attention, generosity, resources and time. The plight of the underprivileged was never far from the consciousness of even the most privileged. As the city brought ever new challenges, church people sought to deal with them. Undoubtedly, some of this was enlightened self-interest; some of it arose from noblesse oblige; but much of it was a response to the love of Christ, a manifestation of his admonition to "feed my sheep." Primarily, they walked as people seeking to be faithful to their Lord, as servants of the Word, and trusting the results of that faithfulness to the workings of the Holy Spirit, aware that: "The wind blows where it wills, and you hear the sound of it, but you do not know whence it comes or whither it goes; so it is with everyone who is born of the Spirit."

I record the gratitude of the First Presbyterian Church in the City of New York to fellow member, Professor Dorothy Ganfield Fowler, for her devoted labor. I also speak the thanksgiving of present church members for all those earlier pilgrims who now "rest from their labors and their works do follow them."

John Brown Macnab

April 1981

Preface

This is the third history of the First Presbyterian Church in the City of New York: the first, a somewhat brief pamphlet, was written by Samuel Miller in 1796, the second, also a pamphlet but more comprehensive in scope, appeared 153 years later under the title, *Faith of Our Fathers,* and was the work of Arthur Wilson Courtney. He was involved in the research for a full-scale volume at the time of his death in 1961. There is evidence in the church archives of still another author's notes for a history of the church, but both date and name of this would-be chronicler are unknown.

First Church has been the "mother" of several of the present-day Presbyterian churches in Manhattan, notably Brick, Rutgers, Fifth Avenue, Madison Avenue, Emmanuel, each of which is the result of combinations with other congregations at various times during the last centuries. The story of Presbyterianism in New York City is one of several expansions and contractions that have allowed the maintenance of a presence amid the fluctuations and changes characteristic of the nation's largest urban population.

The present First Church is the result of a strategic merger in 1918 that brought together three active congregations: Old First, the Presbyterian Church on University Place (it had united with the Mercer Street Church in 1870) and the Madison Square Church, begun in 1854. Each brought a unique and substantial contribution to the merger: Madison Square had the largest endowment; University Place had the largest and most active membership; Old First had the longest history and the most advantageous and valuable location. All three were blessed with far-sighted lay leaders who recognized that forthcoming demographic changes would diminish the effectiveness of each of the churches were they to persist as separate entities. A consolidation of the three, however, gave hope for a single, continuing and strong Presbyterian center in lower Manhattan. To this end the three became one.

The present study attempts to portray various changes and conflicts that marked the life of a particular congregation of Christians during the last three centuries. Often those changes and conflicts were microcosmic versions of what other Presbyterians were also moving through in various parts of the nation. The consistent contention has been between advocates of an evangelical, somewhat emotional and at times anti-intellectual interpretation of the Christian faith and those who wanted one marked by reason, rationality and a minimum of emotion. In the eighteenth century this difference divided Presbyterians into "new side" and "old side" groups; in the nineteenth century it was "new school" and "old school", and in the early twentieth century it became "modernism" as opposed to "fundamentalism." In each instance the evangelical enthusiasts embraced a conservative interpretation of the Bible. One sees a similar situation today in the growth of the "pentecostal" and "born again" adherents at the expense of the older, established churches. In each century, First Church could be numbered with one of the differing groups.

I wish to thank some of those who have aided most in making possible this study of one church's history. Among the several who helped to retrieve and organize the archives that had for so long reposed unattended in the church's basement were: Robert Williams (trained archivist, church member), Mary Warner Reiman (practically-trained archivist, church member), Martha Ludlam Thomson (whose field is interior design but who likes to sort old papers, also a church member) and Donald Quick (building manager of church properties and familiar with various corners where materials were sometimes secluded). He and Mary W. Reiman were also instrumental in having all the historical records of the church transferred to microfilm, courtesy of the Church of Latter Day Saints. John B. Macnab, historian and pastor, served as editor for the final manuscript and also engaged in numerous discussions of its contents during the course of its development. Several other of the church family have given valued assistance in the preparation of the manuscript in its final form: Barbara S. Barr; Joan Hamlin, who typed the major portion of the manuscript; Mary W. Reiman and Charlotte K. Wallace, who also typed other parts. Arthur Ritter, well-known in the field of graphic design, and a church member, has given valuable guidance to the design layout and format. Of course, this book (as with each of the others I have undertaken) owes much to the helpful suggestions, encouragement, patience and understanding support of my husband, Emmett Fowler.

Dorothy Ganfield Fowler

Professor emeritus, Hunter College
and Graduate Center of the City
University of New York

Introduction

New York City Presbyterians who organized as a church in 1716 did so as heirs to almost 200 years of tradition. Moreover they were not the first of their persuasion to establish a congregation in colonial America. Presbyterians had churches on Long Island in the 1640's and somewhat later in New Jersey; in the 1680's and 1690's there were similar congregations in Delaware and on the eastern shore of Maryland and Virginia. Behind these was a history in Europe.

Presbyterian is more accurately descriptive of a particular form of church government than a specific creed or doctrine. The word comes from the Greek for *elder,* or *presbyter* upon whom the church depends for its organization. Creedally and doctrinally Presbyterians find their roots in that interpretation of the Christian faith formulated by John Calvin (1509–1564) whose monumental work, *The Institutes of the Christian Religion,* was first published in 1536.

Calvin hoped by means of the *Institutes* to persuade his king, Francis I of France, of the validity of the Christian faith as interpreted by those who protested excesses in 16th century Roman Catholicism in the hope of reforming the church to pattern it more closely to the New Testament. Forced into exile because of his views, Calvin spent the remainder of his life in Geneva, Switzerland. His *Institutes,* which underwent several revisions, became a major synthesis of Protestant theology.[1]

Geneva was a haven for refugee Protestant scholars from all parts of Europe. As the climate became more hospitable at home and they were able to return, Calvin's ideas gained broad circulation. "Reformed Protestantism," as his interpretation came to be known, spread to the Netherlands, Germany, France, and particularly to Scotland where it became the Presbyterian church under the leadership of the indomitable John Knox.

Knox, often called the "father of Presbyterianism," went to Geneva with his Protestant persuasions when he was forced to leave Scotland by a Roman Catholic monarch, the Queen Regent, Mary of Guise. When he was able to return he successfully established Presbyterianism as the official religion of Scotland. The first general assembly of the new Scottish kirk adopted a Confession of Faith, a Book of Discipline and a Book of Common Order that provided a system of church government and worship.[2]

Calvinism in England was the foundation for the Puritan reformers who wanted to "purify" worship in the established Church of England, divesting it of rituals and ceremonies felt to be too similar to those of Roman Catholicism. English monarchs, titular heads of the church, had little sympathy for such changes and actively moved to resist Puritan reformation attempts. Charles I (1625–1649) was even more insistent than either Elizabeth I or James I on conformity to Anglicanism, and it was during his reign that the migration of Puritans to Massachusetts took place.[3]

As a conflict between Charles and Parliament intensified, Puritan agitation for church reform grew with the other grievances. In 1642, Parliament, without the king's approval, called an assembly to revise Church of England worship. However, Puritanism was not of one mind on the extent to which such reform should go; some saw only the worship as needing change; others saw the necessity for eliminating the episcopal form of government with its bishops and replacing it with a Presbyterian form in which ministers and elders governed.

The Westminster Assembly (named for its place of meeting) began its work July 1, 1643. In the course of its deliberations Scottish commissioners, selected by the general assembly of the Church of Scotland, were added to those appointed by the English Parliament. The majority of the Assembly were supporters of Presbyterianism and created a Confession of Faith, Larger and Shorter Catechisms, the Form of Presbyterial Church Government, and the Psalter (Rous). The result of their labors was presented to Parliament and the Westminster Assembly held its last plenary session on February 22, 1649.[4]

By that time, however, Charles had been removed from the throne, tried, and beheaded. Oliver Cromwell had taken his place as head of state. An independent Puritan, Cromwell was not sympathetic to the Presbyterian supporters and those who sought to make the Church of England Presbyterian were unsuccessful. After the Glorious Revolution (1688) and the accession to the throne of Mary Stuart and William of Orange the Toleration Act was passed granting toleration to the Protestants other than Anglicans but Presbyterianism did not grow in England. William was successful in defeating James II, deposed king of England, and thus Ulster which under James I had been settled with colonists from Scotland, was saved for Presbyterianism. In the words of Dr. Ahlstrom, "The unaltered Westminster Confession (and Catechism) were made normative for the Church of Scotland in 1689, and in due course for American Presbyterians as well."[5]

[1]John Calvin, *Institutes of the Christian Religion,* translated by Henry Beveridge. 2 vols. (Grand Rapids, Michigan, 1966); Hugh Thomson Kerr, ed. *A Compend of the Institutes of Christian Religion* (Philadelphia, 1939); Sydney E. Ahlstrom, *A Religious History of the American People* (New Haven, Conn., 1972), 79–80.

[2]Lefferts A. Loetscher, *A Brief History of Presbyterianism* (Philadelphia, 1958), 33–36.

[3]*Ibid.,* 41–46.

[4]John A. Leith, *Assembly at Westminster* (Richmond, Va., 1973); Henry Sloane Coffin, "The Westminster Assembly," in *The Church Tower,* December, 1945.

[5]Ahlstrom, *Religious History of the American People,* p. 131, n.5; Loetscher, *Brief History of Presbyterianism,* pp. 37ff.

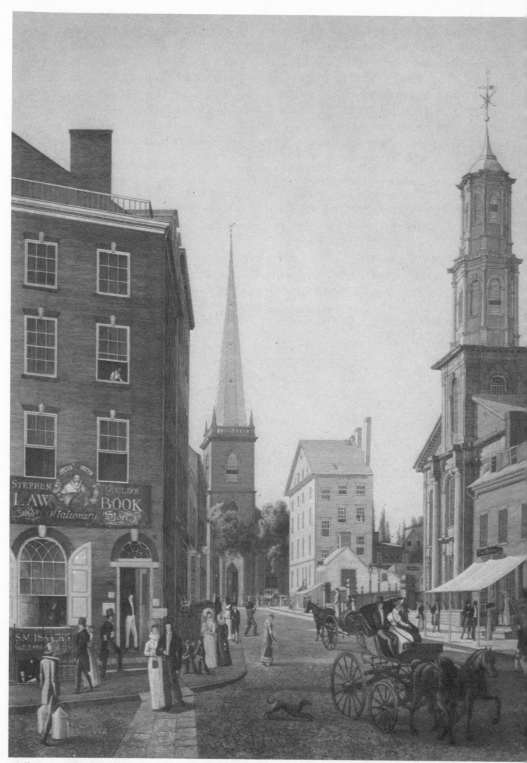

Wall Street, Trinity Church and the First Presbyterian Church (right), about 1825.

CHAPTER ONE

The Church in Wall Street

"New York throughout the colonial period, was distinctly a Presbyterian province," wrote one scholar. Certainly in the early years that statement seems exaggerated for the church had neither recognition nor charter from the Provincial government.

When the British took over New Amsterdam from the Dutch in 1664, renaming it New York, the royal governors recognized the Anglican church as the established church. The Ministry Act of 1693 required provision for a "sufficient Protestant minister" supported by an annual tax on the inhabitants. He was to be selected by the vestrymen of New York City, and their choice was William Vesey, graduate of Harvard University, a Puritan trained by Increase Mather. The members of the assembly who passed the act were mainly dissenters (i.e. those who dissented from the beliefs of the Church of England), who thought they were providing for a dissenting minister. Governor Benjamin Fletcher (1692–1698), however, declared that since only the Anglican church had vestrymen, the act's provision meant an Anglican minister. Vesey was persuaded to conform to the Church of England and went to London to be ordained.[1] In 1697 a charter was granted to Trinity Church and the following year a church was built on Broadway at the head of Wall Street.[2] The Anglican rather than the Presbyterian church became the established church of New York at a time when there were few of either denomination in the city whose total population was about 5,000.

Indeed Presbyterian churches were scarce throughout the American colonies prior to the eighteenth century. Puritans in New England were Congregational. Some of these moved to Long Island in the 1640's and organized churches according to the Presbyterian system. There were a few Presbyterians in Virginia, Maryland, Delaware, and New Jersey, many of whom had come during the Restoration Period in England.

Francis Makemie (statue by Alexander Stirling Calder at The Presbyterian Historical Society)

The "real father of organized American Presbyterianism" was Francis Makemie (1658–1709), an Irishman from Donegal County, Ulster. He was educated at the University of Glasgow, Scotland since "Trinity College in Dublin was closed to Dissenters." He was licensed by the Presbytery of Laggan, came as a missionary to the Barbadoes in 1682, and two years later organized a Presbyterian church at Snow Hill, Maryland, the first in the colonies. When the Anglican church was established in that colony in 1689 a license to preach was required of all dissenting ministers. Makemie received such a license to preach in Maryland and Virginia. He returned to England in 1704 and induced two ministers, John Hampton and George Macnish, to join him in his work in the new world. As itinerant ministers they preached from South Carolina to New England.[3]

Fearing permanent establishment of the Anglican church in the colonies, seven Presbyterian ministers organized the first presbytery in the colonies in 1706. It was "chiefly a *meeting* of ministers . . . to consult the most proper measures for advancing religion, and propagating Christianity." The seven, Makemie, Hampton, Macnish, Samuel Davis, John Wilson, Jedediah Andrews, and Nathaniel Taylor, came from Maryland, Delaware, and Philadelphia. Three were originally from Ireland, one from Scotland, and the rest from New England. Makemie was elected moderator.[4]

Shortly after the establishment of this first presbytery Makemie stopped in New York City on his way to New England. He was offered the use of the Dutch church provided he received the permission of the royal colony's governor, Lord Cornbury (1702–1708). He did not ask the governor, claiming he needed no such authorization since he already held a license. On Sunday, January 19, 1706/7, he preached to a small group of Presbyterians who had been meeting in private homes for several months. Among those present were two merchants, Capt. John Theobalds, builder of a wharf near Pearl Street, and John Van Horne. Others whose names we know were Arthur Young, who had been shipped over from Scotland, and David Jamison (1660–1739), who had been jailed in Edinburgh for joining "a company of religious iconoclasts," the Sweet Singers. He had come to the colony as an indentured servant bound to the Rev. Mr. Clarke, chaplain of the fort. He taught school while he studied law and became recorder of the city council, 1712–1724. Present also was Harris, Governor Cornbury's coachman. The services were held in the home of William Jackson, a shoemaker on Pearl Street. Jackson had been one of the elected vestrymen who had called William Vesey to New York City thinking he would be a Puritan minister. These men were of moderate means. Most of them had two or three Negro servants, probably slaves.[5]

The service was as public as possible; the doors were open and the sermon was printed. It was entitled "The Good Conversation," and was based on Psalm 50:23. Makemie dedicated the printed sermon to "the small congregation who heard the Sermon" and noted that this was the sermon for which "I am now a Prisoner,[6]" undoubtedly referring to what followed its preaching.

Governor Cornbury was incensed. "You shall not spread your pernicious doctrines here," he is supposed to have said. He had Makemie and John Hampton arrested on Long Island where Makemie was to speak in Newtown on the Wednesday following his sermon in New York City. They appeared before the Governor in council chamber, who accused them of preaching in his province without license. Makemie claimed his right to preach under the Toleration Act of 1689. Cornbury maintained that act

James Anderson, first Pastor of the New York Presbyterian congregation.

did not apply to the American plantations. He also said Makemie had violated the Toleration Act when he preached to more than five people in a private house. The Governor further claimed that his instructions from Queen Anne (who was also his cousin) required Makemie to have a special license to preach in New York City. Makemie responded that such instructions had never been promulgated and so were not valid. Makemie and Hampton were put in the custody of Ebenezer Wilson, high sheriff for New York City.

On March 1 they appeared before Justice Mompesson and a grand jury. Charges against Hampton were dropped. He had not preached in the city. Four of Makemie's hearers testified they had heard nothing which disagreed with the doctrines of the Anglican church nor anything against the government. The grand jury voted in quite an unusual manner, according to the narrator of the trial; as they came in from dinner each was asked before deliberation for his vote. Twelve votes for presentment were obtained on the charge of preaching a sermon before more than five persons. Makemie was released on bail and allowed to return to Virginia. His trial was held on June 4; he was represented by attorneys, one of whom was David Jamison, but he also spoke on his own behalf. On June 7 he was acquitted by the petty jury but was required to pay substantial court costs of £83 (equivalent to a minister's annual stipend). This trial was, however, an important landmark in the development of religious liberty in New York.[7]

It was also a factor leading to the recall of Governor Cornbury. The assembly passed and sent to Great Britain resolutions asking for his dismissal. The last of these referred to Makemie, reading: "Resolved, That the compelling of any man, upon trial by a jury, or otherwise, to pay fees for his prosecutions, or anything whatever, unless the fees of the officers whom he employs for his necessary defense, is a great grievance, and contrary to justice." There were many letters of protest. Cornbury was summarily dismissed. The following year the assembly made illegal the assessment of such expenses on an innocent party.[8]

The number of Presbyterians increased, and they continued to meet for prayer in private homes. The time was propitious for them. The colony's new governor, Colonel Robert Hunter (1710–1719), was of Scottish parentage, sympathetic to the Presbyterians and at odds with the minister at Trinity Church who had converted the vestry into a closed corporation, an action which brought dissension in the church.[9]

II

The pressure for a more formal church grew among the Presbyterians and a congregation following the discipline of the Church of Scotland was organized in December, 1716.

The initiators of this action were men of substance and several of them held public office. Most responsible for the move was John Nicoll (1680–1743), a native of Edinburgh, a graduate of its university, who had come to New York in 1711. He was married to a Bostonian, Rebeckah Dowdin Ransford, and they had two children, John and Margaret. Dr. Nicoll was an apothecary, lived on Gold Street near Wall, was listed as a voter in the East Ward, and had served as a deputy constable. Closely associated with him in the church's founding was Patrick Macknight, native of Northern Ireland, a well-to-do merchant and a collector of taxes in the city's South Ward.[10]

It was not exclusively a Scotch-Irish enterprise, and several of those involved were of English lineage. Gilbert Livingston was a young lawyer whose father, Robert, had come from England in

1672 and acquired a large estate near Albany. He was married to the daughter of Henry Beekman, another prominent New Yorker, and had been granted a strip of land at the lower end of Queen Street (now Pearl). He was made a "freeman" of the city in 1716, assessor of the Dock Ward the next year and then became "farmer of excise." He went badly into debt when taxes collected did not equal the sum he pledged to the Crown. His father's death in 1728 left him enough to clear his debt.[11]

The other English family prominently associated with this first Presbyterian church in New York City was the Smiths. William (1662–1736), known as "Port Royal Smith" because he had suffered in the memorable earthquake in Port Royal, Jamaica, had come to New York City near the end of the seventeenth century and was registered as a freeman in 1701.[12] He had married Frances Peartree. Her father, Colonel William Peartree, was a wealthy merchant with a large estate in Jamaica and a profitable trade with the West Indies, and mayor of New York from 1703–1706. Her mother, Anna Litscho (1647–1730), was a daughter of a well-known tavern keeper who had inherited a large lot on the south corner of Wall and Pearl Streets.[13]

William persuaded his youngest brother, Thomas (1675–1745), to migrate to the new country. He was a tallow chandler and evidently had done very well at his trade. His wife (Susanne Odell) belonged to the smaller landed gentry in England. On August 17, 1715, he, with his wife, three sons and two daughters, arrived in New York City. He was shocked that there were neither adequate schools nor a Presbyterian church in the city and was determined to remedy the situation.[14]

The records of the court of general sessions, August 7, 1717, note that an application had been made by Patrick Macknight, and Gilbert Livingston and that it had been ordered:

> that the house Scituate in the East Ward of this City commonly Called & known by the name of Veenvoss' house be & is hereby Recorded a Public Meeting House for the Congregation of Dissenting Protestants called Presbyterians for the Publick Worship of "Almighty God."[15]

The house was located at 144 Pearl Street, south of Wall. The worshippers now numbered about eighty. That fall they called as their pastor the Rev. James Anderson (1678–1740), native of Scotland, member of the Presbytery of New Castle, Delaware. He had been in the city previously and had preached to the group several times. In the call he was promised an annual salary £104. Mr. Anderson wrote to John Sterling, principal of the College of Glasgow, that the little congregation were making great efforts to purchase a site and erect a church on it. He concluded: "I believe by this time you smell my drift. I don't know how to begin to beg any more at your door."[16]

In January 1718/19, Nicoll, Macknight, Livingston, and Thomas Smith purchased land on the north side of Wall Street, east of Broadway, from Abraham De Peyster and Samuel Bayard, giving their joint note for £350. While a building was being erected they received permission to use the City Hall,[17] practically contiguous to the church lot as a place of worship.

A drive for funds to build a church was made. About £600 was raised from people in the city. The legislature of Connecticut made a contribution but the largest sums came from churches in Scotland, primarily through efforts of Anderson's friend, Principal Sterling. Annual appeals by the General Assembly of Scotland were made and money or goods sent.[18] In 1719 and 1722 Patrick Macknight made trips to Scotland to present the congregation's appeal.[19]

The church, commonly called the "Church in Wall Street," was completed and the first service held August 7, 1719. It was a small, rectangular building, sixty by fifty feet, one story high and no steeple. On each side there were three long windows half rounded at the top. The cost was £1500.

Barely had worship begun in the new church when dissension arose, dividing the congregation into its Scottish and English elements. The source of contention was Anderson's rigid theology and discipline, somewhat more severe than the non-Scots desired. In May 1720, some members petitioned the court of quarter general sessions for general permission to hold services in the home of John Barberie on Broadway, near the fort. The petitioners, Thomas Smith, Thomas Grant, constable in Montgomerie ward, William Taylor, constable in the Dock ward, and Samuel Belknap were English Presbyterians. Permission gained, they worshipped there for nine months.

The dissidents appealed to friends in England to find a Presbyterian preacher. They contacted Increase Mather in Boston. They tried unsuccessfully to persuade Nicoll and Macknight to join them. Livingston and Smith conveyed their interest in the Wall Street church property for £175 to Anderson, John Blake, ship carpenter, Joseph Liddle, pewterer, and Thomas Inglis, painter and constable in the Dock ward.[21]

Anderson, Nicoll, Macknight, Liddle, Blake, and Inglis, on behalf of the congregation, in March 1720, petitioned the council to be incorporated "by the name of the Minister, Elders, and Deacons of the Presbyterian Church in the City of New York . . . to worship in after the manner of the Presbyterian church of North Britain [Scotland]." They pointed out that since they were not incorporated they and their heirs were personally responsible for the church's building debt of £2000, construction costs having exceeded expectations. Livingston and Smith objected to the granting of a charter allowing Anderson to remain. They said that he was "very unsuitable for advancing our Interest in New York because severall that joyned with Us after first having forsaken the Congregation upon his Acct and we are also persuaded that he has not been Established among us by very just and Honorable

Methods."[22] The petition for a charter was denied not because of the protest of the Englishmen but due to the opposition of the vestry of Trinity Church. A similar application, made to the new governor, William Burnet (1720–1728), in September 1720 was also denied as was another four years later.[23]

A recent Yale graduate, nineteen year old Jonathan Edwards (1702–1752) came to preach to the English group. He stayed at the home of Thomas Smith and was a close friend of the third son, John (1702–1781) also a Yale graduate who later was minister at Rye, New York. Edwards stayed only eight months (until April 1723).[24]

The loss of the anti-Andersonites put great financial strain on the Wall Street church. Dr. Nicoll made the hazardous trip to Scotland in 1724 to present the case of the church to the General Assembly of the Church of Scotland. Anderson in a letter introducing him to Mr. Sterling said that if they did not get funds soon they would be obliged "to quitt striving and give up our interest in this place." Dr. Nicoll collected over £1000 to apply to the church debt. A bond of £2000, secured by the church building and signed by three ministers of the Presbytery of Long Island, had been issued but could not be found when the minister (Dr. Macnish), in whose possession it was supposed to have been, died. Continuing financial strain provoked more dissension and acrimony. Anderson and some of his supporters accused Nicoll of having the missing bond and keeping it rather than paying off the debt. They also thought he was too close with the money and that some should be used to pay the pastor's salary, who charged him with surreptitiously seeking a new minister and of refusing to be an elder after accepting the position. In such an atmosphere it is hardly surprising that the church was badly in need of elders.

The charges against Nicoll were presented to the Presbytery of Long Island in 1726 and then to the Synod. Nicoll refused to recognize jurisdiction of the church judicatories. The next year he made a full explanation to the congregation which accepted it.

A committee of ministers was appointed to settle the difficulties. The Rev. Mr. Anderson was "obliged to remove" charged with a "spirit of Domination in conducting the affairs of the Congregation and interfering improperly in the management of their temporalities." He went to Donegal, Pennsylvania, where he remained until his death.[25]

The Wall Street Church next embarked on a new course that would define its character for decades. After Jonathan Edwards left them the seceded group returned. Ebenezer Pemberton (1704–1779) was called to be the pastor. He was of the "opposite quarter of theology" from his predecessor.[26] William Smith, the historian, said of him, "He was a man of polite breeding, pure morals, and warm devotion."[27]

It was made clear to the new minister that he was to have nothing to do with the finances of the church. The land and building were conveyed by James Anderson, John Nicoll, Joseph Liddle, and Thomas Inglis, in 1730, to the Moderator of the General Assembly of the Church of Scotland for the sum of ten shillings "lawful money of Great Britain." The General Assembly, August 15, 1732, accepted the property but carefully noted its maintenance remained with the worshippers and declared that they wished the building

be preserved for the pious and Religious Purposes for which the same was designed; and that it shall be free and lawfull to the Presbyterians then residing, or that should at any Time thereafter be resident in, or near the aforesaid City of New-York in America, or others joining with them, to convene in the aforesaid Church for the worship of God in all the parts thereof, and for the Dispensation of all Gospel Ordinances, and generally to use and occupy the said Church and its Appurtenances full and freely in All Times coming, supporting and maintaining the Edifice and appurtenances at their own Charge, as by the said Original deed of Declaration of First May.[28]

The Wall Street congregation numbered no more than seventy to eighty people, about what it had been at the time of organization. The building was in disrepair and the windows had been boarded over. Then in 1739 "God was pleased to visit it, with many other parts of our Land, with a remarkable effusion of the Influences of his Spirit."[29] The 18th Century Great Awakening came to New York's Presbyterians.

It was George Whitefield, noted British revivalist, who was the spark which aroused the Presbyterians in New York City. The English cleric first came to America in 1738 and then returned the next two years to carry on an evangelistic tour of the area between Philadelphia and New York. He held large outdoor meetings (in New York in the "fields"). Pemberton opened the doors of the Wall Street Presbyterian Church to him, the only clergyman in the city to do so. The small church was filled to overflowing. The windows were unboarded and repaired and galleries built.[30]

The Great Awakening caused splits in many churches including the Presbyterian. The "new side" Presbyterians stressed personal religious experiences; the "old side" group tended to a more rational, less emotional position. Although both "sides" subscribed to the Adopting Act of the Synod of Philadelphia (1729) requiring all members of the synod and all ministerial candidates seeking ordination to assent to the Westminster Confession, the "old side" insisted that every line and letter of the Confession was as infallible as the Scriptures and made the synod responsible for maintaining that principle. In 1745 the "new side" presbyteries (New York, New Brunswick and Newcastle) formed the Synod of New York.[31]

The existing churches
in New York City, 1742

City Hall, Wall Street

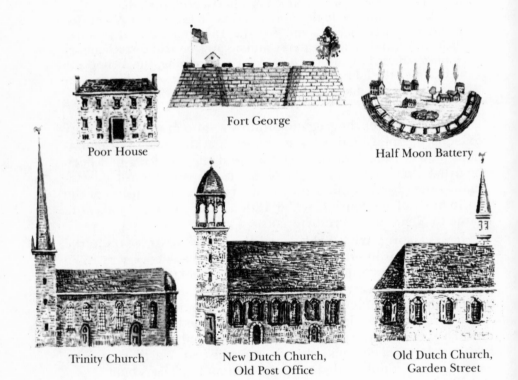

Poor House

Fort George

Half Moon Battery

Trinity Church

New Dutch Church,
Old Post Office

Old Dutch Church,
Garden Street

Wall Street,
Presbyterian
Meeting

Baptist Meeting,
Vandises Street

Lutheran Church,
Broadway &
Rector Street

Quaker Meeting,
Crown Street

Synagogue,
Mill Street

III

The Wall Street Church, as did many "new side" churches, increased in membership. Due to Dr. Nicoll, who for twenty years had taken almost sole care of the temporal affairs of the church and had used his own funds to keep the church out of debt, the church was in good financial condition when he died in October, 1743. Mr. Pemberton, in the memorial service, declared that "while a Presbyterian church subsists in the City of New York the name of Nicoll will ever be remembered with honor, as one of the principal *Founders* and its greatest benefactor." He was buried below the communion table in the Wall Street Church.[32]

Although the deed and declaration of trust of 1732 were to remain in the possession of William Smith, by 1746 control of the property was vested in the hands of eight trustees elected at a congregational meeting by those who held pews or seats in the church. The trustees were responsible for the building and grounds, the letting of pews, and opening of the ground for burials. It was stated that

> Any master of a Family of an orderly life and conversation, who had a pew or Seat in the said Presbyterian Church, and statedly attends upon divine worship in said congregation, shall be deemed qualified to be chosen a trustee.

A trustee was to be elected for a four year term (not to be reelected until one year had elapsed) at an annual election to be held on January 1 or the day following if it were the Lord's Day. They were to meet the first Wednesday of every month at 6 p.m. (5 p.m. in the winter months) and a fine of two shillings was imposed for "every neglect" unless the man had a "reasonable excuse" for his absence. The trustees were to see that no member of the church took interest on a loan from the church; they were responsible for the debt incurred and new trustees, when elected, were asked to promise to bear their "proportion of all risques with the rest of the trustees." It was, therefore, sometimes difficult to get men to take the position. The first meeting of the board of trustees of the Church in Wall Street was held on February 13, 1746.[33]

The second meeting was enlivened by a request from the minister for an increase in salary. It provoked considerable debate. There was only £10 in the treasury. The only sources of revenue to pay the salary were the rental of pews and seats and the receipts from burials, the lots, the rental of the pall and black cloth. When appointed he had been promised £104 supported by collections taken at the Sabbath services. Later pew rentals had increased so he was paid £120, one of the larger ministerial salaries. On the basis that he had no assistant, preached both in the morning and afternoon on the Lord's Day, delivered an expository lecture in the evening and kept up the mid weekly public Catechism sessions, they finally agreed to an increase of £20 so long as he was the sole minister, performed all ministerial services and if absent took care of the pulpit supply.[34]

The relationship between trustee and clergy is frequently delicate and the eighteenth century Wall Street church was no exception. Pemberton was incensed that the trustees met without informing him and without his acting as moderator. They responded by passing a resolution that *"No Minister hereafter have a Power to sit and Act in the Temporal and Secular Business of the said Congregation."* They enunciated an intriguing idea of what amounted to a Trinity of Keys:

> ... the Power in this Church and Congregation, may be considered under a usual similitude, as consisting of *three Keys* to wit the *Key of Doctrinal Instruction,* the *Key of Discipline* and *Government,* and the *Key of the Cash.* The two first, we consider as appertaining to the spiritual affairs of the Church. The latter, as merely secular and temporal. That the first, belongs solely to the Minister by his Office. The second, to the Minister and Elders, either alone or with the Deacons, which we do not determine. That at present, by Reason of the Death of some and removal of others, we have not one lay Elder or Deacon, so that the spiritual power, is now wholly in the hands of the Minister. That as to the *Key of the Cash,* we conceive it entirely belongs to the People. The money is raised by them, and they have the sole right of the Disposal of it. We think it an exceedingly Clear point, that the *purse* is the *Peoples,* and that it is generally so understood, by the Presbyterian Churches, and that their Practice is accordingly .... We would be so far from Establishing the Shadow of a *Papacy* in this Church and Congregation, that we would do all we can to prevent it. We believe, that the whole power of the Keys, in the Hands of the Minister, would prove a dangerous Snare to him ...."[35]

The church was "greatly out of repair" with the roof not keeping out the rain and snow and the fences in bad condition. There was a demand for pews and for more burial ground. An appeal for funds, written by William Smith and personally delivered by Josiah Milliken, was made to the churches in Boston and other towns in New England. Mr. Smith reminded them that they had been recently "saved by God from the hands of Anti-Christian enemies at Cape Breton." He said they had not troubled the people of Boston for twenty years but they did need to enlarge their church and they wanted a steeple and bell to call the people to worship.[36]

The church was rebuilt in 1748. It was railed off from the street, built of hewn stone, enlarged by one-third, with a steeple at the southwest end, 145 feet in height, topped by an ironball and cock. It contained a bell which rang for the first time on September 10, 1748. A memorial stone of black slate was imbedded in the church wall between the two long windows fronting the street with an inscription in Latin written by William Smith:

12

The Wall Street Church, 1748

This Holy House
For the Perpetual Celebration of Divine Worship
First Erected in the Year of Our Lord
1719
Then Thoroughly Repaired
Enlarged and Adorned
In the year of our Lord
1748
Is in This Votive Tablet

DONATED DEDICATED & DEVOTED

By Its Founders
The Presbyterians of New York
For their own and their Children's Use

*   *   *   *   *

Sustained and more Splendidly
Adorned by Harmony and Love
No Less than by the Purity of
Faith—Worship and Behaviour
By the Blessing of Christ
May it Endure for Ages[37]

But once more at the completion of a building the congregation fell victim to dissent and division with the root of the trouble the same as it had been in the 1720's. As earlier, it was the emigrants from Scotland and northern Ireland versus those from South Britain and New England who were more liberal and tended toward the Congregational form of church government. In fact the Wall Street Church did not have the true Presbyterian form of organization for the only lay body was the board of trustees. In October, 1749 two deacons (John Stephens and William Eagles) were selected; they were both members of the board of trustees. Also it was decided that the trustees who were communicants of the church should assist the minister as elders.[38]

Which book was to be used for the singing of psalms was the issue. Psalm singing was an important part of the service. The singing was led by a chorister from the clerk's seat who "lined out" the first line of the psalm and the congregation joined in singing the second line and the rest of the psalm. The trustees voted to substitute Isaac Watts' version for Rouse's "Old Scot's version" (the one adopted by the Westminster Assembly) which they considered "*Low, flat* and *mean.*" A few leading people in the church wanted the *Tate and Brady*, which had recently been adopted by Trinity Church. That the trustees had interfered in the spiritual concerns of the church was as offensive as their choice of psalm book.

The trustees referred the controversy to the presbytery who in turn passed it to the synod, who criticized the trustees for introducing a new psalm book without consulting the congregation but agreed that Watts' book could continue to be used. A committee of ministers (Samuel Davis, Samuel Finley, Charles Beaty) was appointed to assist the congregation in bringing about peace. They directed that elders be elected. In October 1752 David Van Horne (also a trustee) and Israel Horsefield were selected.[39]

Discord continued, however. The focus of displeasure moved to Pemberton and the Rev. Alexander Cummings who had come to the church in 1750 after having served as Pemberton's assistant for nine months prior to his ordination. (He had also married Margaret Nicoll.) The clergy were charged with: delivering a funeral prayer either in the church or at the grave if requested to do so by relatives of the deceased; neglecting formal ministerial visits; failing to emphasize the Westminster Confession and Catechism at baptism; deviating from the Presbyterian form of worship and tending to the Episcopal ritual.

The synod in October 1753 appointed a committee (William Tennent, Aaron Burr, Rich Treat, Charles Beaty, Samuel Davis, D. Bostwick, Elihu Spencer, Caleb Smith, and James Rogers) to meet with the congregation and ministers to attempt to bring about harmony. The outcome was an exoneration of the ministers, who declared that they had not neglected the ministerial visits and the "examining into the Lives and Conversations of the People"; that they were devoted to the Westminster Confession, and that since they prayed at funerals only at the request of the relatives of the deceased that it was not a matter of offense and was practiced by other Presbyterian ministers. As far as the psalm book was concerned the committee felt Watts' version was well adapted for Christian worship. They did not, however, approve of singing anthems on the Lord's Day as that might take the minds of persons from "the important things heard in the House of God." They recommended "mutual forgiveness, moderation and Forbearance towards one another."[40]

Both pastors, however, asked to be dismissed. Cummings pled poor health and moved to Boston, to the Old South Church. Pemberton, upset by the animosities, requested the Synod to give him leave "to remove from this Scene of Clamour & Confusion" and allow him to "spend the remainder of my Days in an Undisturbed Application to the Duties of My Function." He accepted a call to the "New Brick Church," in Boston where he remained until 1774. William Smith, the historian, says that Pemberton resigned "on account of trifling contentions kindled by the bigotry & ignorance of the lower sort of people." The congregation set apart the last day of the year (1753) as a day of humiliation, fasting and prayer.[41]

Several ministers had been invited to assume the pastorate but each refused. It was two years before the vacancy was filled. Finally in July 1755 the congregation, with Aaron Burr, president of Princeton, presiding voted to call the Rev. David Bostwick (1721–1763) of Jamaica, Long Island. A native of New Milford, Connecticut, he had studied at Yale, and received the M.A. from Princeton. He won a majority of votes over Jonathan Edwards of Stockbridge, Massachusetts, even though Edwards was one of the outstanding albeit controversial religious thinkers in colonial America.

Bostwick was reluctant to accept the post but the synod insisted he was badly needed in New York. He accepted the call in April 1756 at a salary of £250 a year and a subscription to the New York Society Library (£6).[42] William Smith described Bostwick thusly:

> He is a gentleman of a mild, catholic disposition; and being a man of piety, prudence, and zeal, confines himself entirely to the proper business of his function. In the art of preaching he is one of the most distinguished clergymen in this parts. His discourses are methodical, sound, and pathetic; in sentiment, and in point of diction, singularly ornamented. He delivers himself without notes, and yet with great ease and fluency of expression; and performs every part of divine worship with a striking solemnity.[43]

A group in the church tried unsuccessfully once more to get the Scot psalm book restored to use, even asking the synod to overturn the congregation's vote in favor of Watts'. The synod refused and the dissatisfied group withdrew to form in September 1756 their own society on Cedar Street; it became a member of the Associate Scotch Presbytery.[44]

Secession of the malcontents restored peace to the Wall Street Church and the congregation grew. The church building was spruced up, the windows and candlesticks cleaned, the walls whitewashed and cushions were bought for the governor's pew. Inscribed over the pew was "Under the auspices of George II, King of Great Britain, Patron of the Church, Defender of the Faith." At his death in 1760 the pew, pulpit and desk were decorated in official mourning.[45]

There was increasing demand for pews and the pew rent was raised so that the best ones rented for £3 a year and the ones in the gallery for £1. The synod passed a resolution that "they who obstinately refuse to pay their pew rents are to be esteemed as not walking orderly and do in fact forfeit yr Pews nor is it Injury done them by the Congregation if they are deprived of them."[46]

Three years after his coming to the Wall Street church, Bostwick said he needed a larger salary since "Providence has given him a large family and Necessaries and conveniences are excessively dear." He pointed out that he had to pay £45 for house rent and his two servants cost £70 and he had extra expenses due to the small pox (he had stayed on the job throughout the epidemic) and the marriage of his daughter. His salary was increased to £300.

Through a legacy of Sarah Floyd and subscriptions of members, the church acquired a manse. The house on Thames Street had an outhouse, kitchen, stable yard, and wells. The title to the property was assigned to John Scott and Peter Livingston who assumed the cost (£1025), a necessity since the church was still unincorporated.[47]

Mr. Bostwick died suddenly in November 1763. He was badly in debt so the trustees voted to pay for a decent burial (£42). The desk and pulpit were draped in black. The money collected at a Sabbath service was given to his widow, and £800 was raised by subscription so she could set up a business to support her family. She opened a boarding house.[48]

V

In the nearly half-century since the founding of the Wall Street Church, the population of New York City quintupled from 5,000 to 25,000. It had surpassed Boston, and in size ranked second only to Philadelphia among colonial cities. It had become a major port, center for commerce, manufacturing, shipbuilding. Whatever the social and civic problems related to this change and growth, there is little indication that the Presbyterians as a church were concerned. Their focus would seem to have been primarily on their personal faith and on the life of the church community, particularly pressed as it was in its early existence.

This is not to imply lack of response to needs within and beyond the immediate fellowship, however. The needy of the church were not neglected. Every year the minister preached a "charity sermon" at which money was collected. Added to the money received from the collections at the Communion table, it formed a special fund for the poor of the church, "which we have always with us," noted William Smith. Those who "have statedly attended publick worship in the said church for 12 months" were considered entitled to relief, a safeguard no doubt designed to avoid support of the unworthy.[49] It was pointed out in the minutes of the trustees that relief from the church should not prevent those in need from receiving aid from the city since poor rates collected by the city vestry were levied on inhabitants in each ward.[50] Presbyterians had organized one of the earliest benevolent agencies in the city—the Scots Society which existed from 1744 to 1753. Then on November 19, 1756, "attired in the wigs and great coats which were the fashion of the day," a small group of Scots formed "The St. Andrew's Society at New-York in the Province of New-York." Its purpose was to care for Scots less fortunate than themselves. On St. Andrew's Day, November 30, members met for a "hilarious feast" at Scotch Johnny's to raise money for the poor.[51]

At least one special collection (£18) was made to promote Christian knowledge among the Indians.[52] Undoubtedly there were additional offerings, for the conversion of native Americans was a major emphasis of the Great Awakening. Repeated wars had dimmed enthusiasm for a mission to the Indians, but the once-lively concern was revived by such as Jonathan Edwards, who ministered directly to them in their own congregations and laid upon the consciences of the converted the necessity for supporting such work. Since the Wall Street congregation under Pemberton's lead had identified itself so thoroughly with the Great Awakening, it seems likely, despite the paucity of official records, that it gave support to its sanctioned causes.

Although accused by critics of anti-intellectualism, the emphasis on religious experience and personal conversion in no way dimmed concern for education. Dartmouth College, which had been started as an Indian mission school by Eleazar Wheelock; the College of Rhode Island (Brown University), Queens College (Rutgers University), and the College of New Jersey (Princeton) were established by enthusiasts of the Great Awakening. In the founding of the latter the Wall Street Church had a direct role.

As early as 1739 Ebenezer Pemberton and the Rev. Jonathan Dickinson of Elizabethtown, New Jersey had sought a charter for a college to educate those of revivalist persuasion, but without success. In 1745 they appealed to Governor Morris for a charter for a college to be established in Newark. He refused. When he died the acting governor, John Hamilton, granted the charter and the college was opened in May 1747. The charter had been "roughed out" and the seal designed by William Smith, trustee of the Wall Street church. He was designated a trustee of the new college, which position he held until his death. Peter Livingston of the Wall Street church became a trustee in 1748. Pemberton was also a trustee and was the first recipient of the Doctor of Divinity degree conferred by the new college. Dickinson became the first president (October 1745–October 1747) and after his premature death was succeeded by the Reverend Aaron Burr. He moved the college to Princeton and a new charter was obtained from Governor Melcher in 1748. The College of New Jersey was aided by gifts totalling £4000 from churches in Great Britain.[53]

Several families who carried major responsibility in the Wall Street Church were also prominent in matters of importance in colonial New York City: among them the Livingstons and the Smiths. Peter Van Brugh Livingston (1710–1792), nephew of founder Gilbert Livingston, was a graduate of Yale (1731) who became a prosperous merchant with his brother, Philip, a privateer in the French and Indian war. He was one of the first trustees when the board was established in 1746. He married Mary, daughter of James Alexander, a prominent lawyer.[54]

William Smith, the merchant, was son of "Port Royal" Smith

18

and Frances Peartree; he was trustee in 1746 but was succeeded the following year by his son, William Peartree Smith. The latter was independently wealthy, a man of leisure, envied by many of his friends. He married Mary, daughter of William Bryant.[55]

The most prominent member was another William Smith (1697–1769), eldest son of Thomas Smith, also a founder. A Yale graduate, he was a zealous scholar, interested in science as well as the classics and was well versed in Greek and Hebrew. He remained at Yale as a tutor and was offered the presidency of the college. He was, however, fascinated by law and was admitted to the bar in New York on May 20, 1724. He acquired one of the best law libraries in the colony. He was appointed attorney general by Governor George Clinton (1748–1753) but was not confirmed by the Crown. He was, however, appointed a member of the Governor's Council in 1753 and served until 1767. In 1754 he was one of the four representatives from New York to the Albany Congress which attempted to win the support of the Iroquois in the conflict with the French. At the conference a plan for intercolonial union, presented by Benjamin Franklin was recommended to the colonial assemblies. Smith was a firm supporter of the plan. Smith became an associate justice of the supreme court of New York, 1763–1769. He married twice; his first wife was Mary Du Bois Het, daughter of a Huguenot refugee from Rochelle France who had come to New York in 1709. The names of fourteen of their fifteen children fill the first page of the Presbyterian church baptismal record, 1720–1790. The Smiths were staunch Presbyterians and practically every Sunday they would be in their pew at the Wall Street church.[56]

It was the pleading of William Smith that led to the disenfranchisement of the Jews in New York in 1738. There was a contest for a seat in the assembly between Adolph Philipse and Cornelius Van Horne. The former was declared elected by the sheriff but Van Horne accused the sheriff of dishonesty in the counting of the votes. William Smith, lawyer for Van Horne, denied that Jews were qualified electors. His speech, based on the Bible, was so emotional that the Jews were thankful that they were only denied the right to vote; they feared a popular attack on them as Smith convinced his audience that the honor of Christianity was at stake.[57]

William Smith and James Alexander were the two most prominent lawyers in New York City. One of their famous clients was Peter Zenger. They had helped him establish his paper, *The New-York Weekly Journal*, to offset the organ of the court party, *The New-York Gazette*, and had contributed articles to it. Zenger got into trouble with the government for his satirical ballads and on January 17, 1735 he was charged with seditious libels.[58]

His lawyers objected at the outset to the court in which he was to be tried. They declared the commissions of Chief Justice De

Lancey and Frederick Philipse were invalid, having been given by the governor without the consent of the council. The Chief Justice declared: "You have brought it to that point, sirs, that either we must go from the bench, or you from the bar." They were disbarred in April 1735. Since the only other prominent lawyer in the city had been retained by the government, friends of Zenger secretly brought Andrew Hamilton from Philadelphia to conduct the case. The trial in City Hall lasted all summer. Hamilton argued a jury's right to decide both the law and facts in the case and if the articles of the newspaper were true it was not libel. Zenger's acquittal by the jury has been hailed as the primary victory for freedom of the press.[59]

Smith and others in his office formed the first lawyers' association in New York City, seeking to elevate the quality of the bench in the colony. It was, however, a restrictive society limiting the number of those entering the profession by agreeing that they would accept no new apprentices except their sons, for the next fourteen years, and after that only one a year. The organization also drew up regulations of fees to be charged by members of the profession. William Smith outlined a course of study for law students.[60]

Smith was interested not only in legal education but also in elementary and college education. In 1732 he with Lewis Morris and James Alexander got the assembly to provide for a "free school" to teach Latin and Greek and practical mathematics. It was under the care of Alexander Malcolm.[61]There were few college graduates in the city; in 1740 aside from the clergy only about a dozen had academic degrees, notably the De Lanceys, the Livingstons, and the Smiths. Massachusetts, Connecticut, and New Jersey had colleges but up to the middle of the eighteenth century New York had none. From 1746 to 1753 money was raised by public lotteries for a college and in 1751 the legislature provided for a board of trustees; seven Anglicans, two Reformed Dutch, and one Presbyterian (William Livingston).

A struggle for control of the college ensued between the Anglicans and Presbyterians. The Presbyterians opposed the establishment of a sectarian college supported by public funds. Livingston in *The Independent Reflector*, a magazine established by some Presbyterian lawyers in 1752, stated that "sound public policy requires the college to admit members of all Protestant denominations 'upon a perfect Parity as to Privileges.' " After the demise of the paper in November 1753 the Anglicans were able to install Dr. Samuel Johnson as president of the college; he was also assistant pastor at Trinity Church.[62]

Classes with seven students began in the vestry room of Trinity in 1753. Trinity offered a large tract of land, a part of King's farm, on condition that the president of the college always be an Anglican and that services follow the English Book of Common

20

Prayer. They petitioned the governor and council for a charter; the Presbyterians protested. The latter maintained that a charter should be given by the assembly and that it should be a "free college," i.e. "be as free as possible from all contracted aims, prejudices and partiality of sectarian zeal." However, Acting Governor De Lancey in 1755 granted a charter to the college. There were protests that the money had been raised by public lottery and should not be used for a sectarian college. The money was divided in 1756; King's College received half; the other half was set aside for the lodgement in jail of crews of infected vessels. The Honorable William Smith, voting in council for the division, jokingly said: "It rids us of a bone of contention by dividing it between the two pest houses."[63]

In 1754 the New York Society Library was established. Prior to this there had been a small library housed in city hall, called the "Corporation Library," largely consisting of religious books given by the Society for the Propagation of the Gospel in Foreign Parts. Interest in it had soon declined. Some public spirited men, among them Presbyterians William and Philip Livingston, William Peartree Smith, John Morin Scott, and William Alexander pledged £600 for the purchase of 700 volumes to add to the "Corporation Library." A subscription of £5 and an annual fee of 10s entitled one to borrow a book but required a deposit with the bookkeeper of one-third the cost of the book. Subscribers elected twelve trustees annually with Anglicans and Presbyterians in competition for the positions. The Anglicans wanted to control the society and have the library serve as the college library. In the first election the Anglicans won a majority of the trustees but in the next election the Presbyterians won a majority. The Society received a charter from George III in 1772.[64] It still flourishes.

In colonial New York City the religious communities were prominent in civic and political activities. In wealth and influence the Anglicans ranked first, followed by the Reformed Dutch, and the Presbyterian, third.[65] Presbyterians opposed the Anglicans on many issues: freedom of the press, public education, a secular college, and a semi-public library.

Large families, immigration from northern Ireland and Scotland and the movement of the population from New England increased the number of Presbyterians, however, and by the middle of the eighteenth century they exceeded in number all other denominations. Their new church—a monument in downtown New York—appeared on many early maps of the city, and its members were soon to play a prominent part in the coming struggle for independence from Great Britain.

[1]Charles W. Baird, "The Presbyterians in the Province of New-York," *Magazine of American History*, III (Oct., 1879), 593–607; Sydney E. Ahlstrom, *A Religious History of the American People* (New Haven, 1972), 215–6; Charles Augustus Briggs, *American Presbyterianism* (New York, 1885), 144–5; Winthrop Hudson, *Religion in America* (New York, 1965), 30–31; Carl Bridenbaugh, *Mitre and Sceptre* (New York, 1962), 117–9.

[2]Benjamin Bullivant, "A Glance at New York in 1697," *The New York Historical Society Quarterly*, XL (January, 1956), 62.

[3]Boyd Schlenther, *Life and Writings of Francis Makemie* (Philadelphia, Pa., 1971), 13–20; E. H. Gillett, *History of the Presbyterian Church in the United States of America* (2 vols., revised edition, Philadelphia, 1873), I:4; Hudson, *Religion in America*, pp. 41–43.

[4]Schlenther, *Makemie*, p. 20; Gillett, *Presbyterian Church*, I: 18–20.

[5]Samuel Miller, *Memoirs of the Rev. John Rodgers* (New York, 1813), 122–7; Edmund Bailey O'Callaghan, ed. *The Documentary History of the State of New York* (4 vols., Albany, 1849–51), I: 395, 398, 404; Richard E. Day, "David Jamison," *Dictionary of American Biography* (hereinafter cited as *DAB*), V: 603–4.

[6]Francis Makemie, "A Good Conversation," *Collections of the New York Historical Society, 1870*, pp. 414–453.

[7]Edward Corwin, ed. *Ecclesiastical Records of State of New York* (7 vols., Albany, 1901–5), III:1669–72; Edward Hagaman Hall, "The First Presbyterian Church of New York," *22 Annual Report* of the American Scenic and Historical Preservation Society (Albany, 1917) 578–80; Schlenther, *Makemie*, pp. 21–25; Francis Makemie, *A Narrative of a new and Unusual American Imprisonment* (New York, 1775).

[8]James Grant Wilson, *Memorial History of the City of New York* (4 vols., New York, 1892), II:78–82.

[9]Corwin, ed. *Ecclesiastical Records*, III: 1673; Hall, "First Presbyterian Church," p. 583.

[10]William Leonard Nicoll, *The Nicoll Family* (New York, 1886), 1–8; *In Memoriam of Dr. John Nicoll*, a leaflet prepared when tablet was unveiled in north narthex, January 11, 1959.

[11]*New York Genealogical and Biographical Record*, v. 84, no. 1–3 (July, 1953), "Gilbert Livingston."

[12]Maturin Delafield, "William Smith," *Magazine of American History*, April–June, 1881, p. 271; William Smith, *The History of the Late Province of New York from its Discovery to the Appointment of Governor Colden in 1762* (2 vols., New York, 1830), I: 231n.

[13]David Valentine, *History of the City of New York* (New York, 1853), p. 240; Wilson, *Memorial History*, II:73n.

[14]Delafield, "William Smith," pp. 272–3.

[15]Isaac Newton Phelps Stokes, ed. *The Iconography of Manhattan Island, 1498–1909* (8 vols., New York, 1916–1928), IV:487; Theodore Fiske Savage, *The Presbyterian Church in New York City* (New York, 1949), 6.

[16]Briggs, *American Presbyterianism*, Appendix, XX, no. 3.

[17]Stokes, *Iconography*, IV:489; New York City, *Minutes of the Common Council of New York, 1675–1776* (8 vols., New York, 1905), III:172.

[18]Gillett, *Presbyterian Church*, I:30–2.

[19]*Ibid.*, I:32; First Presbyterian Church, Journal of Transactions of the Trustees, 1717–1775 (hereinafter cited as Trustee Minutes), p. 1; *The Church Tower*, May 15, November 15, 1931, 19-1.

[20]Hall, "First Presbyterian Church," p. 621.

[21]*Ibid.*, *pp. 622–4*, 627.

[22]*Ibid.*, p. 625; Corwin, ed. *Ecclesiastical Records*, III:2173; Gillett, *Presbyterian Church*, I:37–39.

[23]O'Callaghan, ed. *Documentary History*, III:278–81; Stokes, *Iconography*, IV: 492–3.

[24]Martha Lamb, *History of the City of New York: its Origin, Rise and Progress* (3 vols., New York, 1896), I:518; Ola E. Winslow, *Jonathan Edwards, 1703–1758* (New York, 1940), 85–87; Delafield, "William Smith," p. 275.

[25]Boyd Schlenther, "Presbyterian Church of N.Y. cv. John Nicoll, M.D." *Journal of Presbyterian History*, 42, no. 3 (Sept. 1964), 198–214; (Dec. 1964), 272–85; Briggs, *American Presbyterianism*, pp. 181–4, Appendix, XX, no. 5; Gillett, *Presbyterian Church*, I: 37–39.

[26]First Presbyterian Church, Session Minutes, 1765–1808 (hereinafter cited as Session Minutes), I: 3–4; (historical sketch) Frederick Lewis Weis, *The Colonial Clergy of the Middle Colonies, New York, New Jersey and Pennsylvania, 1628–1776*, Proceedings of the American Antiquarian Society, vol. 66, p. 288.

[27]Smith, *History*, I:258.

[28]Trustee Minutes, I:2–3 (sketch); Indenture, May 16, 1730; Stokes, *Iconography*. IV:516.

[29]Session Minutes, I:5 (statement of the clerk of session in 1807).

[30]*Ibid.*, I:5; Hudson, *Religion in America*, pp. 67–70.

[31]Gillett, *Presbyterian Church*, I:47–58; Lefferts A. Loetscher, *A Brief History of the Presbyterian Church* (Philadelphia, 1957), pp. 58ff; Hudson, *Religion in America*, pp. 61–65; Gordon Trumbull Scoville, "America's Spiritual Revolution," in *The Presbyterian Life*, March 31, 1956, pp. 14–22.

[32]Session Minutes, I:4; Ebenezer Pemberton, *A Sermon Preached at the Presbyterian Church in the City of New-York on the Occasion of the Death of John Nicoll, M.D.* (New York, 1743).

[33]Trustee Minutes, I:4–6, 9–11 (Feb. 13, 20, 1746), 42 (Jan. 4, 1748), 76 (May 3, 1754).

[34]*Ibid.*, I:11–16 (Feb. 20, 1746).

[35]*Ibid.*, I:16–19, 21–25 (Feb. 20, 23, Mar. 4, 1746).

[36]*Ibid.*, I:27–29 (Mar. 13, 1746); Stokes, *Iconography*, IV:595.

[37]Stokes, *Iconography*, IV:605; Smith, *History*, I:258.

[38].Trustee Minutes, I:45 (Oct. 22, 1749).

[39]*Ibid.*, I:51–7 (Jan. 1, 1753), Miller, *Rodgers*, pp. 147–50; Savage, *Presbyterian Church*, pp. 40–41.

[40]Trustee Minutes, I:58–64 (Sept. 24, 1753); copy of Synod minutes in back of book; Session Minutes, I: 6–10 (historical sketch).

[41]Trustee Minutes, I:60–61 (Sept. 27, 1753); Smith, *History*, I:258.

[42]Trustee Minutes, I:88–99 (July 14, 1755), 100–102 (Apr. 16, 1756); Weis, *Colonial Clergy*, p. 185.

[43]Smith, *History*, I:260.

44Trustee Minutes, I:90−99 (Oct. 29, 1755); Savage, *Presbyterian Church*, pp. 199−200.

45Trustee Minutes, I:107−8, 137−8 (June 1, July 6, 1756); Gabriel Disosway, *The Earliest Churches of New York and its Vicinity* (New York, 1864), p. 134.

46Trustee Minutes, I:111−2 (Sept. 30, 1756), 144−5 (Aug. 3, 1762).

47*Ibid.*, I:125−6 (May 1, 1759), 140−1 (Oct. 24, 1761), 144 (Aug. 3, 1762), 146−7 (May 4, 1762); Stokes, *Iconography*, IV:720.

48Trustee Minutes, I:167−9 (Nov. 12, 1763, Jan. 4, 1764).

49*Ibid.*, I:7−8 (Feb. 13, 1746).

50George W. Edwards and Arthur E. Peterson, *New York as an Eighteenth Century Municipality, 1731−1776* (New York, 1917), 297.

51David Baillie Morrison, *Two Hundredth Anniversary, 1756−1956 of St. Andrew's Society of the State of New York* (Philadelphia, 1956), 5−6, 13; Brother Harry M. Dunkak, John Morin Scott and Whig Politics in New York, 1732−1769 (Ph.D. thesis, St. John's University, 1968), 139.

52Trustee Minutes, I:50 (Jan. 2, 1750).

53Alexander, *Presbytery of New York*, pp. 11−22; Gillett, *American Presbyterianism*, I:124−7; L. F. S. Upton, *The Loyal Whig: William Smith of New York and Quebec* (Toronto, 1969), 7.

54John A. Krout, "Peter Van Brugh Livingston," *DAB*, XI:315−6.

55Austin Baxter Keep, *History of the New York Society Library* (New York, 1908), 145.

56Delafield, "William Smith," pp. 264−9; William H. W. Sabine, ed. *Historical Memoirs from 16 March 1763 to 9 July 1776 of William Smith* (New York, 1956), 1−2; Paul Mahlon Hamlin, *Legal Education in Colonial New York* (New York, 1939), 80, 90.

57Smith, *History,* II:46; Lamb, *City of New York, II:*573-4

58Valentine, *City of New York*, pp. 265−6; Lamb, *City of New York*, I:548−56.

59O'Callaghan, ed. *Documentary History*, IV:627; Smith, *History*, II:4−13, 16−22. Two years before they had objected to Governor *Cosby's* change in the court when they defended Van Dam in his demand for salary for the year he was acting governor.

60Hamlin, *Legal Education*, pp. 61−62, 160−1.

61Smith, *History*, II:2; Delafield, "William Smith,: pp. 266−7.

62Smith, *History* II:94, 191−2, 199−200, 238; Theodore Sedgwick, *A Memoir of the Life of William Livingston* (New York, 1833), 70−90; Dorothy Dillon, *The New York Triumvirate. A Study of the Legal and Political Careers of William Livingston, John Morin Scott, William Smith, Jr.* (New York, 1949), pp. 31−40, 78−81, 95; Bridenbaugh, *Mitre and Sceptre*, p. 150.

63Smith, *History*, II:238; Dunkak, Scott, pp. 89−114.

64Keep, *New York Society Library*, pp. 176−7, 535; Lamb, *City of New York*, III:418; Smith, *History*, II:171; Mary L. Booth, *History of the City of New York* (2 vols., New York, 1867), I:319−20.

65O'Callaghan, ed. *Documentary History*, IV, 631.

CHAPTER TWO

Church of the Patriots

In 1765 the Wall Street church came into the hands of a new group of leaders. The old ones either died or relinquished the reins to younger men, often to their sons. A new minister was called who remained until his death in 1811. In addition to the board of trustees, which since 1746 had been the only really organized body and had dominated the governance of the church, there was a session of six elders that held regular meetings with a clerk who kept minutes beginning in January, 1765. There was also a board of deacons, thus giving the church a complete Presbyterian form of government. The result was a period of harmony and growth within the church, a contrast to earlier years. It was, however, the start of a decade of troubled politics in the colony. But within, the ministers and most of the officers were united in support of the colonists' struggle against Great Britain.

On January 17, 1765, the congregation, with the Honorable William Smith presiding, voted to call the Rev. John Rodgers (1727–1811) to be co-pastor with the Rev. Joseph Treat (1734–1797) who had come to the Wall Street church in October, 1762, just prior to Bostwick's death.[1] Rodgers' parents had come from Londonderry, Ireland in 1721, settled in Boston and moved to Philadelphia when he was a little over a year old. At twelve he had been greatly moved by the preaching of George Whitefield and determined to become a minister. He studied with two stalwarts of the Great Awakening—the Rev. Samuel Blair and Gilbert Tennett, pastor of the Second Presbyterian Church of Philadelphia. He received his licensure to preach from the Presbytery at New Castle in October, 1747 and then accepted a call to the St. George church.[2]

While serving there he befriended a young Scotsman, Hugh Knox, who after finishing at Princeton, had been sent by the New

York Presbytery as a missionary in 1756 to the West Indies. In St. Croix Knox was so impressed by the young Alexander Hamilton that he arranged for him to come to New York. Thus Rodgers "was the indirect cause of the entrance of Alexander Hamilton into American history."[3]

The Wall Street Church had earlier called Rodgers to its pastorate in 1754 but he had refused to leave St. George. An ardent supporter of the "new side", he had travelled with George Whitefield on an evangelistic tour in that year. He was moderator of the Synod of New York and Philadelphia in 1763, and was urged by the Synod to accept the second invitation to New York in 1765. He arrived with his family on July 24 and was installed on September 4. In April of that same year he had been elected a trustee of the College of New Jersey.[4]

Mindful of earlier controversy Rodgers chose to conduct all parts of the worship service from the pulpit instead of giving the short, opening prayer, reading the Scriptures and announcing the first psalm from the little desk in front. In addition, at the request of the elders and trustees the pastors adopted the robe worn by ministers of the Church of Scotland — an academic gown with white tabs — "indicating their status as scholars." He also wore black kid gloves and a curled wig. A popular preacher, he used no notes for his sermon, often became very emotional during the delivery, even to the point of weeping. The sermon, the central part of the service, was followed by another prayer, ending with the singing of a psalm. On special occasions the warden took up a collection in a large pewter platter.

In addition to the two religious services on the Sabbath Day and the expository lecture at night, Rodgers instituted weekly catechetical instruction of the children and delivered public lectures on the catechism on Thursday evenings. He made a point of visiting every family of the congregation and encouraged private associations for prayer.[5]

The church had over three hundred communicants. People were admitted to church membership by the elders and ministers either by certificate of dismissal from another church or by profession of faith. A few Negroes were admitted to membership (five in the list of communicants in 1769), and their race was always indicated after the name, e.g. "Sylvia, a Negro Wench," "Holland, a Negro Man," "Hannah, a woman of Color," "Dinah, a free negro woman," "Phoebe, a Negro Woman servant to William Jening."[6] A preparatory service was held on the Friday evening before the communion service.

The Lord's Supper was celebrated four times a year. Tables (four usually) covered with white cloth, containing a silver tankard, four silver beakers, and three silver plates, were set up in the front. The silver beakers, about six inches in height, perfectly plain, were made by Philip Goelet (1708–1748) of New York and

John Rodgers, Pastor, 1765–1811, and strong supporter of the American Revolution

carried the inscription: "Ex dono Annae Peartree, Ecclesiae Christi Presbyterianae apud Neo-Eboracenses, 1730." The silver plates, ten inches in diameter, were inscribed "Ex Dono Peter R. Livingston" and were made by Myer Myers (1723–1796), the outstanding goldsmith in New York City, whose parents had come from Holland and were members of the Shearoth Israel, the earliest Jewish congregation. The tankard was very elaborate. On the side opposite the beaded rat-tail handle was a coat of arms and above the date, "A legacy of Mr. Jeremiah Owen to the Presbyterian Church in New York, 1756." On the lid was a reproduction of a medal struck in 1634 in honor of Gustavus Adolphus "the Protestant hero" of the Thirty Years War. Above was the inscription: "Et vita et morte triumpho." This was the work of Abraham Poutreau.[7]

After an "Action Sermon" (usually about sixty minutes long) the words of the Institution from First Corinthians were read. During the singing of a psalm the communicants, three sets of both sexes at a time, came down the center aisle and took seats on both sides of the narrow tables. After taking a seat the communicant was asked to "surrender" his token by placing it either in a wooden tray or pewter plate or laying it on the table. Tokens, or "Presbyterian checks" signified proper preparation of heart had been made prior to coming to the table, usually by participation in a service of preparation. They were used during the time of John Calvin, as early as 1560. Once the tokens had been collected the elements were uncovered and, the communicants standing, the bread was broken and the wine poured from the tankard into a beaker. The bread was placed by an elder between the two

First Presbyterian Church silver, circa 1730, made by Philip Goelet and Myer Myers, renowned colonial silversmiths

Communion tokens similar to those used in the Wall Street Church

communicants at the head of the table and they broke off a morsel and passed it on; likewise the cup was passed down the table. When this was done the communicants, to the singing of a psalm, returned to their seats and their places were filled by others.[8]

Discipline was strict and the session took seriously its judicature functions. Session minutes contain a variety of cases. One case concerned a man who had joined the group which had seceded from the Wall Street church in 1756 but he now wanted to return because he had been excommunicated by the Scots church: he had occasionally listened to ministers of other denominations. The pastor refused to give him a letter of dismissal because he had not attended the meeting of the session at which his case was to be taken up. The session of the Wall Street church finally accepted him, being of "the Opinion which Mr. Arden maintained in Respect to hearing Orthodox men was becoming the Gospel & not Censurable in the Judicator of any Protestant Church."[9]

There were several cases involving "antinuptial fornication," the evidence being a child "born before the proper time after marriage." For example, Cato, a free Negro, had lived inoffensively until he became a widower and then was found guilty of fornication with a Negro woman who later became his wife. She was an Episcopalian and had had "the Fruit of that Fornication" baptized with a clergyman of that faith. Cato wanted his second child to be baptized in the Presbyterian church. He, however, "appeared Insensible of any Crime therein from his Prejudices of Heathenism whereby he justified that part of his Conduct by his Marrying the Same Woman he had Defiled." The ministers talked with him many times and finally after a year he appeared before the session and professed his penitence and his desire to be "Readmitted into the Communion of this Church, and to have his Child Baptized in the same." The session

> agreed unanimously to Rebuke, & Admonish, & Exhort him before the Session, as tending more to Edification than a more publick Reproof for a Scandal scarce known to any others of the Congregation or People of the City, and having called him in again, he was suitably Rebuked, Admonished & Exhorted before the Session, who received him again into the Communion of the Church.

His child was baptized.[10] Such was the procedure used. It is interesting to note that in most cases it was the man who was brought before the session for this offense.

On the other hand women seemed to have been brought before the session more frequently on the charge of intemperate drinking. Initially two elders were appointed to investigate the charges and prepare a report. If warranted, the accused was summoned to appear before the session following which there would often be a trial with witnesses. In one case witnesses testified to having seen the accused on three occasions when she did not seem accountable. They decided she had been drinking too much, also basing their accusation on the amount of rum she fetched from the grog shop. Her own witnesses declared that they lived with her for several months and had never seen her intoxicated. She did take a little rum "to refresh Nature" every day when she had enough money but only a quart of beer with a gill of rum mixed in it. The session dismissed her "as having forfeited the Right to Sealing Ordinance in the Church until she gives satisfactory Evidence of Genuine Repentence." In another case the woman accused professed "deep sorrow" and she was admonished and exhorted to be "more circumspect in her future Conduct."[11] One man appeared, admitted his sin and promised to "study to walk in his whole future department, in a manner becoming the Gospel of Christ." The session decided that since his conduct had given great offense to his "fellow Professors" he should not "approach the Lord's Table the ensuing Sabbath."[12]

Since the Wall Street Presbyterian Church was not incorporated the trustees themselves were responsible for the church property. In 1765 individual trustees gave their own bond when additional land adjoining the church was bought to increase the burial grounds. The rates for funerals were set by the trustees and varied from £5 for burial in the church to £03 for burial in the church yard; prices for children's graves were less. There were additional charges for the use of the pall and for the sexton inviting guests to the funeral and for attending himself.

Pall bearers at a funeral were given sashes to wear and the following Sunday they attended church in a body also wearing them. Those worn at funerals of notables were white, two or three yards in length. They were placed over the right shoulder and tied under the left arm in a large bow; there was a large rose of the ribbon on the sash. Dr. Rodgers' bow and rose, as minister, were black.[13] The sexton (John Brown) was reprimanded for employing as his assistant a black man; the trustees "being of the opinion that it is improper to Imploy a Negro in that Business."[14]

Because the church was not incorporated, legacies presented particular problems. Anna Peartree had provided in her will in 1730, that the church receive 30s annually for five years. Her daughter and her husband were members of the Wall Street Church and there was no difficulty.[15] Not so when in 1756 Captain Owen left the income from a house on the south side of Maiden Lane near Broadway to be applied toward instruction of poor children of the congregation in reading, writing, and "use of figures." The executor, an Episcopalian, refused to turn the money over to the trustees of the Presbyterian church since the church was not incorporated. The executor also prevented Trinity Church from getting the money and had placed poor Presbyterian children in the care of Presbyterian school masters. During his pastoral visits Mr. Rodgers found many poor children who were receiving no education. He learned of the unused legacy and persuaded the executor to turn it over to six members of the congregation who gave him a bond of indemnity against future claimants (Peter Van Brugh Livingston, William Livingston, William Smith, John Morin Scott, Peter McDougall, and Joseph Hallett). In 1762 Captain John Neilson, commander of a merchant ship blown up off the coast of France, bequeathed "to the Presbyterian Church in New York" £ 100. The executor refused to turn over the money declaring the law knew no such body. (Twenty years later the church did receive the money, but without interest).[16]

The trustees made another appeal (the fifth) for a charter, March 18, 1766. The petition to the King and Council was signed by the ministers of the Presbyterian church "according to the Westminster Confession of Faith, Catechisms, and Directory; agreeable to the Established Church of Scotland." It was signed by William Smith, Peter Van Brugh Livingston, John Smith, Garret Noel, Thomas Jackson, and Nathaniel McKinley (elders); John Stephens and Peter Ryker (deacons), and Thomas Smith, Whitehead Hicks, William Smith, Jr., John Lasher, Joseph Hallet, John Dunlap, Peter R. Livingston, and John Morin Scott (trustees). Governor Henry Moore (1765–1769) and the Council doubted that the Governor's commission vested him with incorporating powers, and so the petition was directed to the King himself. King George III laid it before the Privy Council and they forwarded it to the Board of Trade, who carried the crown's colonial responsibility. They queried Governor Moore about the present state of this "Protestant Establishment" and about the petition of 1759. The King and Council finally decided that there was no need for the Presbyterian church to have a charter or "any other privileges and immunities than it is entitled by the laws of Toleration." It seems that the Bishop of London had opposed the granting of the charter.[17]

By 1766 the congregation had out grown the accommodations of the building and there was growing demand for pews and seats. A committee was appointed to look for new sites. The trustees petitioned the Common Council who proposed two available pieces of land. The first, opposite the old Wind Mill Spot (north side of Chatham Street), was rejected for several reasons: 1) it was too remote for immediate use and the streets would probably not be paved for many years; 2) the street leading to it was so narrow that two or three carriages would obstruct passage; 3) the danger of fire would be great because of wooden buildings in the neighborhood; 4) if the Dutch should build on the site recently granted them the two churches would be so near to each other that the services would conflict. Finally they said that the church there would not "Contribute to the Publick Ornament of the City."

The second proposed site, the "Vineyard Lot," a triangular plot of land at Nassau and Beekman was preferred. It was virgin ground, had no previous ownership, sizeable enough for the church and "Cymetery," and was leased to them by the city for £40 a year in perpetuity. This area adjoining the Commons was being built up and would soon become an important section of the city. The petitioners said that the church with a fence would be "a Great Ornament to the Green whereas it is at Present Entirely useless or Rather a Nuisance as it is now a Receptacle for all the Dirt and Filth of the Neighborhood."[18]

Mr. Rodgers went from door to door for several months soliciting subscriptions for the new church building, which when finished was, according to John Adams, a "very magnificent Building." Constructed of brick, it later became known as the Brick Church, and was opened on New Years Day, 1768.

The Wall Street and the New Church (as it was called at the time) were considered one organization. The two ministers preached alternately on Sunday mornings at the two churches and the Sunday evening service was held at one church one Sunday and at the other the following Sabbath. There was one set of elders, deacons, and trustees, and one roll of 391 communicants.[19]

Although at the north end of the city, the New Church was amid many of the governmental agencies that had been moved to the Commons or Fields (later City Hall Park), including the poor house, erected there in 1734, and a "new gaol" built in 1760, "the finest public edifice of its day." The stocks, whipping post and pillory had been moved there from Wall Street, giving rise to complaints that at times of public executions the sexton opened New Church for spectators resulting in dirt and damaged pews.

William Smith, Sr.,
Trustee.

The trustees ordered that it not be opened except for cleaning and immediately before divine services.[20]

II

New York Presbyterians were largely of the middle class: socially and economically, lawyers, merchants. Some were independent craftsmen, cordwainers, blacksmiths, distillers. Several of the more wealthy had a country as well as a town house. The Hermitage, country place of John Morin Scott was at what is now 43rd Street and Ninth Avenue. William Livingston had an estate at Elizabethtown, New Jersey; Philip and Robert Livingston had homes on Brooklyn Heights; the Smiths had country homes at Haverstraw on the other side of the river.[21]

Politically most Presbyterians were devoted to the colonial cause, not surprising since their traditional form of church government was republican rather than autocratic. The Scotch-Irish particularly had many grievances against England.[22]

A triumvirate of lawyers, each a trustee in the Wall Street Presbyterian Church, were prominent in the pre-revolutionary struggles with the Crown in New York City. All were graduates of Yale College, described by the Tory historian, Thomas Jones, as "a nursery of sedition, of faction, of republicansim," and all entered the firm of William Smith, Sr., as clerks.[23] William Livingston (1723–1790) was the oldest of the three. Admitted to the bar, in October, 1745, he married Susanna French, daughter of a wealthy New Jersey land holder and lived in Water Street until 1758 when he moved to the corner of William and Garden.

Interested in literature he contributed pieces to several papers. His wit, sarcasm and his spare body led to his nickname, "whipping post."[24] In 1770, he with his associates established the Moot, first legal society in the city. For six years their regular meetings were devoted to the consideration of "practical and theoretical problems in law and equity." The prominent members and officers were also Presbyterians.[25]

William Smith, Jr. (1728–1793), son of the firm's founder, was admitted to the bar in October 1750, married to Janet Livingston (cousin of William) and lived at No. 5 Broadway, former mansion of James De Lancey, in the most fashionable section of the city. They had eleven children. Known as a "devout Christian and sincere Protestant," he was reputed to have an annual income of over £2000, more than any other lawyer in New York City. He was also probably the most learned of the group, an historian whose *History of the Province of New York* (1757) was for eighty years the standard history of the province. He and William Livingston published the first digest of the laws of New York from 1691 to 1762.[26]

The most radical and youngest of the three was John Morin Scott (1730–1784). Great-grandson of a Scottish baron, grandson and son of successful New York City merchants, John Morin had been brought up in his mother's French Reform Church. In 1752 he married Helena Rutgers (daughter of Captain Petrus and Helena [Hoogland] Rutgers), who was a member of the Presbyterian church of which John Morin became a trustee in 1761. Admitted to the bar in January, 1752, he developed a prosperous practice.[27] In a crucial case, *Cunningham v. Forsey* (1764), he argued that there could be no appeal on questions of fact from the provincial supreme court to the Governor in Council. He won the case and was upheld by the Privy Council. It was a popular decision for it strengthened the power of colonial courts and diminished that of the Governor.[28] Scott entered politics early, served as alderman from the Out Ward from 1756–1761, and was active on the Common Council.[29]

The triumvirate took the lead in opposition to the encroachment of power by both crown and Anglican church. In 1752 they formed the Whig Club at the principal inn of the city. According to the Tory historian the purpose of this group was "to pull down Church and State, to raise their own Government and religion upon its ruins, or to throw the whole province into anarchy and confusion." Out of these meetings developed a literary magazine, *The Independent Reflector,* that made its appearance on November 30, 1752, with essays on timely topics. It lasted only a year. Printers were afraid to publish it.[30] In one of the last issues (August 16, 1753) Livingston justified resistance to the king on the basis that the monarch had sworn to uphold the laws of England and when he did not allegiance to him ceased. He wrote:

"Whenever a Magistrate acts in Opposition to his political Power, he cannot do Acts as Magistrate. . . . To resist in such a case, is not resisting his Authority, but Force illegal and unauthoritative."[31]

Several of the *Reflector* issues contained attacks on the Anglican church and the possibility of a resident American bishop was a long-standing and inflamatory issue. Anglican clergy had been sent to the colonies by the Society for the Propagation of the Gospel in Foreign Parts, founded in 1701. The church in America was responsible to the Bishop of London. During the reign of Queen Anne (1714) a bill for an American Episcopacy had been drawn up but was dropped after her death. The issue had been raised unsuccessfully again in 1750 by the Archbishop of Canterbury who proposed two or three bishops in America to administer confirmation and ordain priests and deacons.

Samuel Johnson, president of Kings College, urged action in 1766 to establish the bishopric as counteracting the influence of republicanism.[32] This revived an old fear and Presbyterians prepared to unite against such a proposal. Over eighty ministers and elders met in New York City in May, 1766, to establish correspondence with the consociated churches of Connecticut and commissioners of whom John Rodgers was one, were appointed to carry on negotiations. The Great Awakening had taught churchmen the value of establishing communications across colonial and denominational boundaries. The experience was to prove a valuable forerunner for later "Committees of Correspondence" and for the assembling of the Continental Congress. Annual meetings between two groups were held from 1766 to 1775.

The Wall Street Church-Brick Church ministers were among the leaders. Rodgers was appointed to carry on correspondence with dissenters in England. He pointed out that they did not oppose episcopacy as a spiritual office but rather its political and economic power especially since the dissenters in America far outnumbered the Episcopalians. They also had the support in their opposition of the Rev. Archibald Laidlie of the New York Reformed Dutch Church.[33]

In February, 1769 Presbyterians and Baptists of New York City organized the "Society of Dissenters," stating as their purpose:

to unite together for the preservation of their common and respective civil and religious Rights and Privileges, against all Oppressions and Encroachments by those of any Denomination whatsoever.

Presbyterians were represented by Peter Van Brugh Livingston, Samuel Broome, Thomas Smith, Alexander McDougall, Joseph Hallett, William Livingston, David Van Horne, John Morin Scott, William Neilson, John Broome, John McKesson, Peter R. Livingston, and Dr. Benjamin Y. Prime. A standing committee of correspondence, composed of the two Peter Livingstons, Van

Horne, McDougall, John Broome, and Samuel Loudon (a Scotch Presbyterian) was organized to correspond with similar organizations they hoped would be established in other colonies. The articles of agreement "leaked" to the press and the Anglicans labeled it a "Presbyterian plot." According to one scholar this may have "silenced the dissenters for nothing more was heard of the Society after September, 1769."[34]

The dissenters also fought the Episcopal Church claim to establishment with its accompanying right to tax support. An act relieving dissenters from payment of taxes for the support of the clergy of that church passed the assembly in 1769 but was defeated in the council with only William Smith, Jr. voting for the passage. Similar bills in 1770 and 1771 were also blocked. In 1774 Governor Tryon ruled that the Anglican church was established church. The Presbyterians opposed without success.[35]

In political matters most Anglicans supported King and Parliament and most Presbyterians opposed. Professor Levermore noted that the "supreme conception of law and justice which is inherent in the creed of Calvin was the main spring of the whole popular party in New York. ... The lines of cleavage between political parties and religious denominations were virtually identical, and the mutual animosity of the two English churches, Episcopalian and Presbyterian, was the most potent political force in the colony." One of the few Anglicans to support the Whigs was John Jay and he was married to the daughter of William Livingston. The Presbyterians who were loyalists usually held official positions under the Crown.[36]

The struggle focused on control of the assembly, the "center of a vigorous political life." Philip Livingston led the Whigs or the popular party. A prosperous merchant, he entered politics early and served as alderman of the East ward from 1754–1762. By 1758 he had organized the Whig party, sometimes called the Livingston party, and defeated the De Lancey forces. When the Chief Justice died in 1760 the leadership passed to his son, Capt. James De Lancey (1732–1800). The death of George II in the same year necessitated a new election which the Whigs won. They controlled the assembly until 1768.[37]

In 1762 the Livingston controlled assembly sent to London a series of "elaborate and courageous state papers" opposing a taxation program of Chancellor of Exchequer George Grenville. A committee was established in 1764 to correspond with the colony's agent in London and also with committees of other colonial assemblies. On it were two Livingstons, two De Lanceys and a neutral. The Sugar Act of 1764 reduced the duty on foreign molasses but provided for stringent enforcement which irritated merchants who had long evaded any payment of the previous higher duty. This brought forth indignant protests from those affected.[38]

The Stamp Act of 1765, clearly one of the most ill-conceived and ultimately significant Parlimentary blunders in the dealings with the colonies, aroused violent protest. When rumors of the tax reached New York the triumvirate drafted petitions to be sent by the assembly to Parliament and the King. Reaction to the act pointed up striking differences, however, between two members of the triumvirate. William Smith, devoted to the British Empire, proposed there be a parliament for North America with a lower house of delegates elected from each colonial assembly and a council chosen by the King who would serve for life. All requisitions for aid would be sent to this parliament but except in matters of taxation the British Parliament would retain all legislative power. He further proposed a governor general for the colonies. Smith sent his plan to London but to no avail.[39]

John Morin Scott's response on the other hand was far more belligerent. He was said to be the author of a vehement article which appeared in the *New York Gazette,* June 1765, signed "Freeman." A merchant advised the governor that the author "must be a Presbyterian by the tone of the performance," such was their reputation for pugnacity. The article states:

> If, then the interest of the mother country and her colonies cannot be made to coincide, if the same constitution may not take place in both; if the welfare of the mother country necessarily requires a sacrifice of the most natural rights of the colonies—their right of making their own laws, and disposing of their own property, by representatives of their own choosing—if such is really the case between Great Britain and her colonies, *then the connexion between them ought to cease; and, sooner or later, it must inevitably come.*[40]

A Stamp Act Congress with delegates from each colony convened in New York from October 7 to 24. Among New York's representatives were Presbyterian stalwarts, Philip and Robert R. Livingston. A declaration on rights and grievances was passed and sent to the King. At the end of October merchants at a meeting in Burns Tavern resolved not to import any English goods until the Stamp Act was repealed.[41]

Many favored violence to prevent the sale of stamps rather than memorials and petitions. The merchant selected as stamp collector resigned in fear for his life. The first stamps arrived in New York harbor, October 22 and were placed in the fort for safe keeping. A mob gathered and threatened to riot. William Smith, Jr., acted as negotiator between the acting governor, Cadwallader Colden, and the mob. The stamps were turned over to the mayor and deposited in City Hall, and it was during this crisis that Smith was nicknamed "Patriotic Billy."[42]

The rioting was performed largely by unenfranchised mechanics but engineered by more prosperous men such as John Lamb, a liquor dealer, Isaac Sears, a privateer, and Alexander McDougall, a merchant.

McDougall, Presbyterian and a former privateer was probably responsible for securing a large group of sailors to demonstrate.[43] This "radical" group came to be known as the Sons of Liberty or Liberty boys but were referred to by the royalists as the "Presbyterian junto."[44]

The rigor of colonial opposition resulted in the repeal of the Stamp Act, on March 18, 1766.[45] When the news reached New York there was a tremendous celebration with shops, except taverns, closed. Smith and Scott drafted an address of thanksgiving to the King.[46] The Sons of Liberty erected a Liberty pole in the Commons (the first).[47] The Synod of New York and Philadelphia called on the Presbyterians to offer thanksgiving for the repeal and "to fear God," "to honor your king," and pay a due submission to his august parliament."[48]

The Townsend Acts, new tariffs, and efforts to have the colonists pay for the billeting of the British troops needed to protect colonial interests quickly destroyed the short peace. The merchants signed a strict association not to import goods.[49] The following March a committee of inspection of twenty-four, including two Presbyterians (William Neilson and John Broome) was appointed. Times were hard not only because of the boycott but because of the scarcity of money. The Currency Act of 1764 had limited issues of legal tender paper money and by 1768 the old issues had expired. The customs house insisted on coin and there was almost no hard money in the colony.[50]

The election of 1768 for the assembly was a very bitter one between the Presbyterians and the Anglicans. It was the first election in seven years, made necessary because of the passage of the Septennial act in 1743. In this election the radicals supported the De Lancey group. The merchants joined the land owning group, breaking with the Livingstons, and raised the slogan, "No Lawyers in the Assembly." John Morin Scott, whose campaign was managed by Alexander McDougall, was defeated but Philip Livingston was elected and he became speaker of the assembly. Governor Moore dissolved this assembly the following year because it refused to vote supplies for the militia required by the Billeting Act. Livingston suggested a coalition slate but the De Lancey group insisted on three out of the four places so the Whigs put up Philip and Peter Van Brugh Livingston, Theodore Van Wyck and Scott. They urged the defeat of the established church pointing out how the Anglican church attempted to dominate with the Ministry Act, Kings College, the episcopate, and denial of a charter to the Presbyterians. The Livingstons were badly defeated and the De Lanceys became the "popular party." The Triumvirate began publishing *The American Whig*.[51]

The De Lancey controlled assembly passed an act for the provisioning of British troops satisfactory to the Crown. In return the governor agreed to support the currency bill the assembly

Plan of the
CITY OF NEW YORK
1767.

Surveyed by
Bern.ᵈ Ratzen.

SCALE OF FEET
400   1200   2000

Salt Meadows

North River or Hudson

East River or Sound

Part of Long or Nassau Island

Corlaers-Hook

Crown Pt or

Brookland Ferry

Map of New York City, 1767

A City Church   Church of the Patriots

39

Alexander McDougall,
"Son of Liberty"
and Presbyterian Trustee

wanted, issuing £120,000 bills of credit. Handbills addressed "To the Betrayed Inhabitants of the City and Colony of New York," signed a "Son of Liberty" were widely distributed. The author stated that the representatives of the colony had "betrayed the Trust committed to them. This they have done in passing the vote to give the troops a Thousand Pounds. . . . And what makes the Assembly's granting this money more grievous is, that it goes to Support of Troops kept here not to protect but to enslave us." He called for action: "Is this a State to be rested in, when our all is at Stake? No my Countrymen, rouse! Imitate the noble example of the Friends of Liberty in England, who rather than be enslaved, contend for their Right with K—g, Lords, and Commons."[52]

"To the Betrayed Inhabitants" reunited the Sons of Liberty and alienated the masses from support of the De Lancey party. Conflicts between the people and the soldiers took place in various parts of the city. One took place on the grounds of the New Church. The soldiers after great effort cut down the fourth liberty pole (this one had stood for almost three years). McDougall and others petitioned Mayor Hicks for permission to erect another. This was denied by the Common Council (9–6) but one was erected on private owned land near there with money raised by private subscription. It was a symbol of resistance to a standing army.[53]

Two days later McDougall was arrested. He was escorted to the City Hall with a large guard of honor including William Livingston and William Smith's lawyer brothers, John, Thomas, and Joshua. John Morin Scott was his lawyer. He remained in jail for 81 days (February-April 1770). A recent biographer of him says of him:

40

The importance of McDougall's imprisonment to his emerging reputation as a popular leader cannot be exaggerated. Before he went to jail, he had been only one of several local leaders voicing criticism of the provincial assembly's action on the Quartering Act. . . . Imprisonment changed everything. Over night he became a local popular hero, a man who sacrificed his personal freedom to further the libertarian cause.[54]

His stay in jail was hardly a time of undue deprivation. Newspapers reported he entertained 45 gentlemen at dinner one day and 45 ladies at breakfast; that Thomas Smith had sent him 45 pounds of beef, Peter Livingston, 45 bottles of Madeira, and the ministers of the Presbyterian church, 45 pounds of candles. The grand jury indicted him for seditious libel. He was released on a bail of £1000, but never brought to trial for the man who had accused him had died.[55]

McDougall was in jail again in December, 1770 when he refused to answer charges before the assembly. Since he was clerk of the board of trustees of the Presbyterian church the board held their meetings, January 7 and February 4, 1771 in the "New Gaol."[56] McDougall remained in jail until March 4 when the assembly was prorogued with the arrival of a new governor.[57]

The Presbyterians seemed to be on good terms with the new colonial governor. The session of the church passed cordial resolutions on the arrival of Governor William Tryon, July 13, 1771. In 1774 on a visit to Great Britain he promised to do his best to obtain a charter for them. The petitioners drew up a draft of a charter and presented it to the King's attorney but the revolution began before it got out of his hands.[58]

In 1773 disturbances broke out again; this time it was over the Tea Act passed by Parliament, giving the East India Company the right to export tea to the colonies free of all duties but the duty they were permitted to collect in the colonies. The Sons of Liberty, revived, denounced the act. At a mass meeting at City Hall, December 17, an association was formed; the subscribers promised to have nothing to do with the landing of tea and would boycott any who did. "The Committee of Association" of fifteen members was set up to see to the enforcement and to correspond with committees in other colonies and inspectors kept watch on ships suspected of bringing in tea. In January, 1774 the assembly registered a protest against the tea measure and appointed a standing committee of correspondence.[59]

III

After the passage of the Coercive Acts for Massachusetts, closing the port of Boston, May, 1774, the Bostonians appealed for support. The New York committee of correspondence suggested a general congress of the colonies and the establishment of a new committee to bolster Boston's resistance. Now the contest was between the conservative patriots and the Liberty boys (mechanics). Both groups posted notices calling for a meeting to elect a committee. The radicals had suggested a committee of 25 but finally a committee of 51 was nominated. It consisted of 26 loyalists, 7 neutrals, and 18 Whigs, and included such Presbyterians as Philip Livingston, Joseph Hallett, David Van Horne, Peter Van Brugh Livingston, Alexander McDougall, John Broome, and James Jauncey, all of whom were Whigs except Jauncey.

On July 6 the mechanics held a mass meeting in the Fields, presided over by Alexander McDougall. They called for suspension of all trade with England and the election of delegates to the Continental Congress by a "Convention of the Colony," because many of the mechanics did not have the franchise. They put up a slate of five delegates for the Continental Congress: Isaac Low, James Duane, Philip Livingston, Alexander McDougall, and John Morin Scott. The committee of 51 rejected this slate and on July 28 John Alsop and John Jay were elected in place of McDougall and Scott, leaving Livingston the only Presbyterian delegate.[60]

John Adams, on his way to the Continental Congress in Philadelphia stopped in New York, August 20, and had conferences with such prominent Presbyterians as the Smiths, the Livingstons, McDougall, Scott, and Jeremiah Platt. On Sunday he attended services at the Wall Street church and heard Dr. Rodgers preach in the morning and Mr. Treat in the afternoon. He noted that both clergymen were good speakers and preached without notes. Adams said that Peter Van Brugh Livingston ("an old Man, extremely staunch in the Cause, and very Sensible") had described the union formed by the Episcopalians against them and that the Presbyterians had never been able to obtain a charter for their burying ground or the ground on which their church stood. McDougall he described as "a very sensible Man, and an open one. He has none of the mean Cunning which disgraces so many of my Countrymen." He drove with McDougall three miles out of town to have breakfast Monday with the Scotts at their country home. He described it as follows:

> Mr. Scott, his lady and Daughter, and her husband Mr. Litchfield were dressed to receive Us. We satt in a fine Airy Entry, till called into a front room to breakfast. A more elegant Breakfast, I never saw— rich Plat—a very large Silver Coffee Pott, a very large Silver Tea Pott—Napkins of the very finest Materials, and toast and bread and butter in great Perfection. After breakfast, a Plate of beautiful Peaches, another of Pairs, and another of Plumbs and a Muskmellon were placed on the Table.
>
> Mr. Scott, Mr. William Smith and Mr. William Livingston, are the Triumvirate, who figured away in younger Life, against the Church of England—who wrote the independent Reflector, the Watch Tower, and other Papers. They are all of them Children of Yale College. Scott and Livingston are said to be lazy. Smith improves every Moment of his Time. Livingston is lately removed into N. Jersey, and is one of the Delegates of that Province.

Mr. Scott is an eminent lawyer. . . . He is said to be one of the readyest Speakers on the Continent.[61]

The Continental Congress met from September 5 to October 26, 1774 in Carpenter's Hall in Philadelphia. It adopted a Declaration of Rights and Grievances, an Address to the King and one to the people of Great Britain. Of most importance, however, was an Association, an agreement to "pursue a rigid policy of nonintercourse with Great Britain until the grievances complained of should be redressed." Just before the adjournment it issued a call for another meeting in May, 1775 if their demands were not met.[62]

In New York, in November, a committee of sixty was set up to enforce the Association, replacing the committee of 51. In addition to the Presbyterians already on the committee, there were added John Lasher, John White, and Jeremiah Platt, communicants of the Wall Street church.

The provincial assembly, meeting in January, 1775, refused to approve the actions of the Continental Congress or elect delegates to the Second Continental Congress. The committee of sixty took the initiative and suggested a provincial convention to do so. It met in New York City on April 20 and chose delegates to the Congress. The day after the provincial convention adjourned news of the battle of Lexington reached the city. Now, as the historian, George Bancroft notes, "churchmen as well as Presbyterians took up arms."[63]

For days the city was ruled by a mob. The situation proved more than the committee of sixty could handle. A new committee of one hundred was set up. Elected by the freemen and freeholders, it ran the government and put the city in a state of defense, with McDougall responsible for the defense. At least nine of the committee of 100 were prominent Presbyterians (Hallett, Thomas Smith, John and Samuel Broome, John Lasher, John White, Peter Van Brugh Livingston, McDougall and Scott). A motion by Scott, seconded by McDougall, providing for an association which would "engage, by all the ties of religion, honor, and love of country, to submit to the Colonial Congress, to withdraw support from British troops, and at the risk of lives and fortunes to repel every attempt at enforcing taxation by Parliament" was adopted. On April 29 this was presented to the public at the Merchant Coffee House. Thomas, John and Joshua Smith signed at once and McDougall went to William Smith to determine why he had not signed. His answer was that as a member of the Council he felt he could do more good if he remained in the good graces of the governor. The committee of 100 brought order, rigidly enforced the Association and prepared for war.[64]

The New England delegation to the Second Continental Congress was escorted into New York by a grenadier company, led by John Lasher. According to the Tory historian, the delegation was greeted by "the Presbyterian faction and republic party in New York (among which were the two Presbyterian parsons, Rogers and Treat) ... Alexander McDougal, John Morin Scott, Philip Livingston, Peter Van Brugh Livingston, John Jay, James Duane, Isaac Low, William Smith, Thomas Smith, Joshua Hett Smith, Peter R. Livingston, David Van Horne, Donald Campbell, John Van Cortlandt, Isaac Sears, etc.[65]

In June William Smith wrote to Colonel Lewis Morris at the Congress proposing a conciliatory message to the King. First he criticized the action of the First Congress in denying whole legislative authority to Great Britain. He proposed:

> The grand Enquiry therefore should be for a Plan, which discerning her Folly in contending for what she does not really want and cannot execute—and ours in exciting her jealousies, of what she need not fear from our Regard to our own interest, may give Peace and Safety to the whole Empire.

First one should "in the most explicit Manner shew your Loyalty to the King—your Affection to Great Britain, and your abhorrence of a Separation." Lament the present "Calamities so Destructive in both Countries." Declare willingness "to contribute to the exigencies of the Nation" and send delegates from the assemblies to a general convention.[66]

The trustees of the Presbyterian Church had spent so much time on political matters that many meetings had to be adjourned for lack of quorum. Their last recorded meeting was held January 4, 1775. They discussed the debts owed various people and the sending of the delegates to the meeting of the Synod.[67]

The Synod met, May 17, 1775, in Philadelphia a few blocks from where the Second Continental Congress was assembled. A pastoral letter to the churches was composed by John Witherspoon of Princeton University, John Rodgers and David Caldwell of North Carolina, urging Presbyterians to be loyal to the British King. It further urged support of the Continental Congress and stated that if war came the church people should receive it in a "spirit of Humanity and mercy." They continued: "That man will fight most bravely, who never fights till it is necessary, and who ceases to fight as soon as the necessary is over."[68]

The governor dissolved New York's provincial assembly in April, 1775, and in May the voters elected an extra-legal provincial congress, whose first presiding officer was Peter Van Brugh Livingston. Five of the twenty-two delegates from New York City were members of the Wall Street church. This first congress recommended that the Continental Congress appoint Ebenezer Hazard (Presbyterian) as postmaster of New York City which was done. It was difficult to keep a quorum in the provincial congress as many of them were also members of the committee of 100 (the former met in the day time and the latter at night). It was decided therefore to elect a committee of safety of eight to act in the name of the congress (three of them were Presbyterians). The second provincial congress (December 1775 to May 1776) also used the committee of safety which was dominated by Scott and McDougall.[69]

Governor Tryon, who had returned from England in June, 1775, took refuge on a British warship in the harbor. William Smith, a member of the Council, was rowed out to the ship to attend council meetings. Ever the conciliator, he tried to bring a compromise between the British and the patriots, the result being that neither side really trusted him; the British claimed he was leaking information to the Continental Congress and the loyalists, remembering his earlier protests against parliamentary taxation, did not accept him.[70]

IV

November 24, 1775, in accordance with the resolution of Presbytery, was held as a day of fasting and prayer "on account of the melancholy situation of our public affairs." A sermon was preached in the New Church in the morning and in the Wall Street church in the afternoon. The annual collection for the poor was taken.

Many Presbyterians were leaving the city and the last session meeting was held on December 11, 1775. Dr. Rodgers took his family to Greenfield, Connecticut but returned in February 1776 to Greenwich Village as chaplain to General Heath's army from April to November. He held church services in the village all summer.[71]

The Smiths also decided to leave the city. William Smith had sent his library and household goods to his home in Haverstraw and on March 29, 1776 he with four of his children departed by boat for his country home. It was described as a "square, white, two story clapboard house." "The eight large fireplaces were unadorned, built for maximum warmth rather than stylist design. The adzed beams were pinned together with wooden pegs, and they responded in sympathy to the squeak of the wide board floors as Smith paced off his restless indecision." Thomas with his seven children lived near him; Joshua with his two children lived with one of the brothers or in one of the farmhouses. One of their sisters, married to a Scottish colonel, had a house not far distant.

At first it was very quiet there. The whole family drove seven miles inland to attend an English Presbyterian church at the Kakiat cross road. But William Smith soon became restless; writing his journal and letters were not enough to occupy him. He was put on the list of suspected persons by a committee of the third provincial congress (May 14–June 30, 1776). He wrote them a letter explaining that he was "retired" and thought that as a member of the council he should take no part in the unrest of the times. When British ships moved into Haverstraw Bay and harassed the countryside he could watch the activities on the river with a spy glass from his porch. After the death of his daughter,

Elizabeth, he and his family left Haverstraw to visit the Livingston Manor. Later he was parolled there by the provincial congress; it was not exactly confining, however, since the manor consisted of 200,000 acres.[72]

The third New York congress passed a resolution calling for the establishment of a new government stating that the right to form a new government ought to be in the people, thus on May 27 anticipating the step to be taken in Philadelphia some weeks later.

The Declaration of Independence by the Continental Congress was read in the Commons in New York City on July 9 on order and in the presence of General Washington and before a contingent of continental troops. After the reading a mob gathered at Bowling Green and pulled the statue of George III from its pedestal.[73]

General William Howe arrived in New York early in the summer with a large contingent of British troops that far outnumbered the continental forces. He defeated Washington in the Battle of Long Island on August 27, 1776. A strategy conference was held at the home of Philip Livingston on Brooklyn Heights at which Brigadier General John Morin Scott was the only one who protested moving the troops from Long Island to Manhattan. Alexander McDougall, whose regiment had been placed under the continental army in May and had been made a Brigadier General August 9, was placed in charge of the embarkation at Brooklyn Ferry. His job was to draw regiments out of the trenches as boats became available. Not a man was lost.[74]

The British landed in Manhattan on Sunday, September 15, 1776 and the continental army retreated to Harlem (nine miles out of the city) where they were later defeated and Washington retreated to White Plains. By November 16 all of Manhattan was in the hands of the British. The population had fallen to 5,000 but was soon augmented by the influx of loyalists from other parts of the country. Shortly after the retreat of General Washington to Harlem a great fire destroyed one-eighth of the city. Trinity Church and the Presbyterian parsonage were destroyed but the Presbyterian churches were saved. However, during the British occupation the Wall Street church was turned into a barracks and the Brick church was used as a hospital.[75]

Although the city was in the hands of the British and loyalists, the provincial government was controlled by the patriots at their capital at Kingston. John Morin Scott, wounded in the battle at White Plains in October, decided he would be of more use in politics and withdrew from the army in May 1777. He was a leader in the new state government. Advised by William Smith, he was prominent in the drafting of the new state constitution. Dr. Rodgers was chaplain of the constitutional convention and also of the council of safety. Scott was a member of the council of safety from 1777 to 1780. He was secretary of state, 1777–79, a state senator 1777–82, and a delegate to the Continental Congress, 1779–85.[76]

William Smith refused to take an oath to the new state government when summoned in June, 1777 by the council of safety. He declared he was bound by the oath of fidelity to Great Britain. In August, 1778 he returned to New York City and May 4, 1779 was appointed chief justice. The city was under military control however and the civilian courts were not open. Thus he never really served. In April, 1780 he was appointed by Governor Robertson to the advisory Governor's Council, composed mainly of military men. In March, 1782 he suggested the establishment of a civilian government but most of the council were opposed.

He and Joseph Hallet, a merchant, tried unsuccessfully to revive Presbyterianism in the city. Smith tried to get the Hessian convalescents removed from Brick church but the British superintendent of hospitals insisted he needed the facilities. He hoped to persuade Dr. Rodgers to return to preach but that was unlikely. Not only were most of the loyalists opposed to such a possibility but the minister was such a zealous patriot that the British army had put a price on his head. The Tory historian said of him that he was "a person of rigid republican principle, a rebellious, seditious preacher, a man who had given more encouragement to rebellion by his treasonable harangues from the pulpit than any other republican preacher, perhaps on the continent."[77]

William Smith's brother, James (1737–1812) who had received his M.D. degree from the University of Leyden, the Netherlands, and had organized the medical department at King's College, and had served as chairman of the Department of Chemistry and Materia Medica there from 1768 to 1770 had left for England in 1770.[78]

Joshua Hett Smith (1749–1818) who settled in Thomas's house in Haverstraw, the most radical of the brothers when they were in New York City, was active in the Haverstraw militia. His home was visited by Washington, Lafayette and other patriots. It was a relay station for messages from other command posts. On the road from King's ferry to the interior of New Jersey, it commanded a good view of the Hudson and army officers frequented it.

Joshua was a friend of Major General Robert Howe in charge of the new base in the mountains at West Point, thirteen miles from Haverstraw. When Howe was replaced at West Point by General Benedict Arnold in 1780, Joshua became acquainted with the new commander also and acted as a go-between for Arnold and Major John André, aide to a British commander. Joshua had met André in 1775. It was Smith who delivered Arnold's note to André on the British ship in the middle of the Hudson and brought him ashore to meet Arnold. He seems to have been unaware of Arnold's intention to change sides and surrender West Point to the British, and it was at Smith's house that Arnold and André met. Because of that meeting the Haverstraw house would be later designated "Treason House."

André left with plans of the fort in his shoe; he was captured and hanged. Smith was tried on the charge of treason but was acquitted. He was, however, held in the Goshen jail until he escaped to Manhattan in May, 1781. Van Doren says: "Joshua Hett Smith actually deserved his country's thanks for his unintentional share in André's capture and the discovery of Arnold's plot."[79]

Many were the Presbyterians who served in military positions. The Rev. Mr. Treat was chaplain for two militia companies. Major General McDougall was tenth in rank under Washington. After service in the battles of Long Island, Harlem, Germantown, and after Arnold's defection he was put in charge of the Highlands and West Point. He served in the Continental Congress from January to March, 1781 and was elected to the position of Secretary of Marine that year but declined when Congress would not let him retain his army rank and pay.[80] John Broome, John Lasher, and Peter R. Livingston were colonels and John Quackenbos was a captain in the New York militia. Henry Brockholst Livingston (1757–1823), son of William Livingston, was a member of Benedict Arnold's staff in the battle of Saratoga and later an aide to General Philip Schuyler. In 1780 he went to Spain as secretary to John Jay, his brother-in-law. On his return voyage in 1782 he was captured by the British.

Forty more New York Presbyterians served as officers or in the ranks of the continental army, truly a high proportion of the male membership of the churches.[81] Small wonder the American Revolution was called by British author, Horace Walpole, "a Presbyterian rebellion" or as another Britisher expressed it, "Cousin America has run off with a Presbyterian parson."[82]

[1]Session Minutes, 1765–1808, I:1–3 (January 8, 17, 22, 1765); Trustee Minutes, I:158–60 (October 1762). Mr. Treat received a salary of £250 and Mr. Rodgers, £300.

[2]Robert T. Handy, "John Rodgers," *Journal of Presbyterian Historical Society*, XXXIV (June, 1956), no. 2, pp. 69–70; Elwood Starr, "John Rodgers," *DAB*, XVI:75; Miller, *Rodgers*, pp. 12–66.

[3]Letter from Broadus Mitchell (author of biography of Alexander Hamilton), December 13, 1975.

[4]Session Minutes, I:4–5 (February 9, 22), 7 (March 25), 14 (May 7), 17–18 (August 19, 1765); Trustee Minutes, I:175 (January 22, 1765); Miller, *Rodgers*, pp. 73–120.

[5]Trustee Minutes, I:182 (July 26, 1765); Shepherd Knapp, *A History of the Brick Presbyterian Church in the City of New York* (New York, 1909), 36–38.

[6]Session Minutes, I:33 (December 11, 1769).

[7]E. Alfred Jones, *The Old Silver of American Churches* (Letchford, England, MDCCCCXIII), 335–37. The silver is on permanent loan to the Metropolitan Museum of Art.

[8]John Adams, *Diary and Autobiography of John Adams*, edited by L. H. Butterfield (2 vols., New York, 1964), II:131; Session Minutes, I:19–20 (August 25, September 1, 1765); "Sessional Records of Booth Bay, Maine," in *Journal of the Department of History* (Presbyterian Historical Society), XVI, no. 6 (June 1935), 243–48.

[9]Session Minutes, I:18–19, 22 (August 25, 31, October 30, 1765).

[10]*Ibid.*, pp. 15–17 (May 22, June 27, July 25, 1765).

[11]*Ibid.*, pp. 25–27 (June 10, August 26, September 5, November 27, 1768), p. 28 (February 24, 1769).

[12]*Ibid.*, pp. 32–33 (August 24, September 3, 1770).

[13]*Ibid.*, p. 3 (January 17, 1765); Trustee Minutes, I:10 (February 13, 1746/47), p. 183 (September 2, 1765); Knapp, *Brick Church*, pp. 78–79; William Parker Cutler and Julia Perkins Cutler, *Life, Journal and Correspondence of the Rev. Manasseh Cutler, LL.D* (2 vols., Cincinnati, 1888), I:234.

[14]Trustee Minutes, I:185 (February 5, 1766).

[15]Jones, *Colonial Church Silver*, p. 336.

[16]Miller, *Rodgers*, pp. 167–179n; Trustee Minutes, II, 14 (June 12, 1784).

[17]O'Callaghan, ed. *Documentary History*, III:300–307; Corwin, ed. *Ecclesiastical Records*, VI:4046, 4081–3; Stokes, *Iconography*, IV, 705, 763.

[18]New York City, *Minutes of the Common Council*, VII:8–12.

[19]Hall, "The First Presbyterian Church," p. 645; Knapp, *Brick Church*, pp. 17–24, 30, 33; Adams, *Diary and Autobiography*, II:103.

[20]Valentine, *City of New York*, pp. 281–84; Lamb, *City of New York*, I:559; Trustee Minutes, I:218–20 (March 2, 1772).

[21]Virginia Harrington, *The New York Merchant on the Eve of the Revolution* (New York, 1935), 21–25; Adams, *Diary and Autobiography*, II:110.

[22]James Truslow Adams, *Provincial Society* (New York, 1927), 171.

[23]Thomas Jones, *History of New York during the Revolutionary War*, ed. by Edward Floyd De Lancey (2 vols., New York, 1879), I:2–3; see Dorothy Dillon, *The New York Triumvirate*.

[24]John A. Krout, "William Livingston," *DAB*, XI:25–27; Sedgwick, *A Memoir of the Life of William Livingston*, pp. 45–66; George Dangerfield, *Chancellor Robert Livingston of New York, 1746–1815* (New York, 1960), p. 22.

[25]Hamlin, *Legal Education in Colonial New York*, pp. 97, 202; Dunkak, John Morin Scott, pp. 59–61.

[26]Upton, *Loyal Whig*, pp. 23–25; Smith, *History*, I, ix; Richard J. Koke, *Accomplice in Treason: Joshua Hett Smith and the Arnold Conspiracy* (New York, 1973), 17–19; Milton M. Klein, "Rise of New York Bar," in *William and Mary Quarterly*, 1958, pp. 334 ff.; Delafield, "William Smith," p. 418; Richard B. Morris, "William Smith," *DAB*, XVII:357–58.

[27]Dunkak, John Morin Scott, p. 20; Richard B. Morris, "John Morin Scott," *DAB*, XVI:495–96.

[28]Smith, *Historical Memoirs*, pp. 24–28; Klein, "Rise of the New York Bar," p. 351.

[29]Dillon, *New York Triumvirate*, pp. 82–6; Dunkak, John Morin Scott, p. 137.

[30]Charles H. Levermore, "The Whigs of Colonial New York," *American Historical Review*, I, no. 2 (January 1896), 238–51; Jones, *New York in the Revolution*, I:5–6; Bridenbaugh, *Mitre and Sceptre*, 145.

[31]William Livingston, "Of Passive Obedience and Non-Resistance," in *Journal of Presbyterian History*, vol. 52, no. 4 (Winter, 1974), 330–32.

[32]Corwin, ed. *Ecclesiastical Records*, VI, 4084n; Dunkak, Scott, pp. 224–29.

[33]"Minutes of the General Convention of Delegates, 1766–1775," *Journal of Presbyterian History*, vol. 52, no. 4 (Winter, 1974), 339–43; Bridenbaugh, *Mitre and Sceptre*, pp. 271–72; Miller, *Rodgers*, p. 187.

[34]Bridenbaugh, *Mitre and Sceptre*, pp. 278–79; Herbert L. Osgood, "The Society of Dissenters, Founded in New York in 1769," *American Historical Review*, VI (1901), 498–507.

[35]Corwin, ed. *Ecclesiastical Records*, IV:3427–32; Smith, *Historical Memoirs*, I:70; Bridenbaugh, *Mitre and Sceptre*, pp. 330–31.

[36]Levermore, "Whigs of Colonial New York," *AHR*, I:238–39; Smith, *Historical Memoirs*, II:273; Miller, *Rodgers*, p. 206.

[37]John A. Krout, "Philip Livingston," *DAB*, I:316–18.

[38]Levermore, "Whigs of Colonial New York," *AHR*, I:244–46; Alexander Flick, ed. *History of the State of New York* (New York, 1933–37), III:186–88.

[39]Upton, *Loyal Whig*, pp. 51 ff.

[40]Henry B. Dawson, *The Sons of Liberty in New York* (New York, 1859), p. 70; Dunkak, Scott, 182–87.

[41]Harrington, *New York Merchant*, pp. 348–49; Carl Lotus Becker, *The History of Political Parties in the Province of New York* (Madison, Wisconsin, 1960), 26–30.

[42]Upham, *Loyal Whig*, pp. 218, 220; Flick, *Whigs and Tories*, pp. 189–94.

[43]Roger S. Champagne, *Alexander McDougall and the American Revolution* (Schenectady, New York, 1975), 8–9; Daniel D. Haskell, "Alexander McDougall," *DAB*, XII:21–2.

[44]Bancroft, *History of the United States*, IV:9; Dawson, *Sons of Liberty*, pp. 40–1, 105.

[45]Becker, *Political Parties in the Province of New York*, pp. 38–40; Harrington, *New York Merchant*, pp. 326–7.

[46]Flick, ed. *New York State*, III:304–6.

[47]Thomas Wertenbaker, *Father Knickerbocker Rebels* (New York, 1948), 20.

[48]"Resolution of the Synod," *Journal of Presbyterian History*, vol. 52, no. 4 (Winter, 1974), 335–6.

[49]Dillon, *New York Triumvirate*, pp. 102–5; Becker, *Political Parties*, pp. 60–7.

[50]Flick, ed., *New York State*, III:204–6

[51]Levermore, "Whigs in Colonial New York," *AHR*, I:248–50; Dillon, *New York Triumvirate*, pp. 102–5; Smith, *Historical Memoirs*, I:71–2.

[52]Alexander McDougall, "To the Betrayed Inhabitants," in *Journal of Presbyterian History* vol. 52, no. 4, pp. 347–8.

[53]Wertenbaker, *Father Knickerbocker Rebels*, pp. 20–1; New York City, *Minutes of the Common Council*, VII:203–4.

[54]Champagne, *McDougall*, pp. 42–3. Permission of Union College Press.

[55]Jones, *New York during the Revolutionary War*, I:25–8; Dillon, *New York Triumvirate*, pp. 106–23.

⁵⁶Trustee Minutes, I:210 (Jan. 7, Feb. 4, 1771).

⁵⁷Champagne, *McDougall*, pp. 42−3.

⁵⁸Session Minutes, I:45 (August 16, 1771), p. 18 (historical sketch); Miller, *Rodgers*, p. 204.

⁵⁹Flick, ed., *New York State*, III:220−4; Becker, *Political Parties*, pp. 95−109

⁶⁰Bancroft, *History of the United States*, IV:12−13; Barck, *New York City during the War of Independence*, pp. 35ff; Becker, *Political Parties*, p. 112.

⁶¹Adams, *Diary and Autobiography*, II:103, 110. Permission of Atheneum Publishers. (Charles Scribner's Sons).

⁶²Flick, ed., *New York State*, III:245; Edmund Cody Burnett, *The Continental Congress* (New York, 1941), 55−8.

⁶³Bancroft, *History of the United States*, IV:177.

⁶⁴Jones, *New York during the Revolutionary War*, I:43.

⁶⁵*Ibid.*, 45−6.

⁶⁶Smith, *Historical Memoirs*, pp. 228−228c.

⁶⁷Trustee Minutes, I:228 (January 4, 1775).

⁶⁸"A Pastoral Letter," *Journal of Presbyterian History*, 52:4, pp. 378−82; Gillett, *Presbyterian Church*, I:170.

⁶⁹Flick, ed., *New York State*, III:257−65.

⁷⁰Evarts Boutell Greene, *The Revolutionary Generation, 1763−1790* (New York, 1943), 233−34; Barck, *New York City during the War of Independence*, p. 64.

⁷¹Session Minutes, I:60−1 (Nov. 24, 1775); Miller, *Rodgers*, pp. 209, 213.

⁷²Koke, *Joshua Hett Smith*, pp. 22−24; Delafield, "William Smith," p. 424; Smith, *History*, I:xxx. Permission granted by New York Historical Society and by Richard J. Koke.

⁷³Barck, *New York City during the War of Independence*, pp. 39ff; Becker, *Political Parties* pp. 260−5; Flick, ed., *New York State*, III:340−43.

⁷⁴Knapp, *Brick Church*, pp. 67−69; Wertenbaker, *Knickerbocker Rebels*, p. 95.

⁷⁵Knapp, *Brick Church*, p. 69; Barck, *New York City during the War of Independence*, pp. 161−62

⁷⁶Morris, "John Morin Scott," *DAB*, XVI:496; Dillon, *New York Triumvirate*, p. 148.

⁷⁷Upton, *Loyal Whig*, pp. 114−19; Smith, *History*, I:ix; Smith, *Historical Memoirs*, p. 6.

⁷⁸Delafield, "William Smith," p. 278.

⁷⁹Koke, *Joshua Hett Smith*, pp. 31−43; Carl Van Doren, *Secret History of the American Revolution* (New York, 1941), pp. 289−90, 324−38, 352, 428.

⁸⁰Wertenbaker, *Knickerbocker Rebels*, pp. 65−66; Champagne, *McDougall*, pp. 121−28.

⁸¹Knapp, *Brick Church*, pp. 68−69; Francis B. Heitman, *Historical Register of the Continental Army* (Baltimore, 1967), 43−44; R. E. Cushman, "Henry Brockholst Livingston," *DAB*, XI:312.

⁸²Alexander, *Presbytery of New York*, p. 12. James H. Smylie, "Introduction," "Presbyterians and the American Revolution," *Journal of Presbyterian History*, vol. 52, no. 4 (Winter, 1974), 303.

CHAPTER THREE

Restoration and Expansion

A notice appeared in *The New York Packet and American Advertiser:* November 13, 1783:

> The Members of the Presbyterian Congregation are requested, at the desire of some of the late Trustees, to meet at the New Brick Church, this Afternoon at Four o'clock, to provide means for putting their Church in order for Public Worship.[1]

Ever since the King had announced hostilities were at an end in February, Presbyterians had been trickling back into the city while the loyalists prepared to leave. Among those who sailed for England was William Smith, whose family had been connected with the Wall Street church from its founding. He later returned to Canada as Chief Justice from 1785 to 1793.[2]

British troops evacuated the city on November 25, and American troops under General Washington, General Knox, and Governor Clinton marched down from Harlem to witness their departure.[3] The next day Daniel Phoenix (1737–1812), elder, treasurer and trustee of the Presbyterian church welcomed Washington with a patriotic address. Phoenix was also the first city treasurer and held the position of city chamberlain for twenty years.[4]

The State legislature authorized the military council in charge of the Southern District to govern until elections could be held for the Common Council. Broadened slightly, the franchise now included £20 ($50) freeholders, 40s rent payers, and freemen. Even then the proportion of those eligible was less than ten percent; one-third of this number actually voted. Among Presbyterians elected aldermen were John Broome and William Nielson; as assistants, Daniel Phoenix and Abraham Van Gelder. Alexander McDougall was elected to the state senate. He was a state officer in the Society of Cincinnati and the first president of the Bank of New York, organized in 1784. This bank helped create the financial center New York City became, and shortly afterward (1792) the Stock Exchange emerged at 22 Wall Street.[5]

On November 26 the Presbyterians met with their minister, John Rodgers, in Brick Church, less damaged than the Wall Street church, to discuss its repairs. Meanwhile, the vestry of Trinity Church offered use of their chapels on alternate Sundays — St. George, at Beekman and Cliff, and St. Paul. The Presbyterians worshipped there from November, 1783, to June, 1784. At the Congress-recommended Thanksgiving service of December 11, 1783, John Rodgers preached on "The Divine Goodness Displayed in the American Revolution," stating, "Would you reap the fruits of your toils, your losses, and your blood, it is *indispensably necessary* that the federal union of these States be cemented and strengthened — that the honor of the Great Council of the nation be supported, and its salutary measures carried into execution, with unanimity and dispatch, without regard to partial views, or local interests." He sent a copy of the sermon to General Washington.[6]

The city corporation was then petitioned to forgive Brick Church the back rent for the land on which it stood and to reduce the rent from £40 to £21 5s. The Council assented and the church was repaired for £1300 with money raised by subscription. On June 27, 1784, Rodgers preached at the restored church. The pulpit was supported by a single post and crowned with a sounding board. His text — Psalm 122:1, "I was glad when they said unto me, Let us go into the house of the Lord."[7]

The Rev. Manasseh Cutler visited the church on July 8, 1787, and wrote:

Dr. Rogers is certainly the most accomplished gentleman for a clergyman . . . that I have ever been acquainted with. He lives in an elegant style, and entertains company as gently as the first gentlemen in the city. This he may well do, for his salary is 750 pounds a year, and his perquisites upward of 200 more.[8]

At the first session after the peace treaty in 1784, the state legislature passed "An Act to enable all the Religious Denominations in this State to appoint Trustees who shall be a Body Corporate, for the purpose of taking care of the Temporalities of their respective Congregations, and for other Purposes therein mentioned."[9] John Rodgers was chaplain of the legislature at the time Presbyterians were finally permitted to incorporate, a privilege they had wanted for over 60 years. The first congregation to be granted a charter under this act, their seal read, "The First Church in the Commonwealth of New York," with the title of "The Corporation of the First Presbyterian Church in the City of New York."[10]

At a meeting of the male church members in Brick on May 3, 1784, nine trustees were elected, most of whom had served on the board before the congregation's dispersion. The president of the

The Lenox Farm, 1885, located at 71st Street and Madison Avenue, New York City

board was Peter Van Brugh Livingston, member of the first board in 1746.[11] When he left the city in 1786 he was succeeded by Robert Lenox (1759–1839). Born in Kirkcudbright, Scotland, his grandfather had lost the family estate in a card game, so he and his two brothers came to America. He lived with his uncle in Philadelphia, attended school in Burlington, New Jersey, and during the revolutionary war worked as a clerk in an uncle's New York office. He married Rachel, daughter of merchant Nicholas Carmer, and they lived at 59 Broadway with their twelve children. Robert became a commission merchant in a flourishing trade with the West Indies, invested heavily in real estate, and was one of the wealthiest men in New York City. He was the initial president of Mutual Insurance company (the first fire insurance company in the city), an alderman (1795–1797; 1800–1802), president of St. Andrew's Society (1798–1814), and one of the founders of Lying In Hospital.[12]

54

The clerk of the board of trustees was Henry Brockholst Livingston, son of William Livingston, first governor of New Jersey. After the war he studied law and was admitted to the New York bar in 1783, with his office at 12 Wall Street. In 1802 he became a judge of the New York Supreme Court, then associate justice of the United States Supreme Court from 1807–1823. His country estate, Bellevue, was on the East River from 24th to 28th Street. The clerk was not a member of the board, but later Livingston served as trustee from 1809 to 1818 (president from 1813 to 1818).[13]

The treasurer (also not a board member) was John Broome, who served until 1810; he was also an elder. Trained as a lawyer, his older brother, Samuel, encouraged him to enter commercial life. They owned the prosperous importing business Broome, Platt and Co. During the war John served in the army as Lieutenant Colonel and outfitted privateers from Connecticut. He was active in politics; an alderman for several terms, state assemblyman from 1800–1802, state senator in 1804, then lieutenant governor for three terms. President of the New York Insurance Company, the first one of its kind in the state, he was also one of the founders of Tammany Hall and supported Aaron Burr in the election of 1800. His brother was also a member of the board of trustees, on which merchants predominated. The board had three committees: finance, repairs and burial ground, and the charity school.[14]

At their first meeting the trustees decided that a subscription be "set on foot" to be paid annually for three years, since the revenues of the church had been completely exhausted. And the sexton, John Brown, was to continue as collector of pew rents. They agreed that proprietors or those who had rented pews before the war could file their claims with the treasurer and pay rent in arrears in 1776. Pew owners could furnish them as they wished, not with locks, however. If a pew owner died, his widow might have the pew if she wished. If not, the sons had preference according to seniority, the same applying to daughters in the absence of sons. If no applicants, the pew was declared vacant, those unclaimed sold at public auction.[15]

The demand for pews was so great that the Wall Street church was repaired — cheaper than building a new one. The interior had been completely destroyed, only the walls and roof remaining. Two small lots adjoining the church were bought to enlarge the cemetery. The church was opened for services on June 19, 1785, to a capacity crowd. Rodgers preached from Psalm 24: 1, 2:

> The earth is the Lord's, and the fulness thereof; the world, and they that dwell therein; for he has founded it upon the seas, and established it upon the floods.[16]

In 1784, the congregation had decided they could maintain

only one minister, John Rodgers. But Joseph Treat wanted to return, insisting that he was senior minister unless the presbytery dissolved the relationship. A committee was appointed to present the situation to presbytery. Treat had appeared before presbytery in May of that year to acknowledge his sin of intemperate drinking, and professing his sorrow, had been restored to his former standing. He had not, however, returned to the city, nor did the New York City Presbyterians want him back. Finally at a presbytery meeting in Elizabethtown on October 20, 1784, his pastoral relationship with the First Presbyterian congregation was dissolved "apprehending it for the peace and health of said Congregation and for his own comfort." Presbytery advised the congregation to pay Treat full arrears from February 1 to August 1, 1776, although he had taken his family from the city early in the spring and had done little after that.[17]

With the opening of the Wall Street church, a second minister was selected. James Wilson (1751–1799) from Scotland was installed as co-pastor with John Rodgers on August 10, 1785, at a salary of £400. In a visit to New York in 1787 Cutler also assessed Wilson's preaching·

> He uses no notes, nor are they much used by any clergyman in the city. His subject was on Envy. He was sufficiently methodical, but is not a good preacher, nor was there anything extraordinary in his sermon. It was rather a harangue; but he was very catholic in his sentiments.[18]

The internal organization of the Wall Street-Brick church was in full working order again. There were two co-pastors, nine trustees, ten elders, publicly nominated in both congregations for three successive Sabbath days and, if no objections, "accordingly set apart to that office." The same procedure was used in the selection of the four deacons. Several men served both as trustee and elder although some, notably Robert Lenox, thought the practice unwise. Yet he and others continued to serve on the two boards at the same time.[19]

The Presbyterian manse had been burnt during the fire of 1776, and the lot originally willed to the church by John Scott and Peter Van Brugh Livingston was sold for £440. In April, 1786, Trinity Church, noting that the Presbyterian congregations had no convenient homes for their pastors, deeded lots to the Wall Street-Brick church and to the Scotch Presbyterian church on Cedar Street. Income from the lot on the north side of Robinson Street near Great George Street (now nos. 3 & 5 Park Place) was to provide a supplement for the minister's salary. Rodgers, who lived at 7 Nassau Street, refused the supplement, informing the trustees that his present salary was a "decent competency" for his family, and that he wished to assist in relieving the "incumbered situation of the congregation" by appropriating any profits which might arise from the property to pay off the church debt.[20]

Seal of the First Presbyterian Church, 1784

II

Changes in national church organization and the U.S. government were being made at the same time. The Wall Street-Brick church was part of the Presbytery of New York, established in 1738. The Synod of New York and Philadelphia met in Philadelphia in May of 1786 to adopt the following resolution:

> The Synod, considering the number and extent of the churches under their care, and the inconvenience of the present mode of government by one Synod, resolved: that Synod will establish, out of its own body, three or more subordinate Synods, out of which shall be composed a General Assembly, Synod or council, agreeably to a system hereafter to be adopted.

John Rodgers was appointed committee chairman to prepare a plan, the proposal for sixteen presbyteries was also adopted, but the rest of the report was referred to the presbyteries for discussion.[21]

The reports of the 1786 committee on the Revision of the Book of Government and Discipline, chaired by John Witherspoon, aroused considerable controversy in the next two synod meetings. In 1787 the synod adopted the Westminster Confession of Faith, as a standard, merely eliminating the chapter which subordinated the church to civil government, thus conforming with separation of church and state. It also adopted the Larger and Shorter Catechisms of the Westminster Assembly with slight revision. The following year a revised Directory of Worship was also approved, the documents bound into one volume as the "Standard of Our Doctrine, Government, Discipline and Worship."

In May of 1788 the synod also adopted the "Constitution of the Presbyterian Church in the United States of America," thereby settling an ongoing battle between those for the Scottish system and the New England group for Congregationalism. The former won. A General Assembly (the Church of Scotland called theirs a council) headed the structure of four synods and sixteen presby-

Samuel Miller, Pastor, 1793—1813   Robert Lenox (1759—1839)

teries. Each body represented clergy and laity equally, yet the presbytery continued to control ordination of ministers. At the time there were 419 congregations, 177 pastors, and approximately 15,000 communicants.[22]

The first General Assembly met in Philadelphia on May 21, 1789. John Witherspoon preached the opening sermon, and John Rodgers was elected modrator. Further, the psalmody issue that had split the Wall Street church in mid-century was still thriving. A Kentucky representative deplored the fact that the synod had fallen into "pernicious error" by substituting the Watts' version of the psalms for the Rouse versification. This first Assembly also sent a "very felicitous letter" to President George Washington, inaugurated the month before at New York City Hall, practically adjoining the Wall Street church. It was the first religious group to extend congratulations to the new President.[23]

The Wall Street-Brick church was in the Synod of New York and New Jersey, comprising four presbyteries: Suffolk (Long Island), Dutchess County, New Brunswick, New Jersey and the New York. It was the only church in New York City belonging to the latter presbytery.[24]

Since the Rev. James Wilson had left for South Carolina in 1788 because of a lung complaint, the church had only one pastor for two years.[25] Finally on December 2, 1789, the Rev. John McKnight (1754—1823) was installed. He was also appointed professor of Moral Philosophy at Columbia University in 1795, serving as moderator of the General Assembly that same year. His health weakened, probably because of his heavy duties, and a third pastor was needed. The trustees were distressed at "the present destitute state of the Church with respect to Evening Service and likewise at certain times on the Sabbath due to the indisposition of Dr. McKnight."[26]

Impressed by the young Samuel Miller (1769–1850) the few times he had preached, the congregation invited him to become a co-pastor in 1793. His grandfather had come from Scotland and settled in Boston, where he had married a descendant of John Alden. His father John served as a minister in Dover, Delaware. Samuel had no regular schooling until he entered the Academy of Philadelphia (University of Pennsylvania) in 1788. Yet so well trained by his father, he was graduated with "first honors" at the end of one year and then returned to study theology with his father.

Miller's diary paints a graphic picture of presbytery proceedings at the end of the 18th century. In 1791 he presented himself to the Presbytery of Lewes. After an examination into "my experimental acquaintance with religion, and my views in seeking the holy ministry, the Presbytery declared themselves full satisfied, and agreed unanimously to receive me on trial." He was examined in Latin and Greek and preached a homily. Two months later he was examined again in rhetoric and logic, then in the fall sternly tested in his college studies, theology, and sermon delivery. He was finally licensed to preach. There was some hesitation, though, since he had questioned the clause in the Westminster Confession concerning marriage to any close relative of a deceased wife.

At the same time the New York church called him, Miller was invited to replace his deceased father in Dover. He accepted the Wall Street-Brick offer, was dismissed by the Presbytery of Lewes, and joined the Presbytery of New York. Again examined in all his major subjects, he also delivered a sermon and a Latin exegesis. Finally on June 5, 1793, with Rodgers presiding, McKnight preaching, and McWhorter of Newark delivering the charge, Miller was ordained.

A month after his installation he preached his first published sermon on the fourth of July before the Tammany Society, "Christianity the Grand Source and the Surest Basis of Political Liberty." Urging education for children at public expense and questioning the validity of domestic slavery, he also sent a copy to President Washington.[27]

The growing population of New York City encouraged Presbyterians to build another church in the northeastern section. Col. Henry Rutgers, prominent in the Reformed Dutch church and a wealthy brewery owner, deeded land for the church at the corner of Rutgers and Henry Streets. Member of both the trustees and session in 1799, he also imported a bell from England for the new building.[28]

The congregation decided to raise the needed money by a subscription. When the church (a wood structure, 40 by 60 feet) was opened for services on May 13, 1798, all pews were taken immediately, yielding £501 to be added to £2618 from the subscription, toward a total cost of £4542. In 1805 a call was issued to Philip Milledoler, pastor of the third Presbyterian church in Philadelphia. Although part of the collegiate ministry of the three churches, he was exclusively related to the new church, with a salary of $1800. (Note: by this time the church had begun to use dollars instead of pounds.)[29]

As early as 1793 the possibility of separating the Wall Street and Brick churches had arisen because of legal limits on the amount of property a church could own. That year, however, the legislature raised the limit to twice the previous figure, and the concern for separation faded. Raised again in 1802, the new church voted unanimously against separation.

Yet the collegiate ministry remained unsatisfactory. Miller especially urged separation, pointing out that a collegiate ministry was not necessary since the single ministry at a new church on Cedar Street was working very well with John B. Romeyn as Pastor. This church (today the Fifth Avenue Presbyterian Church) was an outgrowth of a mission Sunday School from the Wall Street church, the corner stone laid by Rodgers in 1807 — his last public act.[30]

In December 1808 the session resolved that the congregations vote on separation. On April 6 the Rutgers church vote was unanimous in favor, but the resolution to separate the Wall Street and Brick churches failed by one vote. But with the resignation of McKnight to accept a call in Philadelphia, the separation finally passed on April 12 by a vote of 92 to 77. Already authorized by the state legislature on March 1, the presbytery approved it on April 26. Each building, with its various lots, became the sole property of each church, including burial lots outside the church yards to be divided.[31]

The annuity of £100 from the lots on Robinson Street was given to the senior minister, in this case, Rodgers. He was to continue as minister of both the Wall Street (officially named "The First Presbyterian Church in Wall Street") and Brick Church. Since his health was failing, he had asked to be relieved from preaching an evening service in 1803, and he began taking his sermon notes into the pulpit since his memory was also poor. Rodgers preached his last sermon at Brick Church in September, 1809, and died on May 9, 1811.[32]

As a preacher, Rodgers was not an intellectual but as his co-pastor said, "a moral and religious genius." Likened to the old Puritan divines of the seventeenth century, he spent much time in prayer and fasting, and was particularly systematic in pastoral labor — "preaching, catechising, visiting." Also active in public life, he was trustee of the College of New Jersey, first vice-chancellor of the New York Board of Regents, vice-president of the Society for Promoting Useful Knowledge, a trustee both of the City Dispensary and the Manumission Society of New York.

An organization of special interest to him was the Society for the Relief of Distressed Debtors (he was the first president), a charity founded on January 26, 1787 to supplement rations in debtor's prisons. The group also tried to secure the release of "deserving" prisoners and worked for legislation. They succeeded in getting the Ten Pound Law passed in 1789, which limited imprisonment for those owing less than £10 to 30 days, as well as a law prohibiting sale or use of liquor in prison in 1791. As president of the society, he had solicited a contribution from President Washington and received 20 guineas. And when yellow fever struck the prisons, Rodgers urged the opening of New York Dispensary in 1791.

His funeral was held at Brick Church, and the pulpits of all Presbyterian churches in the city were hung in mourning for six weeks. He was survived by a son, John R. B. Rodgers, an M.D. who later became professor of the Medical Department at Columbia College and served as elder in First Church from 1799 until his death in 1833.[33]

III

At a joint meeting of the session, trustees, and deacons on November 22, 1809, three master builders reported that the walls and roof of the church were unsafe without extensive repairs. Based on this report, it was decided that the existing building be torn down and another erected. While this was done, the congregation worshipped in the Église du St. Esprit on Pine Street.[34]

The new church was opened for services in August 1811, with Miller preaching to a "very crowded audience." Built of brownstone with front pillars ornamented in demi-relief with Corinthian capitals, it measured 97' by 68' and had a very handsome spire. The yard was enclosed with a black iron railing. The inside front of the church formed a semi-circle, with pews along both sides and the pulpit and desk in the center. A large pew to the right of the pulpit and desk was for the session.

The cost of the church was approximately $44,000, made a charge on the pew owners on the ground floor. There were 102 pews, the assessment ranging from $120 to $750 and the annual rental from $15 to $25. Certificates of ownership were awarded to each owner, and one pew was reserved for the pastor and one for the elderly poor. The gallery pews were rented yearly to the highest bidder. Shortly after the church was opened, all pews had been sold and most of the money paid. The trustees decided that since this money had covered the building costs, the church should be used only for the worship of God and for meetings of church judicatories.[35]

The church was presented with new silver utensils by members

William Wirt Phillips, Pastor, 1826–1865. He led the move to Fifth Avenue.

of the board of trustees. In addition to the silver from the early eighteenth century, they had also received a tankard made by Daniel van Voorhis (c.1787) and a silver basin for baptism (1791). In 1812 two large tankards to flank the communion table were presented by William Edgar (an Irishman in the fur trade) and Daniel McCormick. The latter, an auctioneer and director of the Bank of New York, also presented a silver basin and silver plate. Samuel Campbell, a book seller, presented another plate, with two large offering plates given by Robert Lenox and Brockholst Livingston. David Gelston, for many years collector of the port of New York and member of the state legislature, presented a pair of beakers. The value of the plate was cited by weight at $1.25 an ounce; the church silver was declared to be worth $483.[36]

Samuel Miller resigned as pastor of the Wall Street church in 1813 to become Professor of Ecclesiastical History and Church Government at Princeton, the seminary's second full-time teacher.[37] He was succeeded at First Church by Philip Melancthom Whelpley (1794–1824), who had initially wanted to be a foreign missionary but whose health hindered him. Installed April 25, 1815, he was a brilliant preacher.[38]

In 1816 some dissatisfaction surfaced over Whelpley (symptomatic of the dissension in the Presbyterian church which would lead to a split 20 years later), who tended to favor the Hopkinsian doctrines, or the "new Divinity." Samuel Hopkins (1721–1803), a Yale graduate and friend of Jonathan Edwards, rejected Calvin's idea of original sin and believed that "sin was in the sinning." Identifying self-love with sin, he suggested that true virtue consisted of disinterested benevolence. "Regeneration" was the work of the Holy Spirit, and conversion consisted only of the "volitional exercises of the regeneration." He also was much interested in contemporary humanitarian movements; temperance, abolition, and missions.

The pastor of Brick Church also flirted with Hopkins' ideas, but most other New York City Presbyterian ministers denounced them as heretical. Whelpley wrote to some members of the church of his confidence "that the spirit of Christ is still among us," and concerning the doctrines he preached, he did not expect unanimous reception. Rather, they should "search the Scriptures daily, to see if these things are so." A session committee composed of Peter Ludlow and John P. Mumford questioned pew owners and found that only 22 of 177 were dissatisfied with Whelpley. When the Hopkinsian doctrines were brought to the attention of the General Assembly in 1817, it merely urged that the churches act together in spite of differing views.[39]

The church was closed from July to November 1822, and the congregation dispersed "by an afflicting Dispensation of Divine Providence in visiting this City with a Malignant Fever," the last of the severe yellow fever epidemics which the city had suffered periodically. Yet this is not surprising since New York hosted a great number of foreign ships and had no adequate facilities for waste disposal. The Common Council claimed the epidemic had originated in the vicinity of the Trinity church burial ground.[40]

Whelpley died suddenly in July, 1824, and was buried in the minister's vault in the church. The trustees voted to give the widow $1000 in five payments and his mother $500.[41] The church was without a pastor for 16 months but finally on January 19, 1826, William Wirt Phillips (1796–1865) was installed.

Born in Florida, New York, graduated from Union College and Reformed Dutch Seminary, as a student Phillips changed from the Reformed Dutch Church to Presbyterian. Ordained in April, 1818, he was installed as pastor of the Pearl Street Presbyterian Church in New York City. The next month he married Frances Paine Symington.[42]

Phillips came to a church in financial trouble, due in part to the purchase of extra lots in the west rear so that in 1822 the permanent debt amounted to $11,200 and carried at a 7% interest rate. The budget for that year was:

Expenses		Revenue	
Pastor's salary	2500	Rental of pews	1200
Chorister	150	Plate Collections	350
Sexton	200	Burial fees	120
Interest	752	School	30
Insurance, Fuel, etc.	195		
School	130		
Cont.	73		
	$4000		$1700

A trustees' attempt to raise money through a five year subscription, or pledge, was unsuccessful and in an effort to alleviate the deficit the pew valuations were increased and pew owners were charged a higher annual rent.[43]

When on March 31, 1823, the City Common Council adopted an ordinance prohibiting the digging of graves and interment in vaults south of Canal Street, another severe blow was struck at the church's financial resources. Burial lots at North and Forsyth and vaults in the church yard were "sold" on a 999 year lease for $250 each. In 1803 the church rented a hearse and driver (with a black cloth for the horse) for funerals. The burial fee in a vault was $15 and use of the church's velvet pall was an additional $5.

The trustees protested the ordinance (as did Grace, St. George's, Trinity, and Brick churches also) arguing that the church had used the burial ground surrounding the Wall Street church through power granted in the act of incorporation of 1784. Against the Council contention that "the practice of interring the dead within the thickly inhabited portion of our City . . . is injurious to the living," the contrary testimony of several doctors was submitted. They claimed there was no danger to the health of the living from nearby cemeteries. (Many of the medical authorities were members of the Wall Street church.) The ordinance was upheld, however. Accordingly, the church had to pay a fine for his burial in a vault when Philip Whelpley died in 1824.[44]

In 1829 the church found a new source of revenue: the lecture room was torn down and a new building erected, the lower floor divided into offices to be rented to lawyers and the second floor to be used as a lecture room. They had no trouble renting the offices. When they proposed erecting another building, the neighbors at 2 Wall Street protested that they were being deprived of the light and air which the church yard had permitted. The trustees then responded that occupants of those buildings be charged an annual fee for the privilege of the light and air. Consequently, opposition to the new building ceased.[45]

In September 1834, the church was destroyed by fire. The interior was completely gutted, but some items like Dr. Rodgers' pulpit Bible were saved and put in custody of Robert Lenox. The fire insurance companies offered rewards for clues establishing whether the fire had been accident or arson, since no chimney in the neighborhood had been on fire, nor had there been any fire in the church building during the previous three months. (In that crowded section of town, fire was a great hazard and the fire department commissioner urged sextons to ring the church bells whenever one occurred.)

The insurance companies promptly paid the full amount ($20,000), and the church was rebuilt with the same walls. The congregation returned to their own church just one year later. The only major change in the architecture was the substitution of a pointed steeple in place of the tower and dome. Everything seemed propitious. The building pleased the congregation, and the lecture room was the best in the city. And over it were commodious and well arranged rooms for the schools.[46]

IV

In the Calvinist tradition, Presbyterians emphasized education, and one of the important committees of the board of trustees was the charity school. Taking steps to establish the first school, John Rodgers learned of Captain Jeremiah Owen's legacy. There was not enough money, though, so the interest was used to pay for private education of poor youths by Presbyterian schoolmasters. Captain Neilson added to the Owen fund in 1762, and in 1787 a subscription in the church raised £516.[47]

The church received other legacies and had acquired £912 by 1788. The new school was opened on May 1, 1789, for the children of indigent parents. In 1790 a lot on Nassau between Liberty and Cedar was bought and a two-story brick building erected. The school was on the first floor. The master, who received a salary of £100 a year in addition to the use of the building, had living quarters on the second floor. The committee on the charity school interviewed prospective scholars or their families and visited the school once a year to inquire of the student's proficiency. Every year the ministers preached sermons about the school, and collections were taken for support and clothing for needy children. Members of the congregation left money for the school in their wills, and one such donor was alleged to be Elder William Irving (father of Washington Irving).[48]

New York State had a grandiose scheme for public education, and established the University of New York in 1784, headed by a Board of Regents, of which Rodgers was vice-chancellor. At first King's College, later renamed Columbia College, was under the board but soon withdrew. Practically nothing was done to develop a plan for a system of public schools, though there was a nonsectarian, free school for colored boys (1787), one for colored girls (1792), and also one at the almshouse. The only other schools were charities of the churches and private academies.[49] Finally in 1795, the legislature passed an act appropriating £20,000 a year for five years, to be distributed to localities on a quota basis determined by the number of qualified voters, with the locality required to provide an amount equal to one-half the state grant. The trustees of the Wall Street-Brick church petitioned the legislature to make provision for grants to religious organizations with charity schools:

> Impressed with the important Truth that Knowledge is the basis of Virtue, that Virtue on which the Security of our Privileges as a free

People rests, and to render this Knowledge as diffusive as possible, they instituted a Charity School in the year 1789 for the benefit of the Children of their Poor. . . . Nearly 200 poor children have been taught to read write, and the use of figures, Psalmody, and the principles of the Christian Religion.[50]

The legislature did grant £1888 to New York City, of which the Presbyterians received £100 to £200 a year. The church, however, was spending over £500 each year on the school's 50 students. The Episcopalians had 86 charity scholars; Reformed Dutch, 72; the Scotch Presbyterians, 30; Methodists, 30; and the German Lutherans, 20. The largest charity school was the African Free School with 110 students.[51]

In 1805 a group of publicly spirited men, among them Brockholst Livingston, William Edgar, and Samuel Miller, organized the Free School Society (later changed to Public School Society) and in 1809 opened a school on Chatham Street on a lot given by Col. Henry Rutgers. The school was for children whose parents had no religious affiliation and were not, therefore, reached by the charity schools. The purpose of the Free School Society was "to inculcate moral and religious truth without sectarian bias but would also teach what was essentially requisite for the due management of the ordinary business of life."[52]

In 1812 a general school law passed by the New York legislature provided permanent state subsidy for elementary instruction. In New York City the trustees of First Church protested that most of the school fund allotted to the city went to the Free School Society. Because of the protest, the 1813 legislature specified that the appropriation be divided among the Free School Society, the Orphan Asylum Society, Society of Economical School, the African Free School, and the incorporated religious societies with charity schools.

With government aid came government checks, so that in 1823 the superintendent of common schools asked for the statistics of the last eleven years. First Church reported:

average number of scholars	13 per year
total expense for tuition	$1750
received from school fund	$ 354.54

The number of pupils continued to decline as more students went to the "public" schools. The church, therefore, paid tuition for the children and gave up its charity school in 1831.[53]

Unlike the charity school, authorities had little to do with the Sunday Schools, maintained by citizens (probably following the example of Robert Raikes in England, who established the first such school in 1780, nicknamed "the ragged school.") The New York Sunday School Union was formed in February, 1816, to encourage the establishment of Sabbath schools to teach poor children who worked during the week to read, mainly religious tracts.

The first reference to Sabbath schools in the trustee minutes occurred when permission was given in 1817 for the pastor to preach a sermon and receive an offering supporting the Sunday School Society. In the same year separate schools for boys and girls were held at the Wall Street church. Children of the church members, who received their religious instruction at home, were not involved, and, reluctantly, the trustees allowed the Sabbath school children to use "the open space in the gallery of the church at the head of the stairs provided they are not allowed to enter body of the church."[54]

Sabbath schools were criticized for using "that day" for the secular purpose of teaching children to read. The Wall Street church complained that the boys soiled the furniture and defaced the paint in the new lecture room. In 1831 the teachers of the Sabbath schools, dissatisfied with their quarters, left the Wall Street church, but a "Congregational Sunday School" remained. Children of the church members began to attend, and the church assumed more interest in Sunday Schools. The Presbytery of New York, in 1829, directed that the Westminster catechism be used as curriculum.[55]

Presbyterians were quite involved in the intellectual life of the city, and literary clubs were especially popular. The Friendly Society, in which both Dr. Edward Miller and his brother, the minister Samuel, were active, helped publish *The New-York Magazine* from 1790 to 1797. Samuel Miller was author of a two-volume work, *Brief Retrospect of the Eighteenth Century* (1803), a highly regarded, scholarly work which included new literary tendencies in Europe.

The Calliopean Society was founded by William Irving (1766–1821), whose father was prominent in the Presbyterian Church, serving as elder from 1784–1799 and as trustee from 1800–1803. He had his son, Washington Irving (1783–1859), the first American literary man with an international reputation, baptized into the Presbyterian faith in January 1784, when they were worshipping in St. George's chapel. Washington Irving became an Episcopalian and described his father's pastor as "Old Dr. Rodgers, with his buzz wig, silver-mounted cane, well-polished shoes, and shoebuckles."[56]

Rodgers was involved in the Society for the Promoting of Useful Knowledge, of which he became vice-president. The New-York Society Library, founded in 1754 by several Presbyterians and revived in 1788, might be called the first Congressional library, since its headquarters were in City Hall—where the first Congress under the Constitution had met. In 1795 the library acquired its own building. The reading rooms were open to the public but supported by subscriptions ($15), with annual dues of

$1.25. In 1804 the New-York Historical Society was founded with Brockholst Livingston as its first vice-president. One of the popular amusements in the early Federal period was the Waxwork Exhibition at 74 Water Street. And among its prominent figures was John Rodgers.[57]

V

The First Church's register of deaths, 1786–1802, is a fair index of the city's health. At the end of each year a statistical study was made of the sex, age, and causes of death. As expected, the number of yearly male deaths exceeded female, and the number of children's deaths under one year was about one-third of the total. Considering the size of the congregation, the number of deaths per year does seem large, about 100 a year. Although not always indicated, the chief causes were consumption, small pox, and measles. Some of the causes listed have little meaning today. For example, Alexander McDougall died of "nervous decay" at the age of 53.

Apparently there were several fever epidemics from 1794 to 1798 (other sources indicate it was yellow fever). In the latter year, over 200 deaths are listed in the church register, the largest number in the 20 to 40 age group. In 1794 Governor De Witt Clinton appointed Robert Lenox and his father-in-law, Nicholas Carmer, to investigate health conditions. Subsequently, Lenox and John Broome were responsible for purchasing Bellevue to establish a hospital for contagious diseases.[58]

The poor in the church were the responsibility of the deacons, who took care of them with money collected at the communion tables and at special services at which a "charity sermon" was preached each year. In a sermon of 1791, Rodgers developed the stewardship doctrine, "God appointed the rich as 'Almoners' to distribute their abundance among the poor." Besides giving money to the needy, the deacons also bought and stored "chords" of oak wood for their use. Most of the time the amount collected in First Church for the poor (usually about $500) exceeded the needs. At this same time (c.1820), it was estimated that one-tenth of the population received public relief, that 1500 paupers frequented the almshouse, and 300-400 were imprisoned in the city penitentiary.

The church was often called upon to take up collections for the poor in the city. For example, in 1821 with an uncommonly severe winter, the mayor asked the churches to collect for the purchase of wood for the needy. The church raised $167.15 for this crisis. It also contributed to the New York Society for the Prevention of Pauperism, whose purpose was to ascertain the causes of "mendicity" and seek remedies for it.[59]

It was commonly assumed that poverty was the result of laziness, intemperance, or gambling. Therefore, heavy emphasis

December

Lellan — 4th Alexander, Son of Alexr. McLellan, Butcher, Died of a Fit. Aged 2 Months.

heroy. — 8th George, Son of George Macheroy, Sawyer, Aged 6 Weeks

haw — 14th John Shaw, Taylor, Died of a Consumption Aged 40 Years.

rson. — 16th Israel, Son of William Pierson, Carman, Died of a Fit — Aged 18 Years

rson — 21st Hannah, Wife of William Pierson, Carman; Died in Child Bed. Aged 37 Years.

nson — 24th Mary, Wife of Simon Simonson, Shoe Maker; of a Consumption, Aged 27 Years & 9 Months.

Died 1787	No.
Males	62
Females	56
Total	118

Ages	No.
Under 1	36
Between 1 & 2	22
2 " 5	4
5 " 10	1
10 " 20	3
20 " 30	15
30 " 40	12
40 " 50	11
50 " 60	6
60 " 70	6
70 " 80	2
80 " 90	"
Total	118

Diseases	No.
Consumption	19
Decay	6
Apoplexy	2
Inflamation of the Lungs	1
Billous Fever	2
Small Pox	10
Fever	19
Obstruction	1
Black Jaundice	1
Quinsey	1
Asthma	1
Pleurisy	1
Drowned	1
Suddenly	1
Dropsy	1
Flux	1
Dysentery	2
Fits	4
Purging & Vomiting	7
Purging	7
Child Bed	4
Lunacy	1
Shrew	2
Teething	1
Mortification	1
Putrid Fever	1
Cholera Morbus	1
Not Specified	19
In all.	118

Presbyterian Church registry of deaths, New York City, 1787

was placed on character reformation. In 1822 the New York Presbytery created a plan to supply the destitute "with the stated Ordinances of the Gospel," and First Church was assigned the first ward.[60] Even the volunteer interdenominational organizations supported by annual contributions from various churches saw themselves as instruments for correcting social blight. The purpose of the New York Bible Society (1809) initially was to provide Bibles for Sunday Schools and members of the armed forces. Yet small pamphlets, or tracts, seemed to suit the needs of the poor better, so the New York Religious Tract Society (1812–1826) was organized, with Philip Milledoler as president. Visitors, predominantly women, called on the poor with a different tract each month. They reported on their living conditions, as well as the fact that many could not read the tracts presented to them, thus increasing consciousness of the society's ills and needs. The work was expanded and became the New York City Mission and Tract Society (1866–1913).[61]

Seamen were another focus of charitable concern, not wholly surprising since by 1800 New York was the nation's busiest port, as well as the distribution center to the country's interior. Two leaders in its development were Presbyterian elders John Broome and Robert Lenox. Both were active in the Chamber of Commerce; Broome served as president from 1785 to 1790 and Lenox from 1827 to 1839. The Chamber was interested not only in preserving the port's reputation for quality products but also in the people who frequented the port, primarily the sailors. Yearly contributions were taken in First Church for the Society for Promoting the Gospel among the Seamen in the Port of New York (1818) and the American Seaman's Friend Society (1826). The former grew out of the prayer meetings held in the lower part of the city by the pastor and some members of Brick Church. These meetings attracted so many sailors that in the 1820's the Mariner's church, the first church exclusively for seamen, was dedicated (1828). The American Seaman's Friend Society was the first national organization for sailors, and published *Sailor's Magazine*, sent out chaplains, and attempted to find decent housing for sailors when ashore.[62]

The seaman's organization most closely associated with First Church was Sailors' Snug Harbor. In 1790 Captain Robert Richard Randall paid £5000 for 21 acres of land running from Waverly Place to Ninth Street, including the north side of Washington Square. When he died in 1801, he directed that this land be used as a farm to be a "snug harbor" for old seamen. They would, he thought, be able to live from the produce of the farm. The will, thought to have been drawn up by Alexander Hamilton, specified the trustees by title: two officers of the Marine Society, rector of Trinity, and minister of the Presbyterian church. By 1830, when the will was finally settled, the land had become so valuable that it was divided into lots and leased.[63]

By the end of the eighteenth century, American churches had interests beyond the immediate parish. Their horizons extended to the western frontiers of New York, Ohio and other parts of the Northwest Territory. A new enthusiasm for revival, the "Second Awakening," produced concern for evangelism of the American Indian and even an interest in missionaries to foreign countries. For the most part such activity was carried on by interdenominational, voluntary associations formed to meet a specific need.

The Wall Street–Brick Church first became involved in such missionary activity in August 1792 when a collection was taken for missionaries to the frontier, probably in response to a 1791 General Assembly resolution calling for the presbyteries to make a concerted effort to forward yearly mission offerings to the General Treasurer. In 1796 that offering from Wall Street–Brick totaled £38.

Also in 1796, the New York Missionary Society was formed by Presbyterian, Baptist and Reformed Dutch churches for the purpose of promoting mission efforts to the American Indians, with John Rodgers as its first president. In 1805, McKnight was given a leave from his church responsibilities to undertake work by the New York Society with the Tuscarora Indians.[64]

To avoid competition in the formation of new churches on the western frontier of the nation, Presbyterians and Congregationalists created a Plan of Union (1801) that combined their efforts, with each denomination giving recognition and affiliation to ministers of each others's church. The General Assembly established a standing committee on missions in 1802. Elected annually, it appointed and paid the missionaries ($33 a month). Then in 1826, at a meeting in the Brick Church, Dutch, Scottish and Congregational churches formed the American Home Missionary Society. Similar patterns were followed in foreign mission efforts, and annual collections were taken in First Church to support the various boards, often including money to benefit a particular missionary family.[65]

The Plan of Union did not sit easy with the more conservative, orthodox Presbyterians who believed church structure was doctrinal in nature. The influence of congregationalism through contact on the frontier was not to their liking, although in truth the Presbyterian influence proved to be the stronger of the two. The General Assembly meeting in 1837 was completely dominated by conservatives who abrogated the Plan of Union and withdrew from the inter-denominational mission boards to form the Presbyterian Board of Foreign Missions (whose first president was Samuel Miller) and the Presbyterian Board of Domestic Missions. That same Assembly ousted four synods in western New York and Ohio, and the following year the expelled group formed their own General Assembly. Presbyterians were thus divided into "Old School" (the expellers) and "New School" (the expelled).

Although orthodoxy was the visible issue, the church's stand on the abolition of slavery was also involved and certainly a contributing factor in the schism. Those ousted had a high proportion of abolitionists in their number; those who remained did not, including all southern Presbyterian churches. Yet half of the Presbyterian churches in New York City (including First) remained in the Old School fold.[66]

In 1790 New York was the northern state with the largest slave population: approximately 20,000. In New York City the first federal census listed 3,470 Negroes, of which 2,369 were slaves, in a white population of 29,666. Nineteen percent of whites owned slaves, usually only one or two as household servants, however. John Jay's attempt to include in the state constitution of 1777 a prohibition of slavery had failed. He was later instrumental in the forming of the New York Manumission Society in 1785. John Rodgers was on the board of trustees, and Samuel Miller was a member until his move to Princeton.[67]

The united Presbyterian churches in New York had long included blacks—both free and slave—in the membership. The list of those being admitted to the communion table for the first time designated them as, "free negro" or "servant of" a specific member. In all probability the latter denoted a slave. Until 1832 the list of communicants designated blacks, usually as "colored." In that year the First Colored Church was organized and admitted to New York Presbytery with 24 members.[68] An annual offering was taken at First Church for the benefit of the new church.

VII

The period from the end of the Revolutionary War to 1840 was one of growth for Presbyterianism. In 1789 there were four synods, 16 presbyteries and 419 congregations, with 15,000 communicants. By 1837 there were 23 synods, 135 presbyteries, 2865 churches and 220,557 members. During this period several theological seminaries were established, beginning with Princeton in 1812 and extending into the mid-west with Lane Seminary (1829) in Cincinnati and McCormick in Chicago (1836). At the beginning of this period, the Presbyterian church had just formed its national organization, the General Assembly, but by 1837 there were two general assemblies using the same name—one the Old School and the other the New School. And they were almost equal in number of churches and members. For example, the Old School General Assembly comprised 1375 churches with 102,000 members.

The same rate of growth occurred in New York City, with an increase in church numbers as well as their movement north. At the beginning of this period, only the so-called "united Presbyterian church" (Wall Street–Brick–Rutgers) existed, belonging to the General Assembly. Two also belonged the the Associated Reform Synod (Scottish), which joined the General Assembly in 1821. By 1837 there were about 28 Presbyterian churches in Manhattan; half of them including the Wall Street, Brick, and Rutgers churches, remained in the Old School Assembly.[69] In the eighteenth century, the Wall Street church had been a leader in the evangelistic movement of the New Side group, while they turned conservative in the nineteenth. Yet earlier in that century one of their ministers, the Rev. Mr. Whelpley, advocated the "New Divinity." Probably one reason for their remaining in the Old School was their close connection with Princeton Seminary, and another was the most prominent layman and financial contributor in the church Robert Lenox, an arch-conservative in religious matters. He may have influenced the attitude of Princeton Theological Seminary as well since he was a member of the board of trustees from 1829 to 1839, also in charge of their investments.

Thus, the church in the early part of the nineteenth century was ecumenical in its activities. It united with other Protestant churches in forming Bible and tract societies and even cooperated with Congregationalists in missionary projects. By the end of the period the emphasis was on denominationalism. Over two-thirds of the benevolence budget of 1841 ($10,000) consisted of gifts to these boards and to Princeton Theological Seminary.

Although First Church had extended its horizons beyond its own congregation, still it seemed to have little interest in the humanitarian movements of the day, with the exception of some gifts to Negro organizations.[70] Similarly, very little interest was taken in local problems. It still remained largely church-oriented and parochial.

[1]*The New York Packet and American Advertiser* (New York Historical Society), November 13, 1783.

[2]William Smith, *Historical Memoirs*, p. 9.

[3]Pomerantz, *New York. An American City*, pp. 15–21.

[4]Thomas E. Smith, *The City of New York in the Year of Washington's Inauguration, 1789* (New York, 1889) 57; Charles Norris, *Makers of New York* (Philadelphia, 1895), 194.

[5]Pomerantz, *New York. An American City*, pp. 26–8, 69–70, 183, 185; Barck, *New York during the War of Independence*, p. 220; New York City, *Minutes of the Common Council of the City of New York* (19 vols. to 1831) I, February, 1784.

[6]Guy Klett, "Made in Philadelphia. Two Constitutions," *Presbyterian Life*, March 31, 1956 p. 24; Session Minutes, I:18–19 (1807 sketch), p. 63 (July 15, 1784).

[7]Knapp, *Brick Church*, pp. 74–6; Trustee Minutes, II:16–17 (July 30, 1784), 21 June 6, 1785).

[8]Cutler, *Manasseh Cutler*, I:237. Dr. Rodgers' salary was £500.

[9]Trustee Minutes, II:1–7.

[10]Thomas Smith, *New York, 1789*, p. 149; Handy, "John Rodgers," in *Journal of Presbyterian Historical Society*, XXXIV (June, 1956), 73.

[11]Trustee Minutes, II:11

[12]James Lenox Banks, *Genealogical Notes concerning the Banks and Allied Families* (New York, 1938), 54–60; David Baillie Morrison, *Two Hundredth Anniversary, 1756–1956, of Saint Andrew's Society of the State of New York*, 160–1.

[13]R. E. Cushman, "Henry Brockholst Livingston," *DAB*, XI:312.

[14]Trustee Minutes, II:36–7; Norris, *Makers of New York*, p. 235; Pomerantz, *New York. American City*, p. 127.

[15]Trustee Minutes, II:12–14 (May 5, June 12, 1784), 34 (May 2, 1787)

[16]*Ibid.*, 15–6 (June 3, July 20, 1784); Session Minutes, I, 70 (September 1, 1785)

[17]Session Minutes, I:63–7 (July 15, December 4, 1784); Trustee Minutes, II:16 July 20, 1784), 22 (September 12, 27, 1785); Miller, *Rodgers*, pp. 243–8.

[18]Trustee Minutes, II:17 (Nov. 22, 1784), 19 (Mar. 31, 1785); Session Minutes, I:68–71 (June 2, Sept. 1, 1785); Cutler, *Manasseh Cutler*, I:296.

[19]Session Minutes, I:105 (Mar. 4, 1790); Trustee Minutes, II:42 (Dec. 28, 1812), 43 (Apr. 5, 1813). His resolution that it was improper for a trustee to be a member of the session was defeated.

[20]Trustee Minutes, II:26–7 (Apr. 27, 1786), 35 (July 13, 1787), 40–1 (letter of Dr. Rodgers, Sept. 3, 1787), 43 (June 18, 1788), pp. 63–4 (Nov. 30, 1789).

[21]Charles Hodge, *The Constitutional History of the Presbyterian Church of the United States of America* (2 vols., Philadelphia, 1840), I:497–8; Loetscher, *History of Presbyterians*, p. 62.

[22]Ahlstrom, *Religious History*, pp. 375–6; Briggs, *American Presbyterianism*, pp. 364–73; Sweet, *Story of Religion*, pp. 178–9.

[23]Gillett, *Presbyterian Church*, I:268–72, 291.

[24]*Presbyterian Magazine*, I (May, 1851); Alexander, *Presbytery of New York*, p. 31.

[25]Session Minutes, I:84 (Feb. 28, 1788).

[26]*Ibid.*, pp. 97, 98, 101 (July 4, Oct. 1, Dec. 3, 1789); Thomas Smith, *New York, 1789*, pp. 151–2.

[27]Trustee Minutes, II:81–2 (July 18, Sept. 12, 1792); Samuel Miller, *Life of Samuel Miller (2 vols., Philadelphia, 1869), I:33*, 53–62, 87–90; Session Minutes, I:118, 119, 124 (Aug. 23, 29, 30, 1792).

[28]Trustee Minutes, II:111, 112 (June 23, 29, 1795), 116 (Dec. 19, 1796), 117, 121 (Feb. 23, Mar. 27, Apr. 10, June 13, 1797) p. 131 (May 24, 1799), pp. 136–7 (Jan. 1, 1800); Miller, *Rodgers*, p. 269.

[29]Session Minutes, I:219, 222 (Aug. 29, Nov. 19, 28, 1805); Trustee Minutes, II:192 (Aug. 5, 1805).

[30]Trustee Minutes, II:147 (Jan. 6, 1802), 214 (Jan. 10, 1809); Miller, *Rodgers*, p. 271; Knapp, *Brick Church*, pp. 103–4; Session Minutes, II:1–2; Duffield, "Annals," VI:24.

[31]Trustee Minutes, III: pp. 7–9, 17 (Mar. 1, May 23, 1809).

[32]Session Minutes, II:15 (June 13, 1811); Trustee Minutes, III:37 (May 8, 1811); Miller, *Rodgers*, p. 279.

[33]Smith, *New York, 1789*, pp. 15, 149; Miller, *Life*, I:82, 93−4; Raymond Mohl, *Poverty in New York* (New York, 1971), pp. 125−7.

[34]Trustee Minutes, III:24−33 (Aug. 15, 1811).

[35]*Ibid.*, III:285 (picture of interior of church), III:33−5 (June 10, 28, 1811), 36−7 (Jan. 6, 1812); Stokes, *Iconography*, V:1518.

[36]Trustee Minutes, III:78 (Feb. 21, 1792); Session Minutes, I:111 (March 3, 1791); Charles H. Olmstead, "The Old Communion Silver," *The Church Tower*, January 1924, pp. 25−26; E. Alfred Jones, *Old Silver of American Churches*, pp. 337−8.

[37]Trustee Minutes, III:45−46 (June 24, 1813); Session Minutes, II:.31 (Sept. 22, 1813). Dr. Miller had served as moderator of the General Assembly in 1806.

[38]Trustee Minutes, III:57 (March 27, 1816); Session Minutes, II, 35 (March 18, 1814), 37−8 (May 11, 1815).

[39]Session Minutes, II:61−3 (Jan. 22, Feb. 3, 1817); Misc. correspondence of Mr. Whelpley in archives of First Presbyterian church; Gillett, *Presbyterian Church*, II:219−24.

[40]Session Minutes, II:126 (Nov. 21, 1822); New York City, *Common Council Minutes*, IV:576.

[41]Trustee Minutes, III:113, 115 (July 18, Aug. 8, 1824); Session Minutes, II:142−3 (Sept. 2, 1824).

[42]Session Minutes, II:157 (Jan. 25, 1826); Trustee Minutes, III:134, 136 (Dec. 11, 26, 1825).

[43]Trustee Minutes, III, 82−4, 88−9 (May 4, 10, 1822) 151−2 (June 12, 1826), 158−60 (Jan. 8, 16, 22, 1827), 163−6 (May 14, July 2, 11, Sept. 28, 1827), pp. 172−3, 181−5 (Jan. 31, July 1, 1828).

[44]*Ibid.*, II:19 (Mar. 8, 1785), p. 28 (June 27, 1786), pp. 47−8 (July 25, 1788), pp. 164-5 (July 13, 1803), III:92−3 (Feb. 7, Apr. 18, 1823), 118−9 (Feb. 3, 1825); New York City, *Common Council Minutes*, I:378, V:558; XII:811; XIII;25, XIV:576−634.

[45]Trustee Minutes, III:203 (Sept. 1, 1829), 221−2 (Jan. 21, 1831), pp. 259−60, 264, 266 (Jan. 29, 30, June 27, 1824).

[46]*Ibid.*, III:135 (Dec. 16, 1825), 136 (Jan. 21, 1826), 267, 269, 270 (Sept. 15, 18, Nov. 11, 1834), p. 284 (Sept. 5, 1835), 290 (Mar. 30, 1836); Stokes, *Iconography*, V:1729, III:615.

[47]Savage, *Presbyterian Churches in New York City*, pp. 54−5; Miller, *Rodgers*, p. 264; Trustee Minutes, II:47 (July 18, 1788).

[48]Trustee Minutes, II:56−6 (Mar. 15, 24, 1789), 67, 70 (Jan. 23, Feb. 1, 1790), 74−5 (Oct. 25, 1791), 77, 81 (Jan. 24, Oct. 26, 1792), 207 (Nov. 9, 1807), 213 (Nov. 25, 28, 1808), III:47 (Nov. 17, 1813); Session Minutes, II:23−24.

[49]Pomerantz, *New York: American City*, pp. 417, 422.

[50]Trustee Minutes, II:103−4 (March 3, 1795).

[51]*Ibid.*, II:125 (Dec. 25, 1797), 178 (July 7, 1804), 189 (July 16, 1805); New York City, *Council Minutes*, II:404, 586; Knapp, *Brick Church*, p. 88.

[52]Krout, *Completion of Independence*, p. 180; Cubberley, *Public Education*, pp. 67, 87; William Oland Bourne, *History of the Public School Society of New York* (New York, 1879), pp. 2, 110; Trustee Minutes, II:109−10 (May 4, 1795).

[53]Knapp, *Brick Church*, pp. 203−5; Trustee Minutes, II:212 (Aug. 25, 1808), III:19 (Jan. 17, Apr. 2, 1810), p. 40 (May 15, 1812), 105 (May 5, 1823), 229 (May 20, 1831).

[54]Trustee Minutes, III:65−6 (Jan. 15, Mar. 27, 1817), 88−89 (May 11, 1822); Savage, *Presbyterian Churches in New York City*, pp. 54, 59−60.

[55]Trustee Minutes, II:214−5, 217 (June 2, 12, 1830), p. 223 (Jan. 21, 1831) Alexander, *Presbytery of New York*, p. 80; Banks, *Genealogical Notes*, p. 57.

[56]Ahlstrom, *Religious History*, p. 397; Miller, *Life*, I:102, 110, 119; Washington Irving, *Life and Letters of Washington Irving* (edited by Pierre M. Irving, Philadelphia, 1871), IV:313.

[57]Pomerantz, *New York. American City*, p. 432; Thomas Smith, *New York, 1789*, pp. 149, 185.

[58]First Presbyterian Church, Register of Deaths, 1786−1802. Mohl, *Poverty in New York*, p. 127.

[59]Mohl, *Poverty in New York*, p. 160; Session Minutes, I:72−3 (Dec. 22, 1785), 81−83 (Nov. 29, 1787), II:113 (Jan. 19, 1821), p. 136 (Feb. 26, 1824); Still, *Urban America*, pp. 69−70.

[60]Session Minutes, II:125−7 (July 3, Nov. 28, 1822).

[61]Miller, *People are the City*, pp. 40−42..

[62]*Ibid*., pp. 4; Pomerantz, *New York. American City*, pp. 90, 127, 159, 283; Thomas Smith, *New York, 1789*, p. 103; Knapp, *Brick Church*, 240; Trustee Minutes, III:135 (Dec. 16, 1825), 271 (Jan. 9, 1835), 290 (Mar. 30, 1836).

[63]Arthur Bartlett Maurice, *Fifth Avenue* (New York, 1918), 2−3; *The New York Times*, July 28, 1972.

[64]Savage, *Presbyterian Churches in New York City*, pp. 21−22; Gillett, *Presbyterian Church*, I:295, 436; Session Minutes, I:119 (Aug. 30, 1792), 137 (May 2, 1796).

[65]Ahlstrom, *Religious History*, p. 456; Loetscher, *Presbyterians*, p. 69; Gillett, *Presbyterian Church*, I:436−443.

[66]Ahlstrom, *Religious History*, pp. 409, 467−9; Gillett, *Presbyterian Church*, II:553; Hudson, *Religion in America*, pp. 164−5.

[67]S. Miller, *Life*, I:90; Greene, *Revolutionary Generation*, pp. 322−3; Thomas Smith, *New York, 1789*, pp. 122−3; Rosenwaike, *Population History*, p. 24.

[68]Gillett, *Presbyterian Church*, II:257; Alexander, *Presbytery of New York*, p. 45; Session Minutes, II:136 (Feb. 26, 1824).

[69]Gillett, *Presbyterian Chuurch*, II:201, 233, 236, 243, 453−4; Ahlstrom, *Religious History*, pp. 659−61; Loetscher, *Presbyterians*, pp. 78−84; Sweet, *Religion in America*, pp. 292−3.

[70]*Session Minutes*, II:239 (Jan. 11, 1841).

CHAPTER FOUR

Old First
on Fifth Avenue

The opening of the Erie Canal in 1825 secured New York City's position as the leading port of the nation, and the harbor was a "forest of masts" as trade flourished. By 1840, the population of Manhattan had passed the 300,000 mark and that of Brooklyn was nearing 50,000. Packet ships ran regularly to England, the West Indies and the coastal cities on the nation's eastern seaboard. In 1836 2,285 ships entered the harbor, and in 1838 the first steam propelled ocean vessel (The Great Western) made its appearance, albeit steam vessels had long been plying the Hudson River.

In the rebuilding after the great fire of 1834, lower Manhattan became almost entirely commercial. Wall Street was a place of banks, insurance companies, import and export houses and book shops. The New York Custom House replaced the old City Hall and across from it was a new Merchants Exchange, completed in 1841, a gathering place for the business leaders. Trinity Church maintained its stance at the head of the street, however, having been rebuilt for the third time in the 1840's. But the residential population was rapidly disappearing from the area.

The development of mass transit (omnibuses operating on a fixed schedule) in the 1830's provided the population with greater mobility. In 1837 the Harlem railroad ran cars from Harlem to the Bowery, carrying 25,000 passengers each day (but none on Sundays) bringing residents from uptown homes to business establishments at the lower end of the city. The residential area of the city kept moving steadily northward.[1]

It is hardly surprising that such changes meant a declining membership for the Wall Street Presbyterian Church (288 communicants and a lack of sufficient male members to fill necessary church offices) and decreasing financial support. The church had accumulated a large debt as the result of having to rebuild after the fire of 1834 and the financial panic of 1837 that affected many of the members.

The change to a commercial area, however, substantially increased the land value, and sale of the parcel on which the church was situated had the possibility of providing sufficient monies for the purchase of a new site and the construction of a building at a location uptown. On November 3, 1840 a special meeting of the session and trustees appointed a committee to investigate such a possibility.[2]   The Presbytery of New York had suggested consideration of a move to both the Wall Street and Brick Churches since there was no Presbyterian church north of Canal Street. Brick had decided not to relocate. It had a membership of over seven hundred and was in a better location, one not as yet so commercial.[3] A new City Hall had been built in what had been the Commons, now called City Hall Park. The Fresh Water pond or Collect had been drained and that area built up. Opposite City Hall on the west side of Broadway was the new Astor House, a magnificent six story hotel. The Park Theatre had been reopened in 1821. North of City Hall Park, on the corner of Broadway and Prince Street, there was Niblo's Gardens, a fashionable resort with fireworks and entertainment in the summer. On the south side of City Hall Park, near Brick Church, was Park Row where the cheap newspapers were printed. Broadway was still the leading street; in 1836 it had been extended to 23rd Street. It was lined with handsome shops, many with large plate glass fronts.[4] First Church, however, saw the wisdom of the Presbytery's suggestion and decided to explore possibilities of relocating on Fifth Avenue in a growing residential area.

Greenwich Village had become a part of the city in 1821, and after the yellow fever epidemic of 1823 the Council had banned interments in the potters field in the village. Washington Square parade ground was enclosed by a fence and made a public park in 1827. Union Theological Seminary, begun in 1836, was located at 9 University Place, and in the following year the University of the City of New York (New York University) constructed their gray Gothic towers on the east side of Washington Square. A row of houses was built on the north side of the Square in 1833 and the Georgian house of William C. Rhinelander was erected on the northwest corner, 1839–40. The area from Fifth to Fourth Avenues between the Square and 10th Street, Randall's old farm, had been bequeathed by its owner to Sailors Snug Harbor. North of that was the farm of Henry Brevoort whose farm house was on the west side of Fourth Avenue. When the city attempted to cut through 11th Street Brevoort came out with his blunderbuss and successfully prevented the effort. Two Episcopal church congregations moved to the area from lower Broadway, Ascension, in 1841, and Grace, in 1846.[5]

The Wall Street property, however, presented a series of difficulties to the ambitions of First Church. The legality of its sale

78

was questionable since the first property bought had been conveyed to the Moderator of the General Assembly of the Church of Scotland and then deeded back to the congregation (August 15, 1732) but with the proviso that its future use was only to be for religious worship by the Presbyterians of New York. It was concluded, however, that this restriction, which would have made sale to commercial interests impossible, had been removed with the chartering and incorporation of the church in 1784.[6]

The church's legal counsel, S. A. Foot, advised that it was next necessary to hold a meeting of the congregation to approve possible sale and relocation. There was a question as to who was eligible to vote at such a meeting, and it was agreed that only "male members of the congregation who during the preceding twelve months shall have been stated attendants on divine worship and have contributed to its support," were eligible. The congregation met on March 14, 1842 (37 present) and by unanimous vote passed a resolution to the effect that the financial situation of the church made moving essential if the trustees could find no other means of relieving the church from its present difficulties. A committee was selected to find a specific, suitable site.[7]

The church first sold the land on Forsyth and Houston which it had received at the time of the separation of the three churches in 1809. Rutgers church took one lot as it had used up its own burial ground; it was sold to them for $2,880. Another lot was sold to the Second Associate Presbyterian Church for $4,000. These sales were approved by the Court of the Chancery, meeting at the City Hall, June 30, 1842. But because the rest of the Forsyth property had been used as a cemetery it presented problems. What was to be done with the remains of those buried there? It was to be 1866 before the bodies were moved to Cypress Hill Cemetery and the sale was finally completed.[8]

The burial vaults presented a similar stumbling block to the sale of the Wall Street property. Who were the rightful owners of the burial vaults? Foot interpreted ownership as resting with the congregation rather than the lessee. He argued that New York law forbad only "wanton" removal of dead bodies: they could be removed legitimately for other reasons. Furthermore, the City Ordinance of 1823 forbad burial in graves or vaults south of Canal Street, thus making performance of the agreement for burial illegal and excusing the party who ought to perform it. Closing a vault or removing it did not take anything from the lessee since such right was no longer lawful. The city vice-chancellor, however, thought the 999 year lessee had rights to the vault and suggested that the title to the vaults be settled, if possible, by amicable arrangements. Until the matter was resolved no sale of the Wall Street property was possible.

In time an agreement was reached whereby in consideration for $1, a vault owner relinquished right of use and authorized First Church to remove the vaults and bodies. The church agreed to arrange for reburial at the new site, and owners were given the choice of either a new vault or $250.[9]

With the solution of the ticklish issue reached, the trustees proceeded and appointed a committee with authority to purchase land for a new church on Fifth Avenue between 8th and 14th Streets. The purchase of lots between 11th and 12th Streets was completed by the spring of 1844. Some of the owners who sold (a total of seven) wished to stipulate that the land would be used only as a church yard; if used for other purposes the price would be higher. The total paid for the block, 110 by 125 feet in depth, was $52,750.[10]

The building committee pondered the question of moving the old church to the new site at a cost of $32,000 - 38,000. An offer for the building had been made by a group in Jersey City who wanted to erect a Presbyterian church there. It was decided to sell them the church in its entirety - furnishings, chandeliers, carpets, stoves, the iron railing and stone work connecting it with the church - for the sum of $3000. It was moved across the Hudson by boat at 5¢ a load; it took 7,456 loads.[11]

In May, 1844, the Wall Street church was vacated. The congregation temporarily used the chapel of Union Theological Seminary on University Place, close to the new location. The contract for a new building was let on July 4, 1844 and the corner stone (that of the old Wall Street Church) was laid on September 16. In it were placed copies of the Holy Scriptures and the Westminster Confession of Faith, a brief manuscript record of the history of First Church and a copy of the life of Dr. Rodgers by Samuel Miller.[12]

The committee had decided on the Gothic rather than the Grecian style although it was somewhat more expensive. This was the era of enthusiasm for Gothic architecture in American churches. Joseph C. Wells (one of the founders of the American Institute of Architects) was selected as architect and J. G. Pierson as builder. It was said that the church was modelled on the Church of St. Saviour at Bath, England and that the church tower was copied from the Magdalen tower at Oxford. During the construction the local diarist (George Templeton Strong) wrote in July, 1845:

[William Wirt] Phillips's show grows uglier and uglier, and when its tower is finished it will resemble a corpulent Chinese gander with its neck rigid, stout and tall, and its square-built rump and broad expanse of back, sturdy, squat, and not easily to be shaken. A deeply engaged tower in such a dumpy body as this, and a tower of such height and breadth won't improve, as it is risen.[13]

The church was dedicated January 12, 1846. There were only open lots from Fifth Avenue to Broadway and the congregation reached the church by means of a plank walk laid over the soil. There was, however, a large congregation on hand to hear

Phillips preach on "A Memorial of the Goodness of God." He elaborated on the peculiar features of Presbyterianism, its dogma, discipline and organization, showing the Scriptural authority for each. At the afternoon service he gave a history of Presbyterianism in New York.

A reporter for the *New York Herald* thought the building was "an ornament in that portion of the city in which it is situated" and reflected much credit on the architect. He described the interior in more detail:

> The interior of the edifice presents a novel and yet a very agreeable and impressive aspect. It is of the perpendicular Gothic Style, without columns to sustain the long extending arch which makes the seats , in a remarkable degree available and unobstructed. This is a new feature in modern architecture. The slips [pews] are of black walnut of native growth, most beautifully and tastefully carved. ... The ceiling is formed by a system (if it may be so called) of groined arches, with intersecting ribs and pendants forming the keystone of this massive structure. The pulpit is of easy access, and is neatly and tastefully furnished. The heads of the windows have stained glass within tracery, and exhibit much taste in their entire finish.

The First Presbyterian Church in the City of New York, on Fifth Avenue, 11th and 12th Streets, circa 1846

There were tablets of marble to the memory of Robert Lenox and to Dr. J. R. B. Rodgers on either side of the pulpit.[14] The narthex contained the tablet of black marble that had been executed in 1748; it had been found by some workmen in the church grounds of the Wall Street church.[15]

Many years later (1930) an architect, grandson of Trinity Church's Richard Upjohn, described the church as "one of our city's outstanding pieces of architecture." He said not enough credit had been given to the "genius" of Joseph C. Wells; that for years credit had erroneously been given to Richard Upjohn. Furthermore, he saw comparatively little similarity to the church at Bath, calling the design an original "interpretation of the perpendicular Gothic of the period existing in England at the beginning of the fifteenth century." The ceiling was particularly novel, giving an unobstructed view. He stressed the good fortune of the church in owning the entire block.[16]

The move to the new location brought no break in the continuity of organization and the usual election of three trustees took place in May 1846, following the established pattern of returning incumbents to office term after term. Dr. J. Kearney Rodgers, grandson of John Rodgers, was reelected president of the board. At the time of his resignation a year later he described his decision as "one of the most painful of my life."[17]

William Wirt Phillips, of course, continued to serve as pastor until the time of his death, March 20, 1865. He had ministered to First Church for nearly forty years, and had continued to preach despite a long illness until a month before he died. He had been active in many organizations, serving on the governing boards of both the university and the seminary at Princeton, and of New York University. He was a trustee of Sailors Snug Harbor acting for most of the time as secretary of that board. He was Moderator of the General Assembly in 1835 and later President of the Board of Foreign Missions. He had often been plagued by financial difficulties and at one point had had to mortgage his home on Broome and Mercer. At the memorial service for him a somewhat puzzling tribute was paid to him as a citizen who had upheld the Union in the pulpit during the Civil War "at the cost of tender ties." Parenthetically, this is the only reference in the minutes of the session to that conflict. He was buried in vault no. 53 on the north lawn of the church, a donation to his family by the church.[18]

Four years later a Presbyterian church on 15th Street moved to land donated by James Lenox at Madison Avenue and 73rd Street, and renamed itself the Phillips Presbyterian Church in William Wirt's honor. It was later absorbed by the Madison Avenue Presbyterian Church but a Phillips Chapel was maintained within that church.[19]

Frances Symington, Phillips widow, survived him by almost 20 years, and when she died a tablet in her memory was placed on the wall of the sanctuary. She is the only woman to be so memorialized, indicating the esteem in which she was held.

It was to be some nine months before a new pastor was secured, and in December 1865 William Miller Paxton of Pittsburgh was called at an annual salary of $5,000.

In his first annual report to the Presbytery he listed the active members of First Church at 207 after having removed 201 names from the active list for not having attended services for more than two years.[20] A manse for the minister was secured at 49 East 11th Street for $25,000 shortly after Paxton's installation in February, 1866. This need had first been realized when the church moved to Fifth Avenue but the lot on 12th Street was not large enough. The money for the manse purchase was raised by subscription. Paxton remained at First Church until 1884 when he left to accept the chair of Eccelesiastical Homilectical and Pastoral Theology at Princeton Theological Seminary, whose original occupant, Samuel Miller, had also served at First Church.[21]

For two years the church was without a permanent minister, and then a call was issued to Richard Davenport Harlan, the son of associate Supreme Court Justice, John Marshall Harlan. Not since Samuel Miller had one so young been called, (and that call had been to a collegiate ministry). Harlan had just completed his studies at Princeton Theological and was ordained and installed on April 1, 1886. His lack of experience quickly led to strained relations with the church officers, one elder sharing his concern in a letter to George Alexander, pastor of nearby University Place Church. One source of discord seems to have been the construction of a lecture hall for which Harlan said he had raised $28,000 but the trustees had refused to take action on the project. He threatened to resign several times and somewhat suddenly in December 1890 he left to pursue theological studies at the University of Berlin. At the time of his leaving he suggested that First Church and University Place would do well to unite with Alexander as pastor. The churches had joined for services during the summer months. It would be some 28 years before Harlan's suggestion became reality.[22] In September 1891 the congregation issued a call to Dr. Howard Duffield (1854–1941) of Detroit. He belonged to an old Presbyterian ministerial family; an ancestor, Dr. George Duffield, had been a prominent patriot during the Revolution and his father was a professor at Princeton. The new minister was a graduate of both Princeton University and the Seminary. Initially he declined the call to First Church having heard it was not unanimous since the trustees were unwilling to assume the burden of paying a salary of $8,000. Finally Miss Rachel Lenox Kennedy promised to contribute half of the salary. He was installed on December 10; he was to remain until the consolidation in 1918.[23]

Several changes in the church's physical plant began after

OLD FIRST CHURCH
✚ 5th Avenue and 12th Street ✚

HOWARD   DUFFIELD,   Pastor

YOU are cordially invited to
attend Morning Worship at the
Old First every Sunday at 11 A. M.
and the Home Hour Service from
8 to 9 every Sunday evening.

Straight Short Sermons

Best Music in the City

The Seats are Free

The Welcome is Warm

Send us Your address and we
will mail You a Church
Calendar every week.

Howard Duffield, Pastor, 1891–1918.   A Duffield promotion effort, 1910.

Duffield's arrival. A new chapel on 11th Street was constructed,
designed by McKim, Mead and White and built at a cost of
$49,000. It was wired for electricity and opened in December
1893. At the same time a building on the north side of 12th Street,
originally housing a mission school, was sold for $30,000 (the sale
was not completed until 1902).[24] The manse at 49 E. 11th Street
had been sold after Paxton left for the same price at which it had
been purchased, and so in 1895 the house at 12 West 12th Street
was purchased for $50,000 to serve as a new manse. It was a brick
and brownstone mansion originally built for James W. Phillips,
son of William Wirt and Frances Symington Phillips. It had been
occupied from 1866 to 1882 by Thurlow Weed, state boss of the
Republican Party. The interior was particularly impressive with
an octagonal stairwell and a stained glass skylight.[25]

Duffield promoted a full religious program. Services were held
in the morning at 11 a.m. and in the afternoon, following which
came a special prayer meeting in the chapel. A religious service
for children was held on the first Sunday of each month.
Wednesday evening lectures were instituted and in the summer
evening services were held on the south lawn of the church as he
said poor people preferred this. Even during the pastor's vacation
the Wednesday evening service continued, conducted by First
Church's Christian Endeavor Society, the interdenominational
effort to revitalize the Sunday schools that had begun in 1881.[26]

Special efforts were made to increase the attendance at services.
Ushers were provided to aid the seating of strangers as the

84

exclusive pew system began to break down. Visitors were handed engraved cards and were later called on by the elders in their homes. Church posters were distributed throughout the neighborhood — in the hotels, stores, shops and even saloons. The church was open daily for meditation and prayer — one of the few Protestant churches that was — and a 1903–1904 survey showed that 3,462 women and 2,794 men had availed themselves of this opportunity. The church membership increased steadily from 435 in 1896 to 834 in 1915.[27]

Communion services were held five times a year. No tokens were used and session meetings were no longer devoted to discussion of the morals of members. There were a few cases of intemperance and fraud, the most noteworthy case being one in which an elder, who had become custodian of funds raised by women of the church to buy floor covering, deposited the money in his own bank account. It was only with great difficulty that the church was able to obtain the funds after three or four years of trying. He was deposed as an elder and denied the sacrament of the Lord's Supper until he showed "genuine penitence for his wrong doing." In 1912 the use of individual communion cups was instituted. Members no longer went to the front of the church to receive communion but were served in the pews instead.[28]

The bicentennial of First Church's founding was celebrated during the first week of December in 1916. In honor of the occasion the Presbytery authorized general observance in all its

William Carl, long-time organist of the First Presbyterian Church, 1892–1936

churches throughout the city, and official representatives were sent by the Synod and the General Assembly. At the Sunday morning service Duffield, whose enthusiasm and promotional skills were evident in all parts of the program, preached an historical sermon. In the afternoon a former pastor, Richard Harlan, told of his pastorate and the stated clerk of the General Assembly related the work of the other pastors of the church. The service ended with a tribute and prayer by Dr. John A. Marquis, the moderator of the General Assembly. The "anniversary day," December 6th was celebrated with addresses illustrating the work of First Church in various fields: Dr. William Pierson Merrill of Brick Church spoke on "Old First and her Children," Dr. George Alexander, president of the Board of Foreign Missions, on "Old First Church and the Winning of the World," the presidents of Princeton University and the Theological Seminary spoke on "Old First Church and Education." Two speakers represented secular bodies: the presidents of the New York City Chamber of Commerce spoke on "Old First Church and Social Service," and New York's Governor Charles S. Whitman on "Old First Church and the Commonwealth."[29]

This was also the twenty-fifth anniversary of Dr. Duffield's Pastorate and tribute was paid to his services especially in improving the church building itself. The aisles had been paved with marble, an electric lighting system set up, and Westminster chimes installed in the tower.

When he first came to the church Duffield had been struck with the somberness of the sanctuary, with the dark walls and pews. He soon evolved a plan for memorial stained glass windows. The last two were completed just before the 200th anniversary celebration. On the north side the windows represented the various "literary elements in the Holy Scriptures;" Moses for the law, David for poetry, Isaiah for prophecy (designed by Tiffany), St. John for the Gospels and St. Paul for the Epistles. The ones on the South side presented various historical figures who had played a part in the evangelical church. The selection of the windows on the South side is rather peculiar for a Presbyterian church but probably represented the interests of the donors. The first window as one enters the church pictures Peter Waldo, the leader of a twelfth century heretical group, forerunner of Protestantism. James Lenox had been much interested in the Waldensian Society and had, annually, given large sums for their work. The window was donated in his honor. The next window was of Martin Luther, leader of the reformation in Germany in the sixteenth century. Next to him was that in honor of Admiral Coligny, a Huguenot who lost his life in the St. Bartholomew's Day massacre in France in 1572. The last window (designed by Tiffany) shows St. Columba who brought Christianity to Scotland from Ireland, and formed the monastery on the island of Iona. These windows might be said to represent various elements in Protestantism.[30]

II

As the nineteenth century unfolded music played an increasing role in the church service. The session adopted the book of psalms and hymns recommended by the General Assembly of the Presbyterian Church. Musical leadership rested with a quartette. For twenty-five years, until 1870, this quartette was headed by H. Camp and his wife. There being no musical instrument permitted in the sanctuary, the quartette members retired to a room at the rear of the gallery (from which they sang) to get the pitch from a pitch pipe. They then returned to sing.

The trustees recommended in 1855 that the church install a pipe organ, thinking it would attract young people and strangers to the services. The session demurred, undoubtedly because of the opposition of James Lenox, the leading elder and largest financial supporter of the church, who had strong opinions about the sinister influences of such innovations. It was not until 1886 (Lenox died in 1880) that an organ was installed. Aaron K. Belknap's widow (he had been an elder for thirty-four years) and her sister contributed $2,000, one-fifth of the cost, towards the purchase. The organ bellows were powered by a gas engine, and in 1898 an additional pipe organ for the lecture room was given by Albert Remick and his wife.[31]

With the coming of William C. Carl as organist in 1892, the music gained new prestige and emphasis in the life of the church. Duffield, who secured Carl, had met the young man on board ship coming home from Europe. Carl had just completed his study in Paris under the renowned organist, Alexander Guilmant. He added a chorus to supplement the quartette and began a practice of giving organ recitals during the winter. Each recital, however, was in connection with a service of worship, emphasizing the church's distinction from a concert hall. Audience attendance was excellent, frequently numbering as many as 1200.

In 1899, Carl and Duffield founded the Guilmant Organ School, the first of its kind in America, devoted exclusively to the training of organists and choir masters. Carl, of course, was responsible for the musical training and Duffield offered courses in worship, hymnody and theology. On the occasion of the Quadricentennial of the Protestant Reformation (1917), Carl composed a special cantata that was presented at the church. He was twice decorated by the French government and New York University honored him with the degree of doctor of music. He continued at First Church until his death in 1936, at the age of 71.[32]

III

A part of the concern that led to the division of Presbyterians in 1837 into "Old School" and "New School" was an increase in what the conservative Old School group called "the prevalence of unsound doctrine and laxity in discipline." There were other issues, of course, not the least of which was the pressure of abolitionists to have the church declare itself opposed to slavery. In any case, Samuel Miller spoke to the General Assembly of the Old School branch in 1840 on, *The Christian Education of the Children and Youth*. He proposed the essential elements of what would be a program of parochial schools in Presbyterian churches.[33]

Although it was not until 1846 that the General Assembly embarked on such a venture, the session of First Church took such an action in 1844, even before the move to the new location on Fifth Avenue. On April 22 of that year it was decided "that the Session . . . take the necessary preparatory steps to establish a Parochial Free School in connexion with this church." Two weeks later a building was obtained opposite McDougall Street between 8th and 9th streets although it soon moved to a brick building on the north side of West 12th Street. Dr. and Mrs. Sterling were engaged as teachers, and the school opened July 1, 1844. Sterling was also to act as superintendent of the Sabbath school. By September of the same year it was judged a "successful operation" and in November a plan for publicizing it was set forth. Members of the Session were asked to visit it on a regular basis.[34]

In his words to the General Assembly Miller no doubt reflected feelings held by the First Church elders. He spoke of the failure of Presbyterians to provide an adequate Christian education for their children. He described these children as growing up in ignorance, indifferent to the religion of their fathers:

> . . . some becoming profane and impious; others turning aside to various forms of fatal error; and a large majority feeling little attachment to the good old way, in which they ought to have been faithfully and prayerfully trained. And it is painful to recollect that, amidst this unhappy delinquency, the judicatories of our Church have in great measure slumbered over the evil, and have taken no systematic or efficient order for the removal of it.[35]

Beyond the initial months of the school's beginning, little information appears in the church records until December 16, 1847 by which time it is evident that problems had developed. The session minutes of that date report:

> The Session proceeded to consider several matters in relation to the parochial school. A letter was read from Mr. [James] Lenox proposing
> 1. That all pupils shall be required to pay either themselves or thro others and that all who do not pay regularly shall be reported and after a time shall be dismissed from the school — 2ndly that religious instruction must form a part of every day's tuition —
> Every pupil must learn the shorter catechism. Resolved that the Session approve of the foregoing regulations and agree to adopt them — Resolved that it is expedient to employ a male & Female Teacher for the school.

Resolved that a Committee of three in conjunction with the pastor be appointed to confer with Mr. Lenox in relation to the school & to manage its affairs — under the direction of the Session. . . .

Resolved that each member of the Session will consider it his duty to visit the school at least once a month. . . .

Obviously Lenox was not pleased with the school's condition, and this was a matter of concern to him. Parochial education was something he believed in, having given $3,000 to the General Assembly to assist churches that needed help in establishing schools.[36]

Although it is not clear as to what happened to the particular school at First Church, undoubtedly its existence was not a long one—only until 1853. Only 4 per cent of all the Old School churches even had schools, and the median duration of those that were established was three years. It was not a movement of significance and failed to capture the imagination or enthusiasm of any but a few. The support for a system of public education was increasing among Americans and to many Presbyterians the program for parochial education seemed a refutation of that and a formal withdrawal from a society that was growing and expanding rapidly. Even Lenox's determination and the fact that William Wirt Phillips was a member of the General Assembly committee established to promote the venture were not sufficient to keep the school at First Church alive.

For most, the increase of Sabbath Schools, a relatively new institution in American Protestantism, held more promise. In 1853, George Potts, pastor of the University Place church, spoke to a meeting of the American Sunday School Union and discounted the possibilities of expecting either parochial schools or religious instruction in public schools to fulfill the need for the Christian education of children. As he saw it Protestants would do well to give their attention to Sabbath schools in the churches.[37] First Church had two such schools, morning and afternoon, and a Mission Sabbath School as well. This latter was for children of non-church families, and from 1868 to 1885 it was supervised by Elder Latimer Bailey, founder of an importing firm, Allscrop and Bailey. He was a bachelor who devoted his leisure time to church work. The mission school drew children from all parts of the city, and when former students married, Bailey presented them with a family Bible.

One of Duffield's early changes was the consolidation of the church and mission sabbath schools into one with both a morning and afternoon session. The focus had changed; instead of being primarily for the children of poor and uneducated parents, all children were included. The enrollment from 1900–1910 was usually about 500. The pastor's assistant was in charge of the Sunday School although an elder was the superintendent.[38]

In 1908 a conflict arose between Sunday School leaders and the session. The former had decided that instead of the Bible the students should study Josiah Strong's, *The Challenge of the City,* a book whose aim was to arouse churches to social consciousness and responsibility for the increasing problems in urban centers. This was part of the "social gospel" emphasis growing among Protestants. The session refused to permit the study.[39]

With the addition of the facilities on 11th Street in 1893, First Church was able to provide an expanded program of activities and organizations. Portions of the building served as a club room with pool and billiard tables, a kitchen, and a small gymnasium with a physical instructor. There were separate clubs of boys and girls of various ages. It was not until 1914, however, that non-members were permitted into these organizations. The young men had their Old First Fraternity and young women had a similar organization. There were many such clubs and the names changed frequently. In 1907 reports from each were included as part of every annual meeting of the congregation.[40]

IV

Despite the anticipations of relief from financial pressures that stimulated the move to the Fifth Avenue location, such was not the case. The money concerns of the church moved north also. The cost of ground and new sanctuary was almost $120,000. A lecture room, 80 burial vaults, and an iron railing around the grounds brought the total expenditure to $145,809. Only $103,700 of that amount had been realized from the sale of building and grounds at Wall and Nassau, thus leaving a substantial deficit.

Funds for the new church had been secured through the sale of church pews, a procedure somewhat akin to present-day financing of a cooperative apartment building. There were 122 pews listed with a value ranging from $150 to $950 depending on size and location. Purchasers of the pews were charged an annual rental, had to pay for furnishings and cushions in the pew, and could make no alterations as to lining, painting, etc. without permission of the trustees. These rental charges were the major source of current revenue for the church services and program. Occasionally a special subscription would supply additional funds. More frequently the church looked to three or four men to make up the annual deficits: James Lenox, for years the most generous contributor; Aaron Belknap, elder from 1846 to 1871, and Aaron Thompson who served the church as an elder for forty-seven years.[41]

First Church's financial dependence on the Lenox family was both substantial and of long duration. The patriarch of the clan, Robert Lenox, served thirty years as an elder until his death in 1839, eighteen days shy of his 80th birthday. During his life time he had given $2,000,000 to various Presbyterian causes. One of

James Lenox

the city's five richest men, he had invested heavily in real estate. One parcel, "My Farm at the 5 Mile Stone," consisted of thirty acres — Fifth Avenue to Lexington, 68th to 74th Streets. He advised his son to hold on to the land in anticipation of the city's expansion northward when it could be divided and sold as separate lots.

Robert's son, James, described himself as having been "born in the church" and made a public confession of his faith in Christ in 1827. A graduate of Princeton and Columbia, he was admitted to the bar but never practiced law, becoming a partner with his father in the import business — Robert Lenox and Son — instead.

After his father's death he retired from that business and devoted himself to investments, church work, philanthropy and book collecting. His first important book purchase was a copy of *Pilgrim's Progress.* His Bible collection included a Gutenberg Bible, the first to be brought to this country, and he served as president of the American Bible Society for six years, 1866 to 1872. His books were piled high in various rooms throughout the large three story and basement house he built in 1845 at 53 Fifth Avenue, the northeast corner of 12th Street. His unmarried sister, Henrietta, lived in a connecting house and another sister, Mary, married to John Fishbee Shaefe, lived in the same block. A nephew, Dr. James Lenox Banks, lived at 57 Fifth while his parents lived at 72 Fifth. The two corners of 11th Street opposite the church were occupid by another two sisters — Mrs. James Donaldson and Mrs. Davis S. Kennedy. Each of the men, Lenox and Lenox in-laws, was active in First Church, serving as trustee or elder or both. It is small wonder that this family's influence was pronounced in the church's life: they had the power of both money and numbers.[42]

When James Lenox died in 1880 it came as a rude awakening that First Church had no part of his estate: his large fortune was left to the Lenox Library which he had built ten years earlier on Fifth Avenue between 70th and 71st Streets. As if that loss were not enough, Aaron Belknap and Aaron Thompson also died in the same year. It is understandable that the trustees were shortly thereafter to note in their minutes (June 5, 1882): "In consequence of the recent death of some of the prominent members of the church, who have contributed largely to its support, our financial future is uncertain." A committee was formed to impress upon the congregation the need for a Permanent Endowment Fund, noting that the only religious groups to successfully sustain downtown churches were the Episcopal and Reformed Dutch churches, each of whom had large endowments: "Had it not been for Trinity Church and Collegiate Church Endowments, the lower portion of the city would have been given up to Roman Catholics some years ago."[43]

An endowment fund was created, under the supervision of the trustees. Its principal was to be invested in safe, interest-bearing securities, whose income (but none of the principal) was to be applied to the church's support. A book in which contributions to the endowment were recorded was placed in the vestibule of the church building.

By 1895 the endowment, invested in bonds and mortgages, amounted to $30,615. Two additional endowment funds came into being shortly after: the William Moir Fund of $25,000 in 1897 (to which Mrs. Moir added $10,000 in 1906) and the Mary J. Winthrop Fund of $50,000 in 1899. These funds were kept in a separate account at the Institute of the Savings of Merchants and Clerks at Union Square, with the proviso that the principal was to be kept "sacredly intact." The trustees established a committee on investments in 1900.[44]

First Church fared no better with the estates of other Lenox family members than it had with James'. Rachel Lenox Kennedy, who had been contributing half of Duffield's salary, died in Maine in July of 1898. Her will of March 19, 1895, gave $80,000 to the First Presbyterian Church to be invested with the income derived from it to be used to pay church expenses, the first of which was to be the pastor's salary. The will read:

> the above legacy to be paid over to and accepted by said church upon the condition that in case said Church shall at any time cease to be conducted as a Presbyterian Church according to the rules and doctrines of the Westminster Confession of Faith, or Theology as now taught at the Theological Seminary in Princeton, N.J. or shall permit its present form of worship to be essentially changed or shall remove from its present location or permanently cease to conduct religious exercises as a Presbyterian Church at its present location in the manner above set forth, then said principal sum of Eighty Thousand dollars is to be repaid by said Church to my estate.

The will also left $10,000 to Duffield personally, $40,000 to the Presbyterian Rest Home for Convalescents of White Plains, $20,000 to the Presbyterian Home for Aged Women, $10,000 to the Presbyterian Hospital, $15,000 to the New York House and School of Industry, and $10,000 to the New York Female Auxiliary Bible Society.

A Kennedy nephew claimed that no will had been found although her companion insisted it was in a green box in the linen closet at the residence at 41 Fifth Avenue when they left for Maine in June and that her lawyer had carbon copies. The nephew petitioned the court that she had died intestate and he was appointed administrator.

The church engaged the legal services of Richards and Heald to pursue its interests. The Surrogate, however, refused to submit the will to probate on the basis that the original had not been produced and that therefore the money was to be divided between her sister and nephew, her heirs at law. His decision was upheld by the Appellate Division of the Supreme Court and finally in June, 1901 by the Court of Appeals.[45]

Pew rents and endowment income did not produce funds necessary to support the church's work. An envelope system for weekly contributions was revived in 1898 (it had been tried for a short while in 1893). A survey in 1902 showed that 29 of the 94 who paid pew rent also contributed through the envelope system and that 93 non pew renters used the envelope system; that was, however, only 187 out of a membership of 590. Duffield repeatedly appealed from the pulpit for added congregational support, even offering to take a reduction in salary.[46]

In an imaginative move toward easing the economic strain, the trustees arranged a mortgage on the entire real estate of the church to secure a loan of $450,000 with which they proposed to build an apartment house on the site of the manse extending to 11th Street, rising above the chapel building. Income from the apartments for the church's use was their objective.

The pastor learned of this proposal only through an item in a newspaper. Incensed, he called a special meeting of the session (January 29, 1905), who emphatically rejected the possibility of mortgaging the entire property:

> ... It is the deliberate judgment of the Session that in no event and under no circumstances should a mortgage be placed upon the real property of the Church outside of the ground covered by the Manse and the adjacent building lot.

A congregational meeting, May 7, 1905, did approve a mortgage on that property but not the grandiose proposal of the trustees. At a congregational meeting the following year (November 7, 1906) it was decided to hold a corporate meeting each year and to have the pastor and ruling elders thereafter serve as the trustees. The vote was 76−5 in favor.[47]

Part and parcel of the financial strain was a situation similar to that of about a century earlier. Well-to-do Protestants continued to move further north, and in 1906 Duffield launched a campaign to save Old First at its lower Fifth Avenue location. He wrote letters to many prominent people. The New York *World* carried an article, "Shall the Old First Church be Saved?" citing the venerable history: "For almost two centuries the old First Presbyterian Church has been a center of religious influence in New York." It pointed out the service this "beautiful and historic church" was doing in a crowded part of the city, "which being deserted by the rich, is increasing rapidly in population." The article said that it is "architecturally one of the most beautiful churches in the city and stands in the center of the block on Fifth Avenue, between Eleventh and Twelfth streets, with a wide stretch of greensward." In his appeal for aid Duffield wrote:

> Shall the appeal of its history, of its beauty, of its ministry of blessing fall upon unheeding ears? Shall not the lovers of art, the benefactors of the city, the friends of faith, by quick and generous and initial action, lift this ancient church beyond the mischance of change and send it into the third century of its life a great cathedral-like institution for the glory of God, for the honor of the town, and for the good of many souls.[48]

The mayor of New York City responded:.

> I hope sincerely that the friends of the church will make it possible for it to remain where it is. The present building is one of the few old landmarks left; one of the few architectural monuments in the City. More than this, your church is one of the very few restful spots in this busy City of ours. It would be a misfortune were it to disappear, and its place taken by a skyscraper.

Norris K. Jesup, president of the New York City Mission and Tract Society, suggested that one way out of the critical financial condition was the union of Old First and University Place Presbyterian churches. He wrote, however, "The Old First Church to my mind, ought not to be removed. It stands a glory to the civic pride of the City, and as a noble example of church architecture."[49] Among those who answered the appeal was D. Willis James, member of the Madison Square Presbyterian Church, and because of his generous support a program of lectures on modern religious thought and work was established in his name. In 1910 his widow made an additional contribution of $180,000 to the endowment. By 1916 the endowment fund had reached $400,000 and was returning an income of over $15,000 a year.[50]

V

Although resources sufficient to meet current expenses remained an abiding and persistent anxiety, Old First was not devoid of benevolences. Support for these came from special offerings, most of which were designated for the national church organizations: Foreign Missions, Home Missions, Board of Education, Board of the Freedmen as well as interdenominational efforts such as the American Bible Society, the American Tract Society, and the Federation of Churches, forerunner of the Federal Council of Churches organized in 1905.[51]

Within the church membership help for the needy came from offerings on Communion Sundays administered by the board of deacons who also benefitted from a bequest of $9,500 left by Henrietta Lenox for their use. Each summer $200 to $300 was given to the Fresh Air Fund to send children from slum areas out of the city for a vacation.[52]

Only one organization seems to have provoked disagreement in the session: the Anti-Saloon League. In 1904 their request to use the church for a special service and collection was refused, but in 1916 a similar request was granted on the condition that there be no reference to political matters in the service.[53] In the intervening twelve years public support for the temperance movement that would culminate in the adoption of the 18th Amendment had made substantial gain. This was undoubtedly instrumental in the session's change of attitude.

Several charities in the city were favored by First Church, one of them being the Presbyterian Hospital, due in large measure to James Lenox's interest. He had taken the initiative in its organization, donated money for it and given a parcel of land between 70th and 71st Streets for a building. He was on the board of directors whose meetings were held in the lecture room of the church until his death, was the hospital's first president and his words were inscribed on the hospital walls: "For the poor of New York without regard to race, creed or color." In 1875 a church contribution of $5,000 gave permanent access to a bed in the common wards for those in financial need. Similar beds were available at the Manhattan Eye and Ear, Skin and Cancer Hospital and Home for Incurables. These were made possible by the generosity of Jane Hope.[54]

The Presbyterian Home for Aged Women ("pious aged females, members of the Presbyterian churches, who, from adversity or the death of friends, had been left in a state of lonely dependence.") was organized by a group of women meeting in the church's lecture room in April 1866. Again the Lenox family was involved: James donated a lot at 49 East 73rd Street; a sister, Mrs. J. Fishbee Sheafe, was the first directress; Rachel Lenox Kennedy was the financial secretary, and one of the attending physicians was James Lenox Banks.[55]

The oldest group in the church was the Sewing Society. It originated in the Wall Street church and during the Civil War made "Havelocks" and prepared flannels for soldiers. Later they sent boxes of clothing to home missionaries working in various parts of the country. A school to teach children to sew was organized in October, 1897, financed by Elder Albert Remick. Each member was furnished with an apron to be worn at every session of the school and also with a class box. In addition to the sewing they learned songs and memorized Bible verses. At the end of the first season there were 135 scholars and 18 teachers.[56]

First Church had a strong commitment to foreign mission work. Before the Presbyterian Board of Foreign Missions was formed (1837) the Society of Earnest Workers for China was organized at First Church. It financed the Lourie High School in Shanghai. During its first forty years First Church was the largest contributor in the New York Presbytery to the Board of Foreign Missions. The first secretary of the Board and the first missionary sent out by the Board were First Church members. Three of the first six presidents of the Board were pastors of First Church. The first chairman of its executive council, William Wirt Phillips, was succeeded by James Lenox. After Lenox's death the headquarters of the Home and Foreign Mission boards moved to the Lenox home at 12th Street and Fifth Avenue. (When they moved from there in 1893 to 156 Fifth Avenue Rachel Lenox Kennedy dropped them from her will and substituted the First Presbyterian Church). The Woman's Missionary Society of the church, organized in 1892 with Mrs. Duffield as president, was closely associated with the Home Missions Board.[57]

In the immediate neighborhood, the church was particularly concerned about the increasing number of Italian youth and in 1907 an Italian boys club was formed, providing facilities for discussion and games, especially basketball. The Men's League of the church in 1910 proposed renting a house in the Village as a mission with classes to teach foreigners to become "good Americans," but nothing came of the proposal. The church did give financial aid to the Labor Temple at 14th Street and Second Avenue, the first official church agency "to pursue an aggressive social–gospel campaign through the efforts of a paid secretary," whose purpose was "to interpret to the laboring man the Christian answer to the vital problems of the day," through meetings and lectures.[58]

In a variety of ways First Church showed an awareness of needs beyond those of the immediate membership and on at least one occasion the needs invaded the church sanctuary.

March 1, 1914, was a stormy night and the planned Oratorio of the Redemption for that evening had to be postponed. The small congregation was suddenly invaded by a large group of "unkempt, ill clad, rough looking men," of all ages. The ushers showed the men to seats and Duffield suggested they all join in singing some hymns while someone quietly telephoned the police. Duffield gave a brief talk and the police arrived but remained in the vestibule. A young man rose and asked permission to speak. He said that the men had no place to sleep and needed something to eat, that they were willing to work. Duffield said he could not let them stay there but the leader said they would stay even though it meant breaking the law. A member of the board of deacons, Theodore D. Martin, suggested taking the group to the Municipal Lodging House but the men protested. Then he sent a note to Duffield saying that the deacons could give $25 to help out. Duffield closed the service with prayer and went down to talk to the leader, Frank Tannenbaum, who said the men were not begging for aid but were demanding it. Duffield insisted he was not offering charity but an act of friendship in the name of the church. Tannenbaum counted the men (81) and Duffield said the $25 would be enough for lodging as well as food. The men voted to accept it. Tannenbaum did not want to take responsbility for distributing it so Martin accompanied them to an eating place and then to a lodging house. The police never entered the church.

Martin later reported to Duffield that he had accompanied the men across Twelfth toward the Bowery. Tannenbaum suggested he get the money divided and give each man 25¢ but the deacon said he was responsible. As a safeguard against others joining the band of marchers each man was given a red identification check. They stopped at a restaurant at 295 Bowery, and each man received a large portion of bread, cup of coffee, and a plate of beef stew, hamburger, or pork and beans; the charge was ten cents per meal. Those who had been sent ahead to the Salvation Army Hotel on the Bowery reported they had been able to reserve places for all of the men and they checked in eighty of them. Martin paid $16 for the accommodations and turned what was left of the $25 over to Tannenbaum. Martin became convinced that while a few of the men were destitute and worthy of assistance most of the "army" was made up of professional loafers and derelicts who were not interested in working. He believed Tannenbaum was sincere but a "Monomaniac," obsessed by the idea that society owed every man a living at the rate of $3 per eight hour day. He said he preached the "Gospel of Discontent," and attacked the church because it preached the gospel of contentment.

Ten days later Martin received a letter from Tannenbaum sent from Tombs Prison, cell 813. He told how he and his group had been arrested at the Franciscan Church. "I think," he wrote, "that the city made a mistake when they arrested us, and as for the Catholic Church it has but shown itself as we all knew it to be, the blackest, most unscrupulous and damnable institution on the face of the earth."

He wrote: "While our social philosophy and social ideals differ widely we still found something common that night which was strong enough and of sufficient vital interest to make that night one of the most interesting and if I might say one of the most beautiful that I have ever experienced. I take it for granted that it holds true with you, for I doubt very much you ever having gone through such a like experience." He included a list of books for Martin to read. He added, "P.S. with regards to both my friends and enemies in Dr. Duffield's congregation and Dr. Duffield himself."[59]

VI

Unemployment and the depression eased with the out-break of World War I in Europe. The session of First Church immediately took cognizance of the war and in accordance with the President's proclamation set apart November 4 as a day of prayer for peace in Europe. This was a marked change from the attitude in previous wars; in reading the minutes of the church bodies during other wars (War of 1812, Mexican War, Civil War, Spanish-American War) one would not have known a war was going on.[60] Professor Sweet wrote that churches had been accustomed during the Twentieth Century to a crusading role and accepted the United States' involvement as a crusade to make the world safe for democracy. Thus on April 6, 1917, the session passed resolutions on President Wilson's declaration of war. The preamble of the resolutions stated that since in fact the nation had no territorial aims the session avowed accord with the President and recognized the coincidence of the declaration of war with Good Friday. They stated that America also dedicated herself to sacrifice and that First Church would be patriotic and not criticize the national government.

To show its patriotism the Sunday School was directed to salute the national colors at every session and the American flag was displayed in the pulpit. A service flag for members who had volunteered was hung outside the church. A portion of the church lawn was dug up and planted as a "victory garden." The church sanctuary was also closed in 1918 and services were held in the chapel in order to conserve coal. Evening services were held on the South lawn where an outdoor pulpit was dedicated on June 17, 1917. Rooms in the chapel were given over to government work. Duffield was appointed chaplain of the Ninth Coast Artillery and wore a military uniform at service.[61]

[1]Stokes, *Iconography, III:528*−31, 607−15; Philip Hone, *The Diary of Philip Hone, 1828*−1851 (New York, 1910), II:611.

[2]Trustee Minutes, III:318−21 (July 8, Nov. 3, 1840), IV:60−1 (Feb. 23, 1848).

[3]*Ibid.*, III:321 (Nov. 3, 1840).

[4]Stokes, *Iconography*, III:521, 526; Still, *Mirror for Gotham*, pp. 57, 80−1, 93.

[5]Stokes, *Iconography*, III:516−8, 523, 528; Arthur Bartlett Maurice, *Fifth Avenue* (New York, 1918), 35; Henry Collins Brown, *Fifth Avenue Old and New* (New York, 1924), 17−27; Still, *Mirror for Gotham*, p. 96.

[6]Trustee Minutes, III:325−30 (Jan. 3, 1841.

[7]*Ibid.*, 332−3, 350−3, 359−60 (Feb. 10, Mar. 14, 1842).

[8]*Ibid.*, 62−70, 386 (Mar. 31, Apr. 20, May 6, June 3, 1842), IV:163 (Nov. 18, 1861), 172−9 (Apr. 6, 17, 1863), 164, 184 (Feb. 28, Apr. 3, June 26 (1865), 201−3 (Jan. 3, 31, 1866).

[9]*Ibid.*, III:330−2, 354−8, 389−94 (Feb. 10, Mar. 14, Nov. 30, 1842).

[10]*Ibid.*, III:395, 400−2, 407, 411−13, 417 (Apr. 30, July 13, Sept. 9, 16, Nov. 8, 20, 1843), 420−21 (Feb. 7, Mar. 29, 1844), IV:50 (Apr. 30, 1847).

[11]*Ibid.*, III:423 (May 6, 1844), IV:6−7, 9−10 (May 28, Aug. 22, 1844; Savage, *Presbyterian Church in New York City*, pp. 148−9.

[12]Session Minutes, II:252−3, 255−7 (Apr. 22, May 11, Sept. 14, Nov. 29, 1844.

[13]Trustee Minutes, IV:7 (May 28, 1844); George Templeton Strong, *The Diary of George Templeton Strong*, ed. by Allen Nevins (4 vols., New York, 1952), I:240, 267−8.

[14]New York *Herald*, Jan. 12, 1846, 2:3: New York *Daily Tribune*, Jan. 13, 1846, 2:1.

[15]Trustee Minutes, IV:11 (Aug. 22, 1844).

[16]Hobart Upjohm, "Church Building," in *Church Tower*, May 15, 1930.

[17]Trustee Minutes, IV:30 (May 5, 1846), 48 (May 20 1847).

[18]Session Minutes, III:9 (Mar. 31, 1865); Trustee Minutes, IV:188, 191−2 (Apr. 3, May 1, 1865), 197−9 (Jan. 31, 1866).

[19]Arthur Courtney, "One Hundred Years Ago," *The Church Tower*, March, 1946.

[20]Trustee Minutes, IV:206 (Jan. 31, 1866); Session Minutes, III:20 (June 8, 1866).

[21]Session Minutes, III:99−100 (Oct. 12, 1883); Trustee Minutes, IV: 209, 217 (Jan. 31, May 5, 1866).

[22]*Ibid*., III:117−8 (Mar. 5, 1886), 160−1, 165 (May 25, Sept. 28, Dec. 12, 1890; Trustee Minutes, IV:318, letter from Mr. Harlan, Jan. 22, 319−20, letter of Mar. 21, 1891; Elder Charles Jesup to the Rev. Mr. Alexander, April 2, 1890, Alexander correspondence, church archives.

[23]Session Minutes, III:171−6 (Oct. 9, 19, Dec. 1, 1891); Trustee Minutes, IV:322 (Nov. 5, 1891).

[24]Trustee Minutes, IV:336 (Feb. 28, Apr. 15, 1893); Session Minutes, III:196, 198, 200, 205 (Mar. 9, Apr. 21, June 10, Dec. 18, 1893).

[25]Trustee Minutes, IV:292 (May 4, 1885), 350 (Mar. 4, May 2, 1895), 421 (Jan 30, 1902); Glyndon G. Van Deusen. *Thurlow Weed. Wizard of the Lobby* (Boston, 1947), 336−7.

[26]Session Minutes, III:121 (Apr. 30, 1886), 178, 183, 189 (Jan. 7, Mar. 1, Sept. 20, 1892), 206, 211 (Feb. 7, Mar. 3, 1894); Ahlstrom, *Religious History*, p. 838; *The New York Times*, Jan. 6, 1941,15:3−4.

[27]Session Minutes, III:175, 177 (Dec. 1, 14, 1891), 190 (Sept. 20, 1892), 196−7 (Mar. 9, 1893), 247 (Oct. 8, 1896), 327 (Apr. 1, 1900), 415 (Mar. 31, 1905), IV:61 (Mar. 31, 1910), 129 (Mar. 31, 1915).

[28]*Ibid*., III:376 (Nov. 5, 1902), IV:81, 88, 95−6 (Jan. 19, May 29, Nov. 22, 1912).

[29]*The Services in Celebration of the Two Hundredth Anniversary of the Founding of the Old First Presbyterian Church in the City of New York, December, 1916*; Session Minutes, IV:145−6, 151 (Oct. 4, Dec. 10, 1916).

[30]*Year Book*, 1915, pp. 9, 45; *The Church Tower*, March, 1946, pp. 46−7; *Bicentennial Booklet*, pp. 126−33.

[31]Session Minutes, II:275 (Feb. 8, 1848), 279 (Mar. 15, 1849), III:24−5 (Mar. 15, 29, 1867), 46 (Mar. 20, 1871); Trustee Minutes, IV:121 (May 12, 1855), 123 (Apr. 18, 1856), 231 (May 3, 1867), 297, 300 (Dec. 10, May 2, 1886), IV:373 (May 16, 1898).

[32]"William Carl," in *National Cyclopaedia of American Biography* (New York, 1971), XXXV:22; Session Minutes, III:440, 442 (Feb. 7, 28, 1906, IV, 173 (Oct. 3, 1917); *The Church Tower*, Mar. 15, 1932.

[33]Samuel Miller, *The Christian Education of the Children and Youth in the Presbyterian Church* (Philadelphia, 1840).

[34]*Ibid*., p. 22; Session Minutes, II:252, 253, 255 (Apr. 20, 22, May 11, Sept. 14, 1844).

[35]Lewis J. Sherrill, *Presbyterian Parochial Schools, 1846−1870* (New Haven, 1932), pp. 79, 89; Miller, *Christian Education*, p. 22.

[36]Session Minutes, II:273 (Dec. 16, 1847).

[37]George Potts, *A Call upon the Unemployed Talent of the Church* (Philadelphia, 1853), 27−28.

[38]Session Minutes, II:304 (Dec. 12, 1855), III:36 (Dec. 18, 1865), 105−6, 110−2 (May 13, June 11, 1885).

[39]*Ibid*., IV:24 (Mar. 16, 1908).

[40]*Ibid*., III:454−5, 466, 469 (Oct. 14, Nov. 2, 22, Dec. 11, 1906), 474, 475, 477, 479 (Mar. 5, 10, 1907), IV, 14 (Nov. 13, 1907); *The Year Book of the "Old First" Presbyterian Church in the City of New York, 1915*.

[41]Trustee Minutes, IV:4−5, 8 (May 11, June 20, 1844), 24−8 (Jan. 7, Apr. 8, 1846), 39−40, 42 (Feb. 20, 26, 1847), 61−3, 73 (Feb. 23, Apr. 5, 1848), 82−5 (May 25, 1849).

[42] Henry Miller Lydenberg, "James Lenox," *DAB*, VI:172; Brown, *Fifth Avenue*, pp. 27–36; Banks, *Genealogical Notes*, p. 91; Norris, *Makers of New York*, p. 190.

[43] Session Minutes, III:85–7 (Mar. 5, June 11, Dec. 17, 1880); Trustee Minutes, IV, 39–42 (Feb. 20, 26, 1847), 61–3, 73 (Feb. 23, Apr. 5, 1948), 82–4 (May 25, 1849). The library was consolidated with the Astor and Tilden Foundations to form the New York Public Library.

[44] Trustee Minutes, IV:282 (June 15, 1882), 286 (May 7, 1883), 355–6 (May 20, 1895), 362–3 (Apr. 16, 1897), 379 (Mar. 24, 1899); Session Minutes, III:295–6, 298 (Feb. 8, Mar. 19, 1899).

[45] Session Minutes, III:222 (Oct. 8, 1894); Trustee Minutes, IV:376 (Nov. 14, 1898); copy of will, March 19, 1895 in Duffield Correspondence, Church Archives.

[46] Trustee Minutes, IV:330 (Nov. 29, 1892), 435 (May 13, 1902); Session Minutes, III:280 (Mar. 24, 1898), 470 (Dec. 21, 1906).

[47] Session Minutes, III:411, 421 (Jan. 29, May 7, 1905); 459, 463–5 (Nov. 7, 22, 1906).

[48] New York *World*, May 20, 1906.

[49] Mayor George B. McClellan to Mr. Duffield, March 21, 1905, in Duffield Correspondence; Norris K. Jesup to Mr. Alexander, in Alexander Correspondence.

[50] Session Minuutes, IV:22 (Feb. 2, 1908) 56 (Feb. 10, 1910).

[51] *Ibid.*, 297 (Feb. 12, 1899), 407 (Dec. 7, 1904), 338 (Jan. 8, 1901); Sweet, *Story of Religion*, pp. 389–90.

[52] Session Minutes, III:313, 317–8 (Feb. 1, Mar. 18, 1900, 349 (June 4, 1901).

[53] *Ibid.*, III:393 (Feb. 17, 1904), IV:137 (Feb. 11, 1916).

[54] *Ibid.*, III:405, 409 (Oct. 26, Dec. 28, 1904); Trustee Minutes, IV:264 (May 10, 1875); Stokes, *Iconography*, III:763; V:1930.

[55] *Presbyterian Home for Aged Women in the City of New York: The First Hundred Years, 1866–1966.*

[56] *Year Book*, 1893.

[57] *Year Book, 1899;* Mrs. John Finley, "Women of the First Church," *The Church Tower*, Nov. 1956; *The New York Times*, Dec. 22, 1854, 3:3.

[58] Session Minutes, IV:91 (Oct. 25, 1912); *Year Book*, 1907 pp. 45–6; Peter I. Mensus to the Session, June 10, 1910 in Duffield Correspondence.

[59] Session Minutes, IV:112 (March 13, 1914) *The New York Times*, March 2, 1914; Frank Tannenbaum to Deacon Theodore D. Martin, March 10, 1914, in Duffield Correspondence. Later two prominent Catholic laymen became interested in Mr. Tannenbaum and saw that he received advanced education. He ended his career as professor of Latin-American History at Columbia University.

[60] Session Minutes, IV:119 (Oct. 16, 1914).

[61] *Ibid.*, IV:156, 161–3, 165–6, 170, 172–3 (Mar. 21, Apr. 6, 8, 29, Oct. 16, 31, 1917), 176 (Jan. 13, 1918); Sweet, *Story of Religion*, p. 391; *The New York Times*, Jan. 6, 1941, 15:3–4

CHAPTER FIVE

An Emphasis on Missions to Immigrants

"The genesis of the Presbyterian Church on University Place was unique," said one of the ministers of that church. "It had no infancy, no early struggle for existence. Like Athena it sprang into being mature and fully equipped." Unlike First Church it had no long history, no organization; it did not move from one locality to another. It began November 28, 1843, when a "few gentlemen residents in the upper part of the City of New York, impressed with the importance of providing Church accommodations for themselves and others where they might enjoy the privileges of Divine Worship in connection with the Presbytery of New York, met at the home of George Griswold (on Washington Square) for the purpose of considering the practicability of erecting a suitable Church edifice in some convenient neighborhood north of Washington Square."

They immediately took up a subscription and shortly had almost $60,000, with individual contributions ranging from $250 to $6,000. They were incorporated as the Presbyterian Church on University Place; they purchased a site at Tenth Street and University Place, February 21, 1844, and selected as architect Richard Upjohn, who was supervising the construction of Trinity Church. Until the church building was ready, regular meetings were held in the chapel of New York University with the Rev. George Potts as pastor.[1] He was the son of a minister.

Born in Philadelphia in 1802, Potts had come in 1837 to the Presbyterian church on Duane Street shortly after it had moved from Cedar. The Cedar Street Church had been organized in 1808 by a group from First Church who disliked the collegiate ministry system. By 1840, however, Duane Church was losing members as families moved uptown, and about half of the group forming the University Place Church had been members of the Duane church.[2]

On June 12, 1845, the new church, although unfinished, was dedicated. It was of brownstone and was Gothic in style; it followed the beautiful lines of the Salisbury Cathedral in England. It was 146 by 60 feet with a spire 140 feet in height. The roof supported by five columns of freestone gave the interior an impressive appearance.[3]

On October 15, a petition signed by 158 members was presented to the Presbytery of New York; it declared their "sincere attachment to the doctrines and government of the Christian church as maintained by the Presbytery" and expressed the hope the Presbytery would consent to their union under its auspices.[4] Most of the petitioners were of New England origin and included such well known people as James Brown (1791–1877), head of Brown Brothers, "one of the most influential financial houses in the country;" Dr. Horace Green (1802–1866), founder and president of New York Medical College; William Curtis Noyes,

The Presbyterian Church on University Place, 10th Street, New York City, erected 1845

University Place Church Pastor, 1846–1864, George Potts

lawyer; Willard Parker, physician; and Henry J. Raymond (1820–1869), later founder of *The New York Times*.[5] The petition was granted, and three elders and two deacons were elected. The congregation by unanimous vote called Dr. Potts as minister at a salary of $4,000. He was installed on November 26, 1845, and a new Presbyterian church was born.[6]

The church did not have a complex organization. There were very few members on the various boards, and it seems that the deacons and trustees attended the meetings of the session.[7] There was one interesting case brought before the session in its judicature character. A member of the church confessed that "in his business relations he had fallen into scandalous and aggravated sin" and thereby had "greatly wounded the cause of Christ." He had appropriated funds belonging to his employers. Because of the extensive public knowledge of the case, the session decided it was necessary he be suspended from church privileges until "time shall have tested the *sincerity* of his professed repentence." A year later, after his humble confession of his sin and his plea to be restored to enjoying the privileges of the church before he went to a remote part of the country, he was again allowed to receive communion. The decision was read before the congregation at the preparatory service.[8]

There was also an almost humorous dispute between the pastor and the clerk of the session over jurisdiction of the Church Record Book. Dr. Horace Green (elder from 1845–1866) resigned as clerk in May, 1857, and was succeeded by Robert M. Brown (elder, 1856–1860), who immediately took possession of the Church Record Book. A heated correspondence with Potts ensued. The session took up the issue and decided that the clerk should have possession of the book to write up the minutes, "But the Book and the use thereof are for the benefit of the Pastor and the Session, and is their property, subject to their order, at all reasonable times and for all reasonable purposes." They further stated the session should elect a new clerk. Brown resigned but threatened an appeal to the Presbytery. Green took over his old job.[9]

The Presbyterian Church on University Place was composed of very wealthy members — it was said more than in any other New York City church, and they were generous in their contributions to support the Presbyterian boards and similar organizations (1848 - Domestic missions, Foreign missions, Bible Society, Tract Society, Sabbath School, Education, Colonization Society). They were particularly interested in the Church Extension Board which was put on their list in 1867. Its object was to assist new or field churches to become self-sufficient, to purchase places of public worship, and "in general to call out and combine the entire strength of our churches to evangelize this great City." The same year they added the Fund for Disabled Ministers.[10]

Shortly after the church was opened the Ladies Charitable Society was organized. It provided garments for the needy in the mission schools, sent boxes of clothing to missionaries in western America, and during the Civil War made garments and sent books to the U. S. Sanitary Commission, and after the war took up collections for the Freedmen. As usual the deacons had charge of caring for the poor of the church. There were, however, few poor in the parish. One case well illustrates the Calvinist work ethic: the church aided a woman by loaning her a sewing machine (worth $165) so she could support herself and her mother. Fifteen years later after she had proved her diligence, the church decided to relinquish all claim of ownership to the machine. Usually there was an excess of money in the deacons' fund, and money was given to several city organizations, e.g. The Society for the Relief of Poor Widows with Small Children, to the Female Assistance Society, to the New York Magdelene Society and to the New York City Mission Society.[11]

Members of the church were prominent in the formation of interdenominational organizations. The Association for the Improving of the Condition of the Poor (A.I.C.P.) was organized in July, 1843, and was the first to "rally the most intelligent and concerned citizens in a concerted effort to understand the reasons for poverty as well as to meet the emergent needs of the poor themselves." The leader was James Brown, trustee (1844–1877) and elder (1867–1877) in University Place church. Three more of the six founders were also Presbyterians: James Boorman, merchant and founder of the Bank of Commerce, trustee (1836–1842) in the Mercer Street church; James Lenox of First church; and Apollos R. Wetmore of the Madison Square Presbyterian church.

These six men had also been leaders in the New York Tract Society and had learned from the "visitors" of that society about the appalling conditions in which the poor lived. It is possible that the most valuable service the visitors rendered was not in the number of Bibles and religious tracts distributed but in the knowledge of urban blight they gathered in their institutions. Many were stimulated to seek reform and change to remove the obvious inhumanity forced upon those in desperate need.

The A.I.C.P. was the forerunner of professional social work agencies in the city. Volunteers of the organization visited families and referred them to a charitable organization. It also attempted to improve health conditions, opened the first public bath in 1852 and tried to correct the abuses in the tenements.[12] The Young Men's Christian Association grew out of a prayer meeting of seven men in 1852, four of whom were members of the University Place Church. Two of the other three, William E. Dodge and D. Willis James, were members of the Madison Square Presbyterian Church.[13]

II

The mission Sabbath schools were a distinctive mark of the University Place Church. One scholar described these missions as "giving a valuable ministry to people who could not come to the mother church either because of geographical or social distances." Early in the congregation's life (February, 1847) Potts organized such a school in the public school building in 13th Street; it was called the U. P. C. mission. Within two years it had 150 scholars and 15 teachers; by 1857 there were 300 scholars. The first superintendent was Henry H. Bull, a deacon. Prayer meetings for adults were also held in the same building.

Another mission was established in 1854 on Laurens Street (West Broadway), between Prince and Houston. In addition to Sabbath school in the morning and afternoon, preaching services were conducted on Sunday evenings by the Rev. Henry B. Chapin. They also had a meeting for the rougher boys not adaptable to Sabbath School. Prayer meetings were held in the tenements during the week. In 1858 the Laurens mission united with the 13th Street one, and the trustees leased a portion of a building on 140 Sixth Avenue formerly used by the Half Orphan Asylum (to which University Place church had contributed since 1845). The session supervised the new enterprise. The rooms in the building were so commodious it was decided to establish regular preaching services, and the Rev. Charles H. Payson was appointed missionary. He had charge of the school and also preached the gospel (salary - $1,000). In 1860 his place was taken by a student from Princeton Seminary (Mr. Briggs), but times were hard so when he resigned in 1862 preaching was suspended until 1867.[14]

The superintendent of the Mission School from 1863–1868 was Elder Latimer Bailey; in the latter year he asked for a letter of dismissal to join First Church, where he became active in their mission school on 12th Street. The session considered the mission on Sixth Avenue an important function of University Place Church and appointed Joseph M. Greene as missionary to preach there on Sunday evenings as well as supervise the mission. The session appointed one of its members to assist persons attending the Mission School or chapel who were in need of money from the poor fund. This mission was the church's pet charity, and collections for its support were taken every year. Sums of $1,200 each were appropriated for the rent of the building and the salary of the missionary.[15]

The Civil War was a troublesome time for the church on University Place. It was of the Old School and probably somewhat sympathetic to the South. After the split in 1837 Southern Presbyterian churches had belonged to the same General Assembly. Potts, an "elegant preacher," was in failing health and frequently out of the pulpit. Moreover, he seemed greatly disturbed by the war, which was understandable since he had served a church in Natchez, Mississippi, for a dozen years. The congregation suffered: membership was down to two hundred, and many pews were vacant. Potts preached his last sermon in May, 1864, and died September 15.[16]

It was a year before a new minister was installed, May 3, 1865: the Rev. Alfred H. Kellogg of Easton, Pennsylvania. He was young, only three years out of seminary, and at his instigation the number of elders and deacons were increased but with a limited term (three years) for active service. Re-election was allowed, however. Also $9,000 was raised to aid the Morrisania Presbyterian Church (Washington Ave. south of 168th Street) which was then renamed the Potts Memorial Church. Morrisania's pastor was Arthur, son of George Potts. He had suggested the aid as a more fitting memorial than an expensive monument in the cemetery.

Kellogg was a scholar, very much interested in Egyptian studies. This interest seems to have been responsible for his resignation on April 24, 1870, so that he could spend some time abroad pursuing his studies.[17]

III

Following the war, the divisions within the Presbyterian Church came to an end. The Old School and New School groups were reunited in 1869. But Presbyterians in the South maintained their separate status, taking the name of Presbyterian Church of the United States. New York City had thirty Presbyterian churches with nine missions, ranking fourth behind the Episcopalians (57 churches and 22 missions), the Roman Catholics (35 churches) and the Methodists (34 churches and 15 missions).[18]

For the Presbyterian Church on University Place, having just lost its pastor, the time seemed appropriate to entertain the

The Mercer Street Presbyterian Church, 1835, and two of its socially-conscious pastors, Thomas Harvey Skinner, 1835–1848 (above left) and George Lewis Prentiss, 1851–1858.

possibility of a merger with the Mercer Street Church, anxious to move north from its location south of Washington Square. Mercer Street Church had been organized on October 25, 1835, by a group of thirty people who met in a lecture room at the University of New York. They built a church on Mercer Street near Waverly Place — "one of the most beautiful and commodious church edifices in the city," according to a contemporary. Their first minister, the Rev. Thomas H. Skinner, D.D. (1791–1871), had been professor of Sacred Rhetoric at Andover Seminary and was installed at Mercer Street on November 11, 1835. He favored the New School and almost immediately was instrumental in organizing the nondenominational Union Theological Seminary in 1836.[19]

New School Presbyterianism was liberal in its concern for social issues focusing on reform movements such as temperance and abolition, with heavy emphasis on evangelism and "being born again." Thus the elders in Mercer Street Church examined applicants for membership as to their "experimental acquaintance with religion" and if satisfactory they were admitted to membership. The session called for frequent days of fasting, humiliation, and prayer "because of the low state of religion" in the church, and periodically they had a week of evening services. Instead of using the hymn book recommended by the General Assembly, they used Watts' psalms and hymns. They had not only a chorister but also an organ, one of the first in a Presbyterian church.[20]

With a well organized program of visitations, each elder had a number of members assigned to his care by the pastor. A report on the visits was made at the regular weekly meetings of the session. When the visits were completed the members of the session exchanged lists and the visits continued. The membership grew from 277 in 1837 to 403 in 1838 and reached its peak in 1844 with 773 members.[21]

The session of the Mercer Street Presbyterian Church considered several cases of moral transgression by members. In contrast to the eighteenth century when the cases taken up in sessions concerned fornication, intemperance, swearing and petty thievery, those in the nineteenth century more often dealt with irregular business practices. The Mercer Street session was incensed that one of the church members had been guilty of purloining moneys from his employers in Philadelphia and making false entries in the books to conceal the theft. He came to New York, appeared before the session, admitted his guilt but immediately went to London not expecting to return. He could not, therefore, be brought to trial, "yet the honor of the cause of Christ demands that the said [Malcolm] Ives should be cut off from the Communion of the Church," noted the session. It resolved, "that the Pastor publish both his excommunication and the reasons therefor from the pulpit next Sabbath afternoon."[22]

Another member was charged with selling as his own property, and appropriating the proceeds, a home which had been loaned to him by the deacons. He was further charged with attempting to get money by false pretenses. He wrote to his wife's employer and asked for an advance on her wages. He appeared before session and admitted his guilt. He was excluded from the privileges of the church, and a committee was appointed "whose duty shall be to endeavor to reclaim him." He was not "reclaimed," however. Instead of giving evidence of repentance after his suspension, he was convicted of drunkenness and stealing and sentenced to Blackwells Island. The session resolved he be excommunicated.[23]

In another case a bookkeeper was found guilty of forgery while employed with the Bank of Commerce. He met with the session, confessed and repented. But since he had been indicted before a criminal court, the session resolved:

> That in view of the aggravated nature of Mr. William Cutters offence and the great reproach it has brought upon religion, the Session judge that he ought to be suspended from the communion of the church, not withstanding his profession of penitence, and he hereby is suspended until the Session shall revoke his sentence.

It was decided not to have a trial. Three years later he appeared before the session and at his request was restored to all the privileges of the church "in view of the satisfactory evidence of true repentance.[24]

Mercer Street Church was particularly active in recruiting young men for the ministry and frequently had six to twelve candidates. When one of them was expelled from Union Theological Seminary for forging a paper of honorable dismissal from Princeton University, he was immediately suspended from the sacraments.[25]

Although New School Presbyterians were not rigorous in doctrinal matters, the Mercer Street session was alert to any deviation. When having evidence that two women had united with a Roman Catholic church, their names were struck from the record and the action was announced to the congregation. Yet in some cases the Presbytery did not think the church was firm enough. Parke Godwin had been absent from church for some time so a committee waited on him. He informed them "that his religious views had so far changed that he could no longer conscientiously consider himself a member of this, or any other existing Church, and wishing his name to be erased from the roll, the remonstrance of said committee not producing any change in his views it was resolved his name be struck from the rolls. The Presbytery said that the Session should have instituted a trial in due form." In another case Lafayette Bushnell submitted to the session a "paper containing an expression of his dissent from the Doctrinal Standards of the Presbr. Church especially as relating to the doctrines of the Divinity of Christ and atonement." The session voted to exclude him from communion. The moderator of Presbytery criticized the brevity of the minutes as a departure from the technical provisions of the Book of Discipline.[26]

The congregation of Mercer Street Church was economically wealthy and without financial difficulties such as so frequently plagued the First Presbyterian Church. Three of its trustees, Eli Wainwright (1836−1843), James Boorman (1836−1842) and Charles Butler (1836−1839), were responsible for the formation of the Protestant Half-Orphan Asylum in 1835. They rented a house on 12th Street and hired a matron to take care of the forty-nine orphan children. The Society was incorporated by the legislature on April 27, 1837, as "The Society for the Relief of Half-Orphan and Destitute Children in the City of New York." The organization was almost solely a Mercer Street society. In January, 1847, the pastor and Anson G. Phelps represented the church in an association organized to promote city missions.[27]

The Mercer Street Church session was also responsive to requests for help from other churches. They answered the appeal of the Eighth Presbyterian Church in Greenwich Village (at Christopher Street) which First Church had had to refuse. Organized in 1819, it was a church often in financial trouble, and appeals were made to other Presbyterian churches to help to preserve Presbyterianism and prevent their having to merge with other denominations. The Mercer Church resolved (1839):

> That the Session regard the Village Church as occupying a position peculiarly important and interesting and is entitled to the patronage of the Christian Community, and cordially recommend their application to the favorable consideration of the members of this church.

The sum of $100 was taken from the collection made for the American Home Missionary Society and given to the Village Church. Despite such efforts the church finally gave up the struggle in 1841.[28]

Mercer Street also helped out the First Colored Presbyterian Church which had been established in 1822, and took up collections to aid "feeble churches." It was generous to the First German church established in New York City in 1853. The gift enabled them to employ a missionary to labor among the Germans, aided their Sunday School and helped them meet the current expenses of the church.[29] (In 1850 the Germans were the second largest immigrant group entering New York City.)

Skinner resigned in February, 1848, to take a position as professor of Sacred Rhetoric and Pastoral Theology at Union Theological Seminary. His successor at Mercer Street was the Rev. Joseph C. Stiles of Richmond, Virginia, who had been a controversial figure in a church in Kentucky where he had been reprimanded by the Presbytery for preaching against the actions of the General Assembly in 1837 exciding some western synods.[30]

His stay at the Mercer Street Church was only two years. He resigned to become secretary of the American Bible Society.

The congregation nominated the Rev. Mark Hopkins (1802–1887) as pastor. He was president of Williams College, and his reputation as teacher was so highly regarded that a college was defined as "Mark Hopkins on one end of a log and a student on the other." He accepted the call to the Mercer Street Church but later decided against it.[31]

The Rev. George L. Prentiss (1807–1880) of Newark, New Jersey, was installed in 1851. Shortly after he took office a meeting of the congregation was called "to consider our duties in relation to the spiritual necessities of this city and vicinity." The influx of immigrants into New York City had reached more than 200,000 a year. They crowded into the homes left by those who had moved uptown and into tenements. Conditions were deplorable. The church formed the City Missionary Association on November 25, 1851, to "promote the diffusion of the Gospel amongst the spiritually destitute in this city by establishing and sustaining preaching stations and sabbath schools." Every member of the congregation who contributed to the fund became a member of the Association.[32]

At the first meeting of the Association it was decided to have four subcommittees who would explore the area around Broadway and Broome for possible mission sites. Three were selected: the Sixth Street Church which was ready to be dissolved, with the Rev. Franklin S. Howe employed to preach; in the ninth ward on Amos Street, a Sabbath School and a Boys' Meeting were set up but lasted only until December, 1853.[33]

The most successful project was in the eleventh ward at 118 Avenue D., between Eighth and Ninth Streets. Called The Dry Dock Mission because of its location in the shipyard section, it had a flourishing Sabbath School under the superintendency of Judge John L. Mason (trustee of Mercer Street 1836–1842). Union Seminary students were employed to recruit pupils for the school, with transportation provided to teachers at the school. An active Temperance Association was connected with the mission. Although there was a missionary pastor, there was no regular church organization, and so the young people joined either the Eleventh Presbyterian Church, Mercer, or University Place.

The Eleventh Presbyterian Church was sold for a synagogue, and the Rev. Erastus Seymour (1829–1891) was appointed as missionary to the Dry Dock Mission at a salary of $100 a month. Not only were religious services held at the Dry Dock Mission but the sacrament of communion was administered every other month. In this service Seymour was assisted by two elders from Mercer Street Church.[34]

In May, 1858, Prentiss resigned for reasons of ill health. His successor, the Rev. Walter Clarke, resigned two years later giving as his reason declining revenues and the northward movement of the population. The Rev. Robert R. Booth from the Presbyterian Church at Stamford, Connecticut, was called. But the Mercer Street church was losing its congregation, and so in 1867 there was serious concern at the congregational meeting as to the best methods for promoting its spiritual welfare. It was decided to resume both the Sabbath evening meeting and the Wednesday prayer meeting.[35]

The congregation also considered moving and looked for a new site as far north as Forty-sixth Street. Then in the spring of 1870 informal conversations began between representatives of the University Place and Mercer Street congregations as to the expediency of combining the two congregations. The churches belonged to different presbyteries, but this problem was solved when at the order of the General Assembly, July 27, 1870, the four presbyteries of New York were organized into one — the Presbytery of New York, which had been incorporated by the legislature on March 30, 1867. This Presbytery now included 132 ministers and 42 churches.

The union was approved by the two congregations and the agreement was ratified by the Presbytery on September 16, 1870. The edifice of the Mercer Street church was sold for $50,000. The resulting church was named the Presbyterian Church on University Place in the City and State of New York. The united congregation met on September 22 to complete the organization and selected as pastor the Rev. Robert R. Booth at a salary of $6,000. At the time of the union University Place church had a membership of 216 and Mercer Street of 580.[36]

The Presbyterian Church at University Place prospered under the leadership of Dr. Booth, installed October 30, 1870. Church membership increased to 1300 in 1883. The church Sabbath School met at 9:45 a.m., and the pastor conducted a Bible class for adults at the same hour. Services were held at 11 a.m. and 8 p.m. The Young People held a prayer meeting at 7:45 p.m. Communion service was held at 4 p.m. on Sunday afternoons five times a year. Prayer meeting was held on Wednesday evening and a special Bible class conducted by the pastor on Friday morning.[37]

The Board of Trustees of nine members was headed by Dr. Willard Parker. He was succeeded by Robert Lenox Belknap, who remained president until his death in 1896. For the following ten years Thomas Denny was president. There were three committees: church property, pews, and Emmanuel Chapel. The church insured both their pastor and the pastor of Emmanuel with the Society for Promoting Life Insurance among Clergymen.[38]

Suffering poor health, Booth submitted his resignation in 1883 after a pastorate of twenty-two years (thirteen with the new church). A committee of seven was selected to find a new minister, and they settled on George Alexander, pastor of a mission church in a "disreputable suburb" of Schenectady. He was also professor of Logic and Rhetoric at Union College. The committee reported that he was a man of fine appearance, had a good voice and his sermons were not too long. He had been born on October 12, 1843, near West Charlton, New York, had attended Union college (later he was on the Board of Trustees), finished Princeton Theological Seminary in June, 1870, and was ordained the same year. The congregation voted to call him at a salary of $6,000, and he was installed on January 8, 1884. In 1891 he was joined by an assistant, the Rev. Herbert Ford, whose responsibilities included the Sabbath School and "The Weekly Reminder" containing the announcements the pastor ordinarily made from the pulpit. Music was an important part of the service, and the music budget was almost equal to half the pastor's salary. William Adrian Smith had been organist and director of music at University Place church since 1866.[39]

Most of the organizations of the church were devoted to missionary work of some kind. The Women's Home Missionary Society had replaced the Ladies Charitable Society, and the Women's Foreign Missionary Society was formed in 1873. The Light-Bearers Mission Band was formed in 1884 to cultivate the missionary spirit in the young, and shortly after that the Boys' Missionary Society (1886) and the Young Women's Circle (1890) were formed. The Huguenot Auxiliary (1893) was organized to aid the Reform Church in France to carry on home missionary work; it helped support a colporteur in France and distributed Bibles and tracts.[40] The Young Men's Society, headed by Thomas Denny, was responsible for ushering at the evening service, and young men visited hotels on Saturday night to invite transients to services. In 1894 it was suggested that pews for the evening service be free; there was some opposition, and it was resolved that pew holders who objected should give notice and their pew would be reserved as usual. Some members donated money so that certain pews would be free at all services. One of these, Emily Wheeler, had a plate attached to the pew: "As long as the church stands, the stranger within our gates and the poor may feel they have a welcome." The church also maintained a kindergarten on week days and a Children's Hour on Saturday mornings. In 1899 Miss Sarah J. Tibbal donated a home in Ocean Grove, New Jersey, where working women in the church could spend a two-week vacation at small expense.[41]

The sanctuary was modernized in 1884. A new organ and choir loft were installed; glass in the windows was changed; the chandeliers were replaced. High on the wall behind the pulpit was a sign which read: "God is in His Holy Temple — Let all the earth keep silence before Him!" On one side wall were the ten commandments in large blue and gold letters. A parishioner related that when Alexander entered through a small door and took his place at the pulpit, his face seemed "full of peace and joy." In

George Alexander, long-time University Place-First Church Pastor, 1884–1930

Interior of the University Place Presbyterian Church, 10th Street and University Place, New York City

1894 electric lights, donated by the women's organizations, were installed, and a church house — Jubilee Hall — that was later furnished with shower baths and gymnasium was built.[42]

IV

University Place Church had two flourishing missions, one on the lower East side and the other in the west village. In the spring of 1872 the session recommended construction of facilities for a mission in the eastern part of the city and expressed the hope that the congregation would contribute liberally to provide them. A committee was authorized to purchase a site and take subscriptions. By the end of that year $72,650 had been raised; the largest contributor was John C. Green, who had been a member of the board of trustees from 1844–1875 and had served as treasurer for twenty-eight years. He contributed $26,000. James Brown contributed $11,000. A site was purchased on the north side of Sixth Street between Avenues C and D in the 11th ward at the cost of $85,433 with title vested in the University Place church. The new building was dedicated on March 29, 1874. The name of the mission was changed from Dry Dock mission to Emmanuel Chapel.[43]

Erastus Seymour, who in 1864 had come to the Dry Dock Mission and who studied medicine in order to help the people of the congregation, continued as pastor in the new location. Not only were church services held on the Sabbath but prayer meetings on Tuesday and Friday evenings.

Emmanuel's Sabbath School was the largest in New York City and surpassed nationally only by one conducted by John Wanamaker in Philadelphia. The superintendent from 1855 to 1915 was Otis W. Booth. He and his wife, who taught a class, drove down in their coach to Emmanuel Chapel. The vice-superintendent was Thomas Denny, banker and millionaire. His wife and sister also taught classes. Once a year the boys in Miss Adeline Denny's class were invited to her home at 19 West 36th Street. Often they had to walk from the lower East Side for want of money for carfare. Teams of young men combed the district from Houston to 23rd Street from the East River to Third Avenue, ringing door bells to invite the children to the Sabbath School.

In addition to the Sabbath School Emmanuel had an active program of Mothers' meetings for the German immigrants, a Young Peoples' Association, a Helping Hand Committee, and an Industrial School that taught basket making and sewing to girls and woodwork to boys. Bible readers visited the sick and poor of the ward. There was also a trained nurse supported by the Dennys.

For city slum dwellers the Fresh Air projects were a great blessing. The first Fresh Air Fund was established by the New York City Mission and Tract Society in 1868. At Emmanuel one hundred young working women were given the opportunity of two weeks' vacation at Hightstown, New Jersey, at the cost of $7, and the Fresh Air Fund paid their carfare.

The cooking and sewing school was of particular importance. When the pastor of Emmanuel Chapel suggested it be moved elsewhere to keep the place of worship free from secular associations, the session refused. They pointed to the great need for such a school in the neighborhood. It had been housed there for many years, and they regarded it "as a most Christian work in its motives and methods and aims."[44]

A committee of the University Place Church session, consisting of three elders and two from the school, oversaw the chapel. In 1887 Booth and Seymour suggested that four women from the chapel be added to the committee on Emmanuel. Instead the session proposed "it would be more judicious to have a separate committee of female members of the chapel appointed by the session for the work of visitation among the female members of the chapel and for such other ministrations as might be appropriate and under the direction of the Com. on Em. Chapel." Action was postponed because of Booth's opposition to the proposal. Finally in 1892 four women were added to the committee on Emmanuel Chapel.[45]

The chapel grew more rapidly than the church. In 1891 the membership of the church was 700; of the chapel, 952. The church Sabbath School numbered 676 while that of the chapel was 2,260. The chapel depended on the church for financial help, receiving about $3,000 a year plus $1,500 to maintain the building.

Seymour, who had been pastor for twenty-seven years, died in April, 1891. He died in harness: carried home from a prayer meeting, he lay down saying his work was done. His successor, the Rev. Daniel H. Overton, became the stated supply of the chapel until January, 1895, when the Rev. John C. Palmer took over and remained until 1912.

1915 was the peak year for Emmanuel's membership — 1,744 but the same year saw the Sabbath School decline to 1,193 pupils, a reflection of the neighborhood's changing population. The German immigrants were moving to other parts of the city. A factor in their migration may have been the *Slocum* disaster. A fire broke out when the young people of St. Marks Lutheran Church were on their annual excursion up the East River. Over 1000 lost their lives in the fire (64 were from Emmanuel). The effect on the morale of the Germans was devastating. The Germans were replaced by Polish Catholics and Jews. There were few Protestants left in that area.[46]

V

University Place Church's outreach on the west side, the Sixth Avenue Mission, was in charge of Lewis R. Foote. In October, 1873, it changed its name to Bethlehem Mission. The number of churches in the vicinity was increasing so it was decided that the mission should concentrate on its Sabbath School. The work conducted in the Sixth Avenue location was taken over by the New York Presbyterian Church, and the University Place Church moved the Bethlehem program to rooms in the Public School building at 180 Wooster. Bethlehem had a more modest program than Emmanuel and received an appropriation of only $600 a year from the church.

In 1884 the school authorities forbade the use of a public school building for religious instruction and the session decided: "Good impressions made in the S[abbath] S.[school] and religious susceptibilities awakened there could not be crystalized for want of means adapted to such an end -Nor could effective and permanent influences for good be exercised upon the godless multitudes among whom the work of the mission lies." So room was acquired at 222 Thompson between Bleecker and West Third, and a student from Union Seminary was employed to take charge.[47]

In March, 1889, Alexander presented University Place's congregation with the necessity of providing a permanent home for the Bethlehem Mission. By September, $50,000 had been sub-scribed by the members of the church, property at 196 Bleecker Street purchased, and a chapel was dedicated on February 14, 1890. A committee headed by Frederick A. Booth, clerk of the session and treasurer of the trustees, supervised the work of the mission. Booth served in this capacity for twenty-one years until his death in 1913. For three years Christopher Humber, M.D. of Wichita, Kansas, was in charge of the Mission. When he resigned the church's pastoral assistant, the Rev. Herbert Ford, took over the work, and under his auspices communion was served at Bethlehem for the first time in twenty years. Regular church services were held on Sunday and Thursday evenings. Members were received into the membership of Bethlehem Chapel, and their names were also carried on the roll of University Place Church. There were 138 members of the chapel and 300 in the Sabbath School.

When Ford became pastor of the Presbyterian Church at Palisades, New York, in March 1900 the Rev. G. H. Simonson took his place. From 1904–1912 the assistant pastor of the Spring Church, Joseph W. Miller, was in charge.[48]

As the area's population increased in density and conditions of overcrowding mounted, people appeared less inclined to go to church. University Place Church noted:

> Such conditions have led many churches to throw much of their strength into what has been called institutional work. Their aim has been to draw the surrounding community into friendly relations with the Church by ministering to their natural craving for amusement, for recreation, for social pleasure, or for instruction in gainful arts. . . . (But)
>
> Partly through force of circumstances, partly in consequence of convictions gradually formed we have been led to emphasize the spiritual mission of the Church—rather than her social mission—to make our primary appeal to the religious craving rather than to the physical and social cravings of the people.[49]

The Mission, however, was not without many social and intel-lectual activities. Lectures and socials were held in the chapel, and there was complaint that the young people were too hilarious. Four workers were connected with the Mission, one of whom was supported by the New York City Mission and Tract Society. The teachers taught not only religion but also arithmetic, writing and reading, and in 1905 there were classes in typing and stenog-raphy. The Free Kindergarten Association of New York used certain rooms for their work, paying $8 a month towards the cost of the extra cleaning. The Mission also had an active circulating library. In 1908 a gymnasium was outfitted and there was physical training for girls, a baseball nine and a basketball league for boys. Those who were not members of the mission were charged one cent an afternoon for use of the gym; the money was used to buy basketballs. In 1903 a branch of the Penny Provident Bank was established to receive the savings of the children; they varied from one cent to one dollar deposits. Every summer a boat was chartered for a day's excursion up the river. The mission also furnished the ice (200 pounds a day) for the neighborhood fountain, consisting of a pipe and cup.[50]

In the 1890's the population around the mission became heavily Italian as immigrants from Northern Italy moved into the section west of Broadway. Only about three percent of them were Protestant but many were without a church affiliation although baptized in the Roman Catholic faith. Bethlehem adapted its work to this growing group and in 1896 an Italian class was formed at the mission led by a Mrs. Perenti. In 1899 services in Italian were begun on Sunday afternoons, led by Eleanor M. Pendleton, the New York City Mission Society worker. The Mission committee refused to appropriate funds for her work. Although in sympathy with the effort, they were not willing to provide money for a worker not under their supervision.[51]

Emily Wheeler felt strongly the need for Christian work among the burgeoning Italian populace and offered University Place leaders $50,000 toward that end. Mrs. Edith P. Stimson also contributed a large sum for the same purpose. The house next to Bethlehem Chapel (198 Bleecker Street) was purchased for $35,000, and services for adults in Italian and for children in English began in June 1904. Carlo G. Barbuto was missionary for work with the Italian people and those recommended by him and examined on the catechism by the session of the University Place Church, were received as members of that church on confession of faith. Communion services in Italian were also held in the mission house, with elders of University Place serving the elements.[52]

The building at 198 Bleecker was named "The Memorial House" and was run by a special committee of three women and four men with Emily Wheeler as its dominant force. She contributed $29,000 as basis for an endowment whose income was used for work at Memorial House. She was instrumental in establishing a milk station to provide bottled milk for sick babies. She paid to have a door cut through to the chapel building to make room for a day nursery. The enrollment was 44, the maximum number the facilities could maintain, with a cook, nurse, and matron. A doctor from the Board of Health visited the nursery each day. The near-by public school sent over several children, whose mothers worked, to receive a hot meal in the middle of the day.

The work with the Italian immigrants flourished. By 1910 there were fifty to sixty present at worship, and at the last communion service in that year, six new members were received. All offerings received at the Italian services were used for the mission. In 1911 a summer Bible school was held with a student from Auburn Seminary in charge; this was the first one in the city. The average attendance was 180. The yard was opened in the summer and girls used it in the morning and the boys in the afternoon.[53]

In 1916 Miss Wheeler offered to meet the expenses for a new building needed to provide more room for the Sunday School and recreational activities. It was decided to replace 196 Bleecker with "a building better adapted to the needs of the work." In January, 1917 the Rev. F. J. Panetta ended his work at the mission, and the Rev. Thomas Barbieri was appointed to take charge of the Italian speaking congregation. The Bethlehem and Memorial House committees were combined and took responsibility for all the work on Bleecker Street. The area was almost solidly Italian, and Bethlehem concentrated on their needs.[54]

VI

At the same time women were playing an increasing role in the life of the home church on University Place. In 1915, Alexander formed the Pastor's Aid Committee, all of whom were women, with Mrs. Thomas Denny as the convenor. They had a hospitality committee to welcome and visit strangers. Invitations to attend church services were placed in the nearby Martha Washington Hotel. Mrs. Denny sent her carriage to bring the elderly to communion services. A Helping Hand committee aided needy families with clothing, bedding, milk and eggs and even with the payment of rent. In some cases they tried to find better apartments for poor families living in unfit quarters. There was a committee on literature that distributed books and magazines. When the United States became involved in war in 1917, the women of University Place decided that the church was "sort of a humanitarian and patriotic center and many are looking to it for guidance." They formed a chapter of the Red Cross Auxiliary at the church to make surgical dressings, hospital garments, etc., and contributed a Ford ambulance, which was given to the Red Cross.[57]

But the area around University Place Church had become increasingly mercantile. The church which had been composed of such wealthy men began to experience financial pressures. A permanent endowment had been started in 1891 with $60,000. By 1915 it had reached $223,409.53, including the funds earmarked for the chapels. The combined revenues from pew rents ($4,000), endowment ($6,900) and offerings ($5,400), however, did not cover expenses. Alexander offered to take just half his salary, and the salary of his assistant, the Rev. Thomas Guthrie Speers (appointed in May, 1916), was only $1,500 (in March, 1917, he was made an associate minister at $2,500 but shortly after that he left to become a chaplain in the United States army).[56]

Many of the trustees and elders who had helped form the

church died early in the twentieth century, and it was difficult to find men to fill the positions on the boards. It was especially difficult to get a quorum for meetings of the board of trustees, and it was decided that an executive committee of five would take care of the investment of endowment funds and all expenditures. More and more there was discussion of a union with First Church, which was only two blocks away. They had held joint services in the summer and on special holidays. There was much surprise when a third church decided to join in the merger, the Madison Square Presbyterian Church at 24th Street and Madison Avenue.[57]

[1]George Alexander, "History of the University Place Presbyterian Church," *The Church Tower*, January, 1925, p. 11; University Place Presbyterian Church (U.P.) Session Minutes, I:1−2 (Nov. 28, 1843).

[2]Alexander, "University Place Church," *The Church Tower*, Feb. 1925, pp. 7−8; U.P. Session Minutes, I:131−6; Savage, *Presbyterian Churches in New York City*, p. 142.

[3]Stokes, *Iconography*, V:1791.

[4]U.P. Session Minutes, I:2−3.

[5]Alexander, "University Place Church," *The Church Tower*, Feb., 1925, p. 7; Frank R. Kent, "James Brown," *DAB*, III:126−7; U.P. Session Minutes, I:154 (Dec. 7, 1866).

[6]U.P. Session Minutes, I:9−12.

[7]*Ibid.*, I:8.

[8]*Ibid.*, I:45−6 (Dec. 7, 1848), 55 (Dec. 31, 1849), 56−7 (Jan. 11, 1850).

[9]*Ibid.*, I:87 (May 4, 1857), 112−7 (Oct. 8, Nov. 16, 1859), 125 (Jan. 10, 1862).

[10]*Ibid.*, I:42 (Sept. 29, 1848), 163 (Apr. 18, 1867), 191−3 (Apr. 18, June 11, 1869).

[11]*Ibid.*, I:83−4 (Jan. 21, Feb. 4, 1856). 92 (Nov. 16, 1857), II:94 (May 7, 1873); *Services Commemorative of the Fiftieth Anniversary of the University Place Presbyterian Church*, Nov. 24−28, 1895, p. 135.

[12]Alexander, "University Place Church," *The Church Tower*, Feb. 1925, p. 21; Miller, *People are the City*, p. 59; Carroll Smith Rosenberg, *Religion and the Rise of the American City. The New York City Mission Movement* (Ithaca, 1971), p. 247; Robert R. Rowe, "James Boorman," *DAB*, I:443; Kent, "Brown," *DAB*, III:126−7.

[13]Alexander, "University Place Church," *The Church Tower*, Feb. 1925, p. 21; James Grant Wilson, *Memorial History of the City of New York* (4 vols., New York, 1892), III:441.

[14]Miller, *People are the City*, p. 98; *Fiftieth Anniversary*, pp. 207−9; U.P. Session Minutes, I:92 (Nov. 16, 1857), pp. 98, 106 (June 7, Nov. 5, 1858), 121 (May 11, 1860), 139 (Nov. 13, 1862).

[15]U.P. Session Minutes, I:125 (Mar. 7, 1863), 153 (Sept. 17, 1866), 159−63 (Feb. 8, Mar. 16, Apr. 18, 1867), 179−81 (Feb. 17, Apr. 10, 1868).

[16]*Ibid.*, I:136 (Sept. 1864); Alexander, "University Place Church," *The Church Tower*, Feb. 1925, p. 13.

[17]Alexander, "University Place Church," *The Church Tower*, Feb. 1925, p. 21; U.P. Session Minutes, I:143−7 (Mar. 2, 30, Apr. 6, 1865), 161−3 (Apr. 13, 1867), 199−204 (Mar. 8, 1870), Savage, *Presbyterian Churches in New York City*, pp. 178−9.

[18]Miller, *People are the City*, p. 67; Ahlstrom, *Religious History*, p. 468.

[19]Mercer Church Session Minutes, I:1−2 (Oct. 8, 25, 28, Nov. 5, 11, 1835); *Fiftieth Anniversary*, pp. 22, 56−9.

[20]Mercer Church Minutes, I:8, 9, 12, 25−43 (Feb. 22, Mar. 2, Apr. 22, Oct. 27, Dec. 28, 1836), I:53 (Apr. 20, 1838), 85 (Nov. 25, 1839), 87 (Jan. 15, 1840).

[21]*Ibid.*, I:17 (Sept. 21, 1836), 30, 40 (Feb. 10, Oct. 6, 1837), 64 (Oct. 24, 1838), 170 (May 26, 1844).

[22]*Ibid.*, I:95−8 (Apr. 3, 1840).

[23]*Ibid.*, I:119−22 (Oct. 29, Nov. 12, 19, 1841), 141 (Dec. 16, 1842).

[24]*Ibid.*, I:203−5, 208−10 (Oct. 31, Nov. 7, Dec. 5, 15, 1845), 212 (Jan. 7, 1846), 258−9 (June 10, 1848).

[25]*Ibid.*, I:269 (Jan. 19, 1849), 461−2 (Mar. 29, 1860), 508 (Feb. 6, 1862).

[26]*Ibid.*, I:138 (Dec. 2, 1842), 192 (Dec. 13, 1844), 202 (Oct. 20, 1845), 291 (Apr. 2, 1849), 507, 522 (Feb. 2, Oct. 30, 1862).

[27]*Ibid.*, I:229 (Jan. 15, 1847); *Fiftieth Anniversary*, pp. 76−7; David S. Muzzey, "Charles Butler," *DAB*, II:360.

[28]Mercer Session Minutes, I:78, 85 (Apr. 3, Oct. 18, 1839); Savage, *Presbyterian Churches in New York City*, p. 139; First Church Trustee Minutes, III:87 (May 11, 1822).

[29]Mercer Session Minutes, I:101 (June 5, 1840), 305, 307, 311 (Apr. 4, May 30, Nov. 21, 1851), 317 (Apr. 5, 1852), 331 (Mar. 4, 1853), 410, 412 (Feb. 4, Apr. 1, 1858), 444 (Mar. 10, 1859); Record of Executive Committee of City Missionary Association Connected with Mercer Street Presbyterian Church, Jan. 27, 1855; Savage, *Presbyterian Churches in New York City*, p. 154.

[30]Mercer Session Minutes, I:241, 256 (Feb. 12, May 4, June 2, 1848); Gillett, *Presbyterian Church*, II:539−40; *Fiftieth Anniversary*, pp. 56−9.

[31]Mercer Session Minutes, I:297 (Oct. 15, 1850), 303 (Jan. 17, 1851).

[32]*Ibid.*, I:305 (Apr. 4, 1851); *Fiftieth Anniversary*, pp. 72−3; City Missionary Association, pp. 3−4; William Walker Rockwell, "George Lewis Prentiss," *DAB*, VIII, 189−90.

[33]City Missionary Association, Dec. 8, 20, 27, 1851, Jan. 10, Mar. 27, 1852, Dec. 24, 1853, Apr. 15, 1854.

[34]*Ibid.*, Jan. 10, 1852, Jan. 14, 18, 1854; Mercer Session Minutes, II:7 (June 8, 1865); *Dry Dock Mission, Emmanuel Chapel and Emmanuel Presbyterian Church, One Hundredth Anniversary*, pp. 7−8.

[35]Mercer Session Minutes, I:422−3 (Apr. 19, 23, 1858), 437, 440 (Jan. 7, Feb. 9, 1859), 469 (Dec. 19, 1860).

[36]*Ibid.*, II:140, 144 (June 9, July 31, 1870); U.P. Session Minutes, I:205−9, 211−2 (May 5, Sept. 16, 1870), II:1−7 (Sept. 18, 22, 1870; Alexander, "University Place Church," *The Church Tower*, March 1925, pp. 13−14; S. D. Alexander, *Presbytery of New York*, p. 141.

[37]Alexander, "University Place Church," *The Church Tower*, March, 1925, p. 21; The University Place Church Year Book, 1885; the use of individual communion cups and unfermented wine was adopted May 31, 1914 (see Session Minutes, IV:280).

[38]U.P. Session Minutes, II:56 (Apr. 1, 1872); Trustee Minutes, II:25−6 (Mar. 24, 1884), 38, 41−2 (Feb. 24, May 18, 1885), 145 (Apr. 6, 1896).

[39]U.P. Trustee Minutes, II:2–10, 14–15, 21–22 (May 28, Nov. 7, 1883), 99 (Mar. 19, 1891); U.P. Session Minutes, 337, 341, 345 (July 2, Nov. 3, Dec. 6, 1883); *U.P. Year Book*, 1890–1891, pp. 6–7.

[40]*U.P. Year Book*, 1896–1897, p. 27.

[41]*U.P. Year Books*, 1887–1888, p. 25, 1899–1900, pp. 41–2, 1903–1904, p. 37; U.P. Session Minutes, III:132 (Sept. 27, 1894), 246 (June 16, 1899); U.P. Trustee Minutes, II:126 (Oct. 29, 1894), 175 (Mar. 16, 1899). Mr. Denny was trustee at Mercer Street Church, 1868–70 and at University Place, 1870–1874, 1889–1906.

[42]U.P. Trustee Minutes, II:28–9 (Apr. 16, 1884), 104 (June 7, 1892), 122 (Mar. 12, 1894), 309 (Apr. 1914), 314 (Feb. 11, 1915); *The Church Tower,* April, 1925, p. 10; *U.P. Year Book*, 1895–1896, p. 8; letter to Ruth McLaren, 1977.

[43]U.P. Session Minutes, II:18 (Dec. 8, 1870), 96, 109 (May 14, Dec. 11, 1873), 113 (Mar. 25, 1874), 148–55 (May 13, 1875).

[44]*Dry Dock Mission, One Hundredth Anniversary*, pp. 12, 32–3; U.P. Session Minutes, II:349 (Jan. 10, 1884), III:184 (Feb. 18, 1887); *U.P. Year Books*, 1885, p. 25, 1892–1893, p. 34, 1902–1903, p. 49.

[45]U.P. Session Minutes, II:309 (June 1, 1882), 425 (Apr. 14, 1887), III:43, 49 (Mar. 29, Apr. 29, 1891), 82 (Oct. 26, 1892).

[46]U.P. Session Minutes, II:354 (Mar. 6, 1884), 440 (Jan. 26, 1888), III:44–5, 51 (Apr. 22, May 28, 1891), 141 (Feb. 28, 1895), IV:221 (Nov. 20, 1912); *U.P. Year Book*, 1906–1907, pp. 44–45; *The New York Times,* June 16, 1904, 1–6.

[47]U.P. Session Minutes, II:58 (May 8, 1872), 114, 121–2, 130–1, 134, (Feb. 23, Apr. 9, Oct. 8, Dec. 3, 1874), 362, 370 (June 12, Dec. 4, 1884).

[48]*Ibid.,* II:462 (Mar. 22, 1889), III:6, 7 (Sept. 6, Oct. 13, 1889), 94, 106 (Mar. 23, Sept. 21, 1893), 261 (Mar. 1, 1900), IV:248 (July 2, 1913); U.P. Trustee Minutes, II:115 (Nov. 6, 1893).

[49]*U.P. Year Book*, 1897–1898, p. 9.

[50]Minutes of Bethlehem Chapel Committee, Nov. 9, 1891, Sept. 6, 1893, Jan. 3, 1894, June 29, 1898; U.P. Session Minutes, III:131 (June 16, 1889) *U.P. Year Books*, 1899–1900, pp. 67, 69, 1903–1904, pp. 49, 69.

[51]Bethlehem Chapel Minute Book, Sept. 16, 1896, Dec. 27, 1899, May 16, 1900; John B. Macnab, "Bethlehem Chapel: Presbyterians and Italian Americans in New York City," *Journal of Presbyterian History*, v. 55, no. 2 (Summer, 1977), 145–160; Rosenwaike, *Population History of New York City*, p. 83.

[52]Bethlehem Chapel Minute Book, June 1, 1904, June 3, 1908; U.P. Trustee Minutes, II:229 (Feb. 17, 1904), 252 (Apr. 10, 1907), 258–9 (Dec. 1, 1908); U.P. Session Minutes, III:372 (Mar. 23, 1904), 427 (Oct. 26, 1905).

[53]Minutes of Memorial House Committee, June 1, 1900, Sept. 15, 26, Dec. 30, 1910, Oct. 13, 1911; U.P. Session Minutes, IV:42 (Sept. 25, 1907); *U.P. Year Book*, 1911–1912, p. 74.

[54]Minutes of Memorial House Committee, Jan. 16, 1914, Jan. 5, 1917; U.P. Session Minutes, IV:262 (Jan. 7, 1914), 340 (Oct. 18, 1916), 346 (Feb. 21, 1917), U.P. Trustee Minutes, II:260–1 (Dec. 1, 1908), 321 (Oct. 24, 1916).

[55]Small notebook entitled, "Pastors Aid of the Presbyterian Church on University Place," in Alexander correspondence, church archives.

[56]*U.P. Year Book*, 1889–1890, p. 6; U.P. Trustee Minutes, II:312–3 (Feb. 11, 1915); U.P. Session Minutes, IV:355 (Mar. 7, 1917).

[57]U.P. Session Minutes, IV:396 (July 3, 1918); U.P. Trustee Minutes, II:187 (Dec. 4, 1899).

CHAPTER SIX

An Institutional Church: Madison Square Presbyterian Church

"The rapidly changing American city was responsible for creating the institutional church. It was an attempt to give the church a wider function, in the face of the growing needs for social and moral usefulness in congested city areas," writes historian W. S. Sweet.[1] Although not the first such church in New York City the Madison Square Presbyterian Church was one of the most active institutional churches after the Civil War. Its beginning was explained in the minutes of its session:

> The continued Change, & rapid increase of population rendering necessary the establishing of a new Presbyterian Church in the vicinity of Madison Square, in the City of New York, an arrangement was entered into between the Pearl Street, and Central, Presbyterian Churches, whereby the former, became merged in the latter, with a view to the sending forth a Colony therefrom, to unite with members of sister churches, in the projected enterprise, with the Rev. Mr. Adams, D.D. for their pastor.[2]

The Pearl Street Church was established in 1800 in a section of the city which at the time was considered the suburbs; it was almost on the banks of the "fresh water pond," and those coming from the eastern part of the city had to cross bridges to get to the church. It began as an offshoot of the Presbyterian Church formed by a group of Scots who had seceded from the Wall Street Church in 1756. William Wirt Phillips was pastor of the Pearl Street church from 1818 until he went in 1826 to the First Church. The Central Presbyterian Church, organized on January 8, 1821, had its place of worship on Broome Street that it occupied on May 7, 1822. The Rev. William Patton, D.D. was its first pastor. He was succeeded by the Rev. William Adams (1807–1880), a descendant of Henry Adams of Braintree, Massachusetts and William Bradford of Plymouth. He had studied at Yale and Andover Seminary.[3]

As people moved uptown in the 1840's, the membership of both churches declined severely. Adams called a meeting of the male members of Central to decide what should be done. A committee recommended on January 21, 1853, the uniting of Pearl Street and Central to form a new church to be established in the upper part of the city. The recommendation was approved, and the new congregation held the first service in the Union Theological Seminary on University Place, on February 13, 1853. On March 3 they formally organized with 142 members, most of them from Central, elected five elders and three deacons, and by unanimous vote elected Adams pastor at a salary of $3,000. On March 6, the new church was received into the Fourth Presbytery of New York, an outgrowth of the Associate Reformed Presbytery that had been made up originally of ministers from Scotland and Ireland. In 1822 it had become a part of the General Assembly of the Presbyterian Church, and in the split of 1838 it joined the New School General Assembly. Adams was a leader in the New School group and moderator of its assembly in 1852.[4]

A certificate of incorporation was recorded in the County Clerk's office on December 8, 1853. The new church was to be called "The Madison Square Presbyterian Church, in the City of New York." Nine "discreet" men were elected trustees for a three year term. In the center of the seal was a wreath of vine leaves with grapes and the motto, "Her Planting," surrounded by the corporate name of the church.[5]

The site selected for the new church was the southeast corner of Twenty-fourth Street and Madison Avenue, facing Madison Square, which had been successively a potter's field for victims of yellow fever (1794), an arsenal, a haven of refuge of the Society for Reformation of Juvenile Delinquents and a parade ground. In 1847 the area had been formally opened and named in honor of President Madison. Fifth Avenue had been cut through to Twenty-third Street in 1837 and was crossed by Broadway at that point. A road house called Madison Cottage on the northwest corner of Twenty-third Street was replaced by Franconi's Hippodrome in 1853. Six years later the Fifth Avenue Hotel was built there — a white marble, six story palace, with the first passenger elevator in the city.[6]

New York City had grown very rapidly. In 1850 the population was over 500,000 with the northern boundary of 34th Street. The distributing aqueduct at 42d Street and Fifth Avenue brought pure water from the Croton reservoir providing an adequate supply of this essential. The streets were kept clean with center sewers; thus plagues were curbed and fires contained. For some time the city had had paved streets, gas lights and public transportation (with blacks segregated from whites). North from Washington Square were the impressive brown sandstone residences of leading citizens. Fifth Avenue was called in the local guide book of 1853 "the most magnificent street on this continent, if not in the world."[7]

A lot, 175 feet on 24th Street and 74 feet on Madison Aenue, was purchased from Henry Dwight, Jr., for $50,500. Ground was broken for the church April 18, and the corner stone containing a copy of the Bible printed that year and a copy of *The New-York Times* of that date was laid July 12, 1853.[8] The new church was described in *The New-York Daily Times:*

> The building is Gothic in its style, and the characters of the ornamentation modern. The roof is divided into small, square panels, which are exquisitely painted. The roofing is somewhat peculiar in its character and very elegant. The gilding and painting, though rather profuse, are so judiciously applied that they give an air of lightness to the interior of the edifice, without detracting in any material degree from the general and appropriate effect. The building altogether, is certainly one of the finest of its kind in the city.[9]

Ground glass was placed on the outside of the windows on the South side of the church to exclude the rays of the sun "incommoding the congregation." Silk curtains were hung in the music gallery where the organ was located. The church was valued at $141,000. The vacant lot on 24th Street next to the church was given by Dwight to Adams who built a house there with its beams inserted into the side wall of the church. The church was dedicated December 24, 1854, and in spite of "exceedingly inclement weather" there was "a crowded and most respectable congregation."[10]

A notice advertising the sale of pews at auction was placed in the newspaper: 220 pews — 154 on the ground floor, valued at $135,000. The best pews sold for $1,000 each.

Annual rentals (8% of the value of the pew) were assessed on the owner and collected by the sexton, for a commission. One member became quite incensed at the demands of the sexton for payment of the rent. He had received the pew as part of his inheritance when his father died. He moved out of town and although he remained a member of the church he never used the pew. He expected the sexton to rent seats in the pew or to sell it. Instead he continued to receive bills for rent. He felt the sexton was remiss. He finally turned the pew over to the trustees, considering it a dead loss of over $1,000.

Ownership of pews posed another problem especially when there was a demand for seats. There were over 971 sittings, of which only 38 were free. It was suggested that pew owners permit strangers to occupy seats in their pews if there were any vacant ones at ten minutes after eleven. Those who were opposed could inform the sexton, and their pew would be reserved for them.[11]

126

William Adams, Pastor of the Madison Square Presbyterian Church, 1853–1874

Charles H. Parkhurst, Madison Square Pastor, 1880–1918, and social reformer

II

Although less actively involved than in earlier years in the oversight of the ethical and moral practices of the membership, the session was not indifferent to member's activities. There was no escape when scandal rocked the church in 1859. The case concerned Henry Dwight, Jr., a major contributor to the building of the church who was a member of the board of trustees, 1853–1857. An exchange dealer, he had borrowed money from Brown Brothers giving stock of the Chicago and Mississippi Railroad as collateral. Unable to pay his debt, the stock declined in value, and Brown Brothers became involved in the reorganization of the railroad which became known as the Chicago, Alton and St. Louis Railway. In December, 1855, Dwight was indicted for conspiracy to defraud the creditors of the railroad by means of certain leases. He pleaded not guilty, and the case was disposed of by a *nolle prosequi* proceeding.

In the spring of 1856 he was again accused of conspiracy to defraud; this was due, he said, to the instigation of several members of the church, notably Charles Gould, trustee, and W. S. M. Blatchford, an elder. He was arrested and again indicted. He asked Dr. Adams to secure a trial for him by the session, since he was a member of the church in good standing. The session refused on the basis that the Book of Discipline made no provision for a member demanding a trial; a trial could be brought about only on a charge by a member of the session or by the session itself. Dwight wrote: "I asked the Session of your Church to give me a Fish - they have sent me a Serpent. I asked an investigation. They have sent me advice."

In 1861 he again asked for a hearing by the session. The indictment was discontinued in May but rumor was widespread. The session decided to try him "for said alleged offence upon the ground of General Rumor or Common Fame." The vote was five to four. A committee of two was appointed to prepare charges against him and conduct the case. On October 17, 1861, the trial began and the session was enjoined to "recollect and regard their high character as Judges of a Court of Jesus Christ and the solemn duty in which they are to act." The committee reported:

> Common Fame charges Henry Dwight a member of this Church with the Sins of Perjury — of Defrauding others by false and fraudulent representations — of embezzlements — and other Frauds, to the manifest injury of his own Christian standing and reputation and to the flagrant reproach of the Church of Christ.

Charles Gould, president of the Chicago, Alton and St. Louis Railroad, was called as witness as he had been the one who had accused Dwight in 1858. He refused, saying that he had instituted judicial proceedings in the courts and he thought that was where such charges belonged and he had no wish to revive the proceedings. Finally on May 18, 1862, the session by unanimous vote decided that none of the seven specifications had been sustained by the evidence presented. They passed the following resolution:

> In recording their judgment upon the charges alleged by Common Fame against W. Henry Dwight, the Session in justice to themselves & the accused hereby bear testimony to the frankness, with which, during the progress of this protracted trial, Mr. Dwight answered all the questions that were propounded to him, & made all the explanations that were desired of him (many of which were corroborated by documentary evidence) & do hereby express their unanimous opinion, that he has not only vindicated himself from the several accusations in which he has been tried, but that his vindication, has been ample, and complete.

The session requested that the pastor announce this to the congregation at the close of the communion preparatory service.[12]

Gould resigned as trustee in October, 1862, asked for a letter of dismissal from the church and a certificate to the Plymouth Church of Booklyn where Henry Ward Beecher was pastor. The session called him before them (March 5, 1863) and pointed out that the affidavit he had filed against Dwight in 1858 was at considerable variance with the testimony presented at the latter's trial. The session refused to grant the letter of dismissal until Gould explained the discrepancies. Gould refused. After a year he withdrew from the Presbyterian church and asked that his name be stricken from the membership list of the Madison Square Presbyterian Church. He did not join the Plymouth Church.[13]

128

While the quarrel between Dwight and Gould was before the session, another disagreement between two prominent members of the church also came to their attention. George D. Phelps, president of the Delaware, Lackawanna and Western Railroad Co., 1854–1857, declared that William E. Dodge, a member of the railroad's Board of Managers, had presented a report to stockholders of the corporation affecting Phelps' public and private character. Unable to get satisfaction from the Board of Managers, of which he was no longer a member, Phelps attacked those he considered responsible for his situation, William E. Dodge and James Brown of Brown Brothers. He wrote long open-letters to each in the public press.

Since Dodge was a member of the Madison Square Church, Phelps brought charges before the session. He accused Dodge of lying, of conspiring to ruin him by allegations of official malfeasance, and of distributing a report when he was a member of the Board of Managers which greatly mortified and injured him. The session refused to take cognizance of the charges. Phelps then appealed to the Fourth Presbytery protesting that there had been "no proper or fair investigation of the said charges," that he had had no opportunity to appear in person and that there had been "manifestation of great prejudice and partiality in the case on part of certain members of the session." The Presbytery rejected his appeal on the basis that the session, a court of first resort, had not instituted a trial. Finally, March 5, 1864, Phelps asked for a letter of dismissal from the Madison Square Church.[14]

III

The Madison Square Presbyterian's board of deacons in addition to the traditional role of care for the poor, also had charge of the communion service, responsibility of the elders in most Presbyterian churches. The service was held on Sunday afternoons at four o'clock. Elders and deacons entered in a body, and the congregation rose during the procession. The elements were passed through the aisles by the deacons. There was some complaint about the large bills for the wine "especially as the quality had been complained of, at late communion service." Unfermented wine was served in the mission chapel.[15]

The main function of the deacons, however, remained the care of the church's poor, and a deacons' fund was maintained for this purpose. Members in need were "entitled to receive assistance from the deacons' fund". The expenses for those who could not pay when in such institutions as the Half Orphan Asylum, Home for the Incurables, Home for Aged Women, Bloomingdale Asylum, Institute for the Blind, were met by the church. Small monthly allowances were given to help out with the rent of those living at home or for their board with another. The fund helped provide coal, clothing, and especially funerals.

Madison Square Church seems to have been particularly generous not only "as regards the Deacon's Fund, but toward all those Benevolent Associations & enterprises on behalf of which appeal had been made to the congregation", receiving among others a special collection to aid families of disabled soldiers during the Civil War.[16]

Shortly after the church was dedicated the session minutes stated:

The Madison Square Presbyterian Church & Congregation, having been signally favored of Providence, in the prosecution of their enterprise, considered it their duty & privilege to engage in efforts to extend the blessings of the gospel, to the destitute around them.

They rented a few rooms near the church and invited children in the neighborhood directly east of the church to Sabbath School. Largely from Irish Catholic families attracted by the novelty, those who responded proved so unruly that the police had to be called.

Rented quarters also proved quite unsatisfactory, and in 1857 it was decided to buy lots and erect facilities. A mission, a neat brick building, was erected on Third Avenue between Thirtieth and Thirty-first streets "for the purpose of gathering in the ignorant & neglected children, & youth, in that vicinity for instruction on the Sabbath, & also to provide a place for public religious worship." The building, capable of accommodating five or six hundred, was completed at the cost of $14,500 by the end of 1857 and dedicated on January 11, 1858.[17]

The pastor, in November, 1857, had organized a Young Men's Association which in addition to their own personal activities (prayer meetings, lectures, social functions) took a particular interest in the mission and arranged for systematic visitations among the poor. Eight of their membership were elected annually to oversee the work of the mission. The same members served for years. The first chairman of the Mission Committee was William E. Dodge, Jr. (1827–1903), who was also superintendent of the Mission Sabbath School. Two others who served as chairman for many years were D. Willis James (1832–1907) and Theodore Roosevelt, Sr., (1832–1878).

Both Dodge and James were grandsons of Anson G. Phelps (1781–1858), who had founded in 1833, with his sons-in-law, Phelps, Dodge and Company. Located on Cliff Street, the firm dealt in metals and soon branched out to include both mining and railroads. Each of the grandsons became a partner in the firm, and James, who lived at 40 East 39th Street, was by the age of thirty sufficiently wealthy to devote much of his time to philanthropy. He served on the Mission committee several of the years between 1859 and 1894. He was elected a deacon in 1861 and an elder and trustee in 1885.[20]

Theodore Roosevelt, Sr., had an import glass business at 74 Maiden Lane but was more interested in charitable causes. His home was at 28 E. 20th Street and he was a member of the Madison Square Presbyterian Church. He served on the Mission Committee from 1859 to 1874 and was elected chairman six times. Theodore Roosevelt, Jr., later President of the United States, was baptized in "Dr. Adams's Presbyterian church" on April 21, 1860. In his *Autobiography* he told how his father would drop him off at the Madison Square Church Sunday School on his way to teach a class at the Mission Sabbath School. Members of the committee, especially the chairman, were expected to attend not only the Sabbath evening service but also many of the weekly services at the Mission.[21]

Sabbath School was held at the Mission at 9 a.m.; the average attendance was 400. Boys and girls met in the afternoon to sing and to listen to remarks made by the superintendent. On Saturday mornings the girls attended Industrial School, where they were taught to sew (in 1870 the attendance averaged 175). Forty young people from the church visited the area from Lexington and First Avenue and from 26th to 35th streets to invite non-church going adults to attend the chapel services and "to gather their children into our Mission School." Worship services were held for adults in the morning and evening. Those admitted to communion had to be passed on by the session of the parent church, for they were placed on the membership roll there as well as at the chapel. Prayer meetings were held on Tuesday and Thursday evenings at the Mission, and family prayer meetings were held in the tenement houses. Each one had its own leader, generally a member of the Young People's Association. There was difficulty with one leader who "deems himself endowed with marvelous and special Heavenly Gifts which lift him above the necessity of all human assistance and even of any particular regard for the Word of God. In fact he is what is termed a perfectionist." In 1858–1859 the Rev. William Hough conducted the services and administered the sacraments, and was succeeded in 1860 by the Rev. Charles H. Payson.[22]

In 1860 the building was enlarged to provide a place for social gatherings, including weekly lectures and musical programs. By 1866 the pastor suggested that the building was too small, accommodating at most five hundred people. Since the chapel opened, 299 members had been admitted, and by 1870 the membership reached 435. The Mission Committee decided that they could do nothing about enlarging the chapel at that time, the property being mortgaged at $11,000 and the mortgagee (Anson P. Stokes) having called for payment. By contributions from the members of the Mission Committee the mortgage was paid off by May, 1868.[23]

A large number of German immigrants had moved into the neighborhood, and many of their children attended the Mission

Sabbath School, representing about two hundred of the families. In 1868 it was decided to hold religious services and administer the sacrament of the Lord's Supper at the Mission Chapel in the German language. The Germans were listed separately on the register of church members and were later considered a German branch of the church. Rev. Martin A. Erdmann, German missionary in the employ of the City Tract Society, conducted the services and in 1870 became pastor of the German branch, serving until his death in 1877.

The Germans presented some problems as Mr. Erdmann reported at the end of the first year of his pastorate. Those who were fourteen or over when they came to the United States considered themselves already members of the Christian church and expected that status in the Presbyterian church here. If they were not so recognized because they had not been converted in the Presbyterian mode they might leave and go back to the Catholic or Lutheran churches from whence they came, he wrote. An even more troublesome problem was their attitude toward Sabbath observance. Although the pastor agreed that their behavior violated the Fourth Commandment and therefore they were sinners, he thought it was better to have them come to the Presbyterian church where they would hear a "better Gospel than they hear from their unconverted preachers and priests. At first we must have the people and afterwards try to make the best of them by the Grace of God," he argued.[24]

Payson continued to be dissatisfied with the status of the Mission. He wanted a new building, and some of his congregation subscribed to a building fund. Most of the expenses of a new building, however, would fall to members of the parent church. Having just paid off the mortgage on the present building, they were unwilling at that time to go into debt. Payson wrote in April, 1870: "Twelve years of experience have convinced me that Missions as now conducted have clogged the wheels of Presbyterianism in our city the last quarter century. They hinder or prevent the growth of all new organizations, foster pride, increase pauperism, & beggary and in fine degrade rather than elevate. Such results do not belong legitimately to Christ's work." At the same time he presented his resignation.[25]

The Mission Committee persuaded him to continue his pastorship and they began plans for a new mission. Four lots on Thirtieth Street between Third and Second avenues were purchased for $50,000, and the Mission Chapel was sold for $41,250.

A new brick building, called The Memorial Chapel of the Madison Square Presbyterian Church, was dedicated March 28, 1875. All seats were free, but they decided to pass baskets on Sunday and take up money in envelopes so the Chapel would pay part of their expenses. Over half of the expenses were paid by the parent church, and evidently there was growing resistance on the part of church members to carrying such a large share — although special pleas for the Mission work were made from the pulpit, and a circular letter and a subscription book were sent out.

Payson died suddenly of pneumonia, the result of having been out in a severe snow storm, January, 1877. He was succeeded by a graduate of Union Theological Seminary, Edgar H. Elmore, but his health was such he needed a milder climate. He resigned in 1885 to become professor of English literature at Maryville College in Tennessee.[26]

The Mission committee decided that the time was ripe for separation. The people of the church were no longer active in the work of the chapel and many were opposed to the large expenditures. It was pointed out at a committee meeting that New York church life was unique in that the "wealthy class meeting in congregations apart from those of moderate circumstances and the poor again distinct from either of the other two classes — as to place of worship." They realized that the worshippers at the chapel were too poor to carry on the work without help and decided to try to find a pastor who would have the qualifications to carry on an independent church. They brought in the Rev. Jesse F. Forbes, who had been pastor of the First Congregational Church at Warren, Massachusetts. He was received into the Presbytery, and an independent church with 277 members was organized on January 21, 1886, and named the Adams Memorial Presbyterian Church in honor of William Adams, who had died on August 31, 1880.

Although an independent church, their resources were small and the Madison Square Church continued to contribute to their support ($3,000 a year).[27] The Adams Memorial Church grew and by January, 1888, had a membership of 407. In spite of the fact that almost one hundred scholars had left their Sabbath School when the German branch was formed into the Zion German Presbyterian Church with the Rev. Louis Wolferz as pastor, the Sunday School had an enrollment of between 800–900 and an attendance of over 600. The church had three prayer meetings a week and weekly meetings for Gospel and Temperance work at the Stearns Silk Factory (213 East 42d Street) for which Mr. Stearns bore the expense. Before long Adams Memorial Church was faced with the same problem experienced by the old established churches, i.e., members moved to other locations as they became more prosperous.[28]

IV

While the Mission Committee was so heavily involved in work on the east side, Madison Square Church had had a change in leadership. Adams had been elected president of Union Theological Seminary and had resigned in the spring of 1874. During his pastorate the church had increased in membership to 1486 and had a budget of over $50,000.[29] The Rev. William Jewett Tucker of Manchester, New Hampshire, became pastor in May, 1875, but remained only four years and resigned to become professor at Andover Theological Seminary.[30]

The Rev. Charles H. Parkhurst (1842–1933) succeeded Tucker. He had been invited to preach at a Presbyterian church in New York City by D. Willis James, who had attended services at the Lenox, Massachusetts church where Parkhurst was pastor. James wanted members of the Madison Square Church to hear Parkhurst without it being too obvious he was a candidate for the Madison Square pulpit. Three days later he received an informal invitation to become the pastor. There was some opposition in the New York Presbytery — he was a Congregationalist who when asked what he thought of the Presbyterian system of government admitted he knew very little about it. He was, however, accepted.[31]

Installed at Madison Square Presbyterian Church on March 9, 1880, Parkhurst immediately took steps to become informed on all activities of the church. He asked that monthly reports be made to the session from each department. His report to Presbytery in 1882 (the first one where the statistics of the church were separate from those of the chapel) listed a church membership of 703 with 140 in the Sabbath School; the budget was $31,629. His salary was $8,000, and the music budget was over half that sum. He brought in his brother, Howard E. Parkhurst, as music director. In the familiar pattern, a quartette furnished the music.[32]

V

Women were very active in the Madison Square Church, and in 1891 it was proposed that some be deaconesses. This proposal was rejected. The women were primarily involved in the social work of the church, particularly the Third Avenue missions. In 1882 the various women's societies were organized into the Ladies' Association with Mrs. Parkhurst as president. It combined the Ladies Home Missionary Society, The Ladies Foreign Mission Society, The Ladies Employment Society, Industrial School and Band of Ministering Children. The next year the Loan Relief Society was added. The first two organizations were usually found in the churches but the others were peculiar to an institutional church.[33]

The Employment Society grew out of the activities of the women during the Civil War when they worked together on garments for soldiers. Theodore Roosevelt, Sr., suggested they combine this work with the Mission and provide sewing for women who needed to earn money while their men were in the army. The work continued after the war, and the Society was organized in 1872. The women of the church bought the material, cut out the garments and distributed them to the women at the

The Madison Square Churches—old (*right*) and new—Madison Avenue at 24th Street, 1906.

Third Avenue Mission, often having to teach them to sew. They in turn received money for their week's work. This activity not only enabled them to earn some money but also gave them some social contacts. About seventy-five women were usually involved in the program. Dr. Adams had noted that the "Employment Society had done more to make the mission on Third Avenue possible than any one influence he knew of. . . . We have tried to make the women feel that is a business institution, and that they must earn what they get so far as possible."[34]

The Loan Relief Society, incorporated in 1883, was a unique organization for a church, as indicated in the constitution:

> Its object shall be to devise methods for assisting the poor to help themselves; to loan money in small sums upon good security to those temporarily disabled by misfortune, and articles necessary for the comfort and recovery of the sick; to supply medical attendance and medicine gratuitously when needful, or to secure their purchase for the poor at a low rate; to visit the sufferers in their homes, and thoroughly investigate into the nature of their distresses. Also to tender legal aid and protection, to give counsel and advice, and to help those who are oppressed and defrauded.

The variety of committees give an idea of the work of the Society: visiting committee, coal committee, legal aid committee, loan committee.

The committee on coal was one of the most successful. They bought wholesale coal in the summer months when it was cheapest and sold it to the poor of the church and mission at the same low price. The legal aid committee helped the poor to secure damages for injuries, to make landlords liable for repairs, to force employers to give women who had been discharged the pay due them, and with similar violations.

Out of the visiting committee grew the Ladies' Visitation Society and Bureau of Information. Each member took one or two mission families under her care, visited them from time to time, and gave such aid and encouragement as was necessary. Since jobs were often the greatest need, the Bureau of Information was formed in 1891. Its aim was to procure jobs for members of the Mission. They kept a job registry of the unemployed, investigated references, tried to get them in touch with members of the church who wanted help. Most of the jobs were domestic, and more than half of them were in the country.[35]

The church had many other organizations. Out of a sewing class grew The Helping Hand Society, organized in 1891, which sought to "teach the mothers of the Church House Mission to make garments for themselves, to bring them into pleasant association and give them one-half hour of practical and religious instruction." It grew rapidly and soon had fifteen classes. Since many of the women had young children "the Creche" was organized to take care of those who came with their mothers. The

136

Needle Work Guild secured and distributed garments to the poor. The Fresh Air work, organized by the Young People's Society in 1880, found places for children to go outside the city during the hot weather; in the beginning they stayed with farmers in Connecticut but later a permanent home was established at Fort Montgomery on the Hudson River. From 1882 to 1904 over six thousand children benefitted from this work. Money for the project and for poor and sick children was raised by the Band of Ministering Children organized in 1882.[36]

Two of the best known organizations of the church were the Boys' and the Girls' Clubs. The Boys' Club was an attempt to domesticate "the rather incorrigible element of our East Side population." The leaders were volunteers, and the activities included gymnastic drill, field athletics, orchestral training, and carpentry. In addition there was "as much in the way of intellectual illumination and moral and religious suggestion as the peculiar features of the situation render feasible." The Girls' Club grew out of a Bible class at the Mission. The work consisted of a Young Woman's Gospel meeting, three Bible classes, and classes in cooking, dressmaking, singing, gymnastics, machine sewing, embroidery, millinery, basketry, and music.[37]

The Madison Square Church House,
corner of 30th Street and
Third Avenue,
New York City, 1901

VI

Parkhurst was interested in wider horizons for the congregation of Madison Square Church beyond those of the church and the Mission. During a visit to Europe he became acquainted with the missionary work of Dr. Robert McAll among the Protestants in France and later was president of the National McAll Association. The McAll mission became one of the annual benevolences of the church, and a branch of the association was formed at the church.[38]

Parkhurst was also active in the Evangelical Alliance. It had been formed in 1846 to bring about cooperation among various denominations of the Christian religion. Adams had supported the program and in 1873 had participated with the Dean of Canterbury Cathedral, a minister from Geneva, one from India and others in a joint communion service. The organization was almost dead when it was revived by Josiah Strong, pastor of the Central Congregational Church in Cincinnati, Ohio, in 1886. He became general secretary of the organization, and William E. Dodge, Jr., of Madison Square Presbyterian Church was the president. The Alliance held interdenominational conferences in 1887, 1889 and 1893, the eventual outgrowth of which was the Federal Council of Churches organized in 1908. It was not only an advocate of ecumenism but also of the social gospel. Josiah Strong in his book, *The Twentieth Century City* (1898), was one of the first to present the viewpoint that the Christian Church should help solve urban problems, and with this viewpoint Parkhurst was in thorough agreement.[39]

He held a conference at his home on November 15, 1886, proposing a replacement for the Third Avenue Mission that had become the Adams Memorial Church. A new mission committee was established, rooms were rented at 386 Third Avenue, and the services of Mr. and Mrs. Charles Ballou obtained as missionaries. The church appropriated $10,000 for the work.

Many changes in location and personnel hindered the growth of the work. It was decided in 1891 to build facilities suitable to house all departments of the work and to act as a settlement house. The Madison Square Church House was incorporated with its own Board of Trustees headed by Parkhurst. The building and land and furnishings, which cost approximately $150,000, were turned over by the building committee to the trustees, March 30, 1901.[40]

A description of the building gives an idea of the scope of the work. On the first floor was the auditorium where were held evening gospel meetings. There also the Employment Bureau conducted its activities and the Helping Hand Society and other organizations held their meetings. On the second floor was the kindergarten room, a medical clinic including one for alcoholics, and rooms for Bible classes and conferences. The third floor contained a large library consisting of over 4,000 volumes, including books in German and French, and the Girls' and Boys' club rooms and classrooms. Both of these clubs had professional leaders. On the top floor there was a gymnasium with dressing rooms and showers, and on the roof a playground for the children. In the basement the Workingmen's Christian League had their club room, and there was space for manual training and wood work.

The work was supervised by a Gospel Committee headed for years by Henry N. Tifft. The House was open daily from nine a.m. to nine p.m., and activities were scheduled for almost every hour. Provision was made for free baths for men and women during those hours. The house attracted ever increasing constituents; it gave the people in the neighborhood somewhere to go in the evenings. The roof of the Church House furnished some respite from the heat in the summer.[41]

Although St. George's Episcopal Church at that time was hailed as the epitome of the institutional church, the Madison Square Church House carried on the same activities. It was, however, separated from the parent church by several blocks. The pastor of St. George's, the Rev. W. S. Rainsford, predicted that eventually the State would take over the functions performed by the institutional church, and that prediction has been largely an accurate one.[42]

[1]Sweet, *Religion in America*, pp. 373–4.

[2]Madison Square Presbyterian Church Session Minutes, I:1

[3]Savage, *Presbyterian Church in New York City*, pp. 127–8; Frederick Torel Persons, "William Adams," *DAB*, I:101–2.

[4]M.S. Session Minutes, I:1–6; Alexander, *Presbytery of New York*, pp. 88, 96.

[5]Madison Square Presbyterian Church Trustee Minutes, I, Dec. 8, 1853, Dec. 12, 1854. (no paging)

[6]Brown, *Fifth Avenue*, pp. 53–65; Maurice, *Fifth Avenue*, pp. 86–90.

[7]Stokes, *Iconography*, III:634–9; Still, *Mirror of Gotham*, p. 126, 157.

[8]Memo. as to Madison Square Presbyterian Church Property and Window Rights, Nov. 18, 1953; Minutes of the Building Committee, July 12, 1853; *The New York Times*, Dec. 17, 1906, 6:4 (it gives the date of the *Times* in the corner stone as July 13, 1853).

[9]*New-York Daily Times*, Dec. 25, 1854, 3:4.

[10]M.S. Session Minutes, I:24 (Dec. 24, 1854); M.S. Trustee Minutes, I, Feb. 8, Apr. 25, 1855.

[11]M.S. Trustee Minutes, I, Dec. 9, 12, 1854; Fred H. Dodge to Mr. Woodruff, treasurer, May 24, 1880, in Misc. correspondence, church archives.

[12]M.S. Session Minutes, I:62–9 (Feb. 12, 1859), 102–6, 117–47. (Apr. 30, May 7, 10, 14, 15, Oct. 17, 18, 28, Nov. 5, 11, 18, 20, Dec. 3, 7, 16, 30, 1861), 148–164 (Jan. 8, 15, 27, Feb. 4, 24, Mar. 4, 10, 17, 24, 31, Apr. 10, 17, 21, May 6, 12, 18, 20, 23, 1862); John A. Kouwenhoven, *Partners in Banking, 1818–1968* (New York, 1968), 75, 118.

[13]M.S. Session Minutes, I:157–8 (Oct. 20, 24, 30, 1862), 178–9, 182–92, 206–7 (Mar. 12, 17, 20, 31, Apr. 10, Nov. 6, 1863); 222–3 (Oct. 21, 1864).

[14]M.S. Session Minutes, I:152, 157, 162–6 (June 5, Oct. 20, Dec. 17, 22, 26, 30, 1862, 169–71, 194, 199–200 (Jan. 27, Apr. 21, May 19, 1863). File of correspondence, church archives.

[15]Minutes of the Board of Deacons of the Madison Square Church, March 29, 1854, Apr. 3, 1868. (no paging)

[16]*Ibid*., Apr. 2, 1856, June 3, 1857, Feb. 4, 1858, Dec. 6, 1861, Nov. 29, 1864, Feb. 3, Mar. 31, Oct. 1, 1865, Dec. 5, 1868, Apr. 5, 1872, May 30, Dec. 5, 1873.

[17]M.S. Session Minutes, I:54 (Apr. 1, 1858); M.S. Trustee Minutes, May 20, 1859.

[18]M.S. Session Minutes, I:151 (May 23, 1862); Mission Book. Young Men's Association of the Madison Square Presbyterian Church in the City of New York, 1858–1859.

[19]M.S. Mission Book, Apr. 8, 1858; Miller, *People Are the City*, pp. 219–20.

[20]William Bristow Shaw, "Daniel Willis James," *DAB*, IX:573–4; H. W. Faulkner, "Anson Greene Phelps," *DAB*, XIV:525–6.

[21]M.S. Mission Book, Jan. 2, 1866, Nov. 15, 1871; Theodore Roosevelt, *Autobiography* (New York, 1914), pp. 9–10.

[22]Mission Book, I, Nov. 9, 1865, Nov. 23, 1869; D. J. Egleston, Report of Mission Committee May, 1870 in Correspondence file, church archives.

[23]M.S. Mission Book, I, Apr. 12, 1866, Jan. 28, Apr. 17, May 8, 1867, Feb. 11, 1868.

[24]Report of M. A. Erdmann, Apr. 1, 1870, Apr. 1, 1871, in Correspondence file, church archives; M.S. Session Minutes, II:29 (Feb. 2, 1871), 52 (Jan. 2, 1872), 82, 84 (Apr. 3, 8, 1873).

[25]Mission Book, II, Apr. 8, 1870. Charles H. Payson to the committee.

[26]*Ibid.*, II: Nov. 15, Dec. 18, 1871, Jan. 29, Mar. 27, 1872, May, 1874, Apr. 10, 1875; M.S. Session Minutes, II:177, 188 (Jan. 24, May 10, 1877).

[27]Mission Book, III, Apr. 2, 1884, Nov. 2, 1885, Feb. 1, 1886, Jan. 25, 1887; M.S. Session Minutes, II:255 (Sept. 3, 1880), III:61 (Mar. 1886).

[28]M.S. Mission Book, II, Nov. 15, 1877, III, Jan. 25, 1888; M.S. Session Minutes, III:62 (Feb. 28, 1886).

[29]M.S. Session Minutes, II:91, 93 (Oct. 1, 16, 1873), 99, 105 (Jan. 5, Apr. 5, 1874).

[30]M.S. Session Minutes, II:130, 135 (Mar. 29, May 12, 1875), 233, 234 (Sept. 10, Oct. 3, 1879).

[31]M.S. Session Minutes, II:244, 247 (Jan. 30, Feb. 2, 1880; Charles H. Parkhurst, *My Forty Years in New York* (New York, 1923), 59–62.

[32]*Ibid.*, 66–7; M.S. Session Minutes, 267 (Mar. 3, 1881), 284 (Apr. 1, 1882).

[33]*Year Book, Ladies's Association of the Madison Square Presbyterian Church*, 1887; M.S. Session Minutes, III:131 (Jan. 29, 1861), 163 (Dec. 4, 1893).

[34]Charles H. Parkhurst, *A Brief History of the Madison Square Presbyterian Church and its Activities* (New York, 1906), 85–8; *Madison Square Presbyterian Church Year Book*, 1893, pp. 45–7; M.S. Deacons Minutes, Jan. 29, 1888, Nov. 29, 1891.

[35]Parkhurst, *Madison Square Presbyterian Church*, pp. 89–96; *M.S. Year Book*, 1897, pp. 60–64.

[36]Parkhurst, *Madison Square Presbyterian Church*, pp. 97–100; *M.S. Year Book*, 1896, pp. 62–3.

[37]Parkhurst, *Madison Square Presbyterian Church*, pp. 105–8.

[38]*Ibid.*, pp. 43–4; *The Church Tower*, March, 1936, p. 33.

[39]M.S. Session Minutes, II:92 (Oct. 5, 1873); Hopkins, *Social Gospel*, pp. 115, 159–60; Ahlstrom, *Religious History*, pp. 802–4.

[40]M.S. Session Minutes, III:206A (1895 Report); Parkhurst, *Madison Square Presbyterian Church* pp. 47–55.

[41]*M.S. Year Book*, 1902, pp. 14–29.

[42]Hopkins, *Social Gospel*, pp. 154–6.

CHAPTER SEVEN

Charles H. Parkhurst:
Crusading Pastor

There was nothing in Charles H. Parkhurst's background to indicate he would become one of the outstanding civic reformers in New York City and would help bring about the defeat of Tammany Hall in the election of 1894. In his autobiography he said that he had "looked upon New York as a kind of Jerusalem, a sort of holy city, a monumental exhibit of the finest product of modern civilization." He was, therefore, shocked by the gambling, vice and crime in the city.[1] He called a special meeting of the session on January 3, 1881, and explained his reasons for calling it:

> the consideration of measures for more effective action in promoting the work of the church in its aggressiveness against the powers of evil in the world, in the quickening of life of the Church, for the advancement and increase, and for the revival of interest in the same wherever its influence may be extended.[2]

He felt a responsibility for the young men in the church and hated to see them surrounded by such temptations as existed in the Tenderloin, which was just across the square from the church. As a young man he had exercised initiative in his teaching methods and had continued to use unusual methods in spite of the reprimands of school boards. His religion had always been an integral part of his life, and he saw the church as a social force. Perhaps his lack of theological training led him to action rather than to dialectical expositions. He had great physical and moral courage and independence and was very stubborn. His assurance of his being right made him willing to accept the scorn and criticism of the press and government leaders — probably even of some of his parishioners, although most of them seem to have supported him.

His weapon was the pulpit, and at that time he was one of the most brilliant and effective preachers in New York City. A future colleague said of him: "I vividly recall hearing him preach in later years - his full gray beard, his bespectacled but piercing eyes, his close reading of his manuscript, the utter absence in his delivery of any trick of the orator, and yet his strange fascination which kept his audience fairly on the edge of their pews."[3] Parkhurst had, from time to time, touched upon the subject of crime in New York, so in November, 1890, he was invited to become a member of the Society for the Prevention of Crime. It was an organization composed of civic leaders but had contented itself with small results. At the death of Dr. Howard Crosby, Dr. Parkhurst became president of the society on April 30, 1891. He accepted the position on condition "that we cease occupying ourselves with cutting off the tops and applying ourselves to plucking up the roots."[4]

Sunday, February 14, 1892, he began his attack on the city government. The church was comfortably full; in the congregation was the Republican boss of New York State, Thomas Collier Platt, who directed his activities from the Fifth Avenue Hotel across Madison Square from the church. Present also were a few reporters, as "Dr. Parkhurst frequently made good copy." He began, "Ye are the salt of the earth. This, then, is a corrupt world, and Christianity is the antiseptic that is to be rubbed into it in order to arrest the process of decay; an illustration taken from common things, but which states at a stroke the entire story." He then declared that the municipal government was rotten and that the officials blocked all efforts at reform by protecting owners of saloons and houses of prostitution. He declared the officials were "a lying, perjured, rum-soaked, and libidinous lot." He denied bringing politics into the pulpit. It was not the concern of the church what administration was in power but it was the concern of the church to strike at iniquity. He summed it up as follows:

> The only object of my appeal this morning has been to sound a distinct note, and to quicken our christian sense of the obligatory relation in which we stand toward the official and administrative criminality that is filthifying our entire municipal life, making New York a very hotbed of knavery, debauchery and beastiality, in the atmosphere of which, and at the corrosive touch of which, there is not a young man so noble, nor a young girl so pure, as not to be in a degree infected by the fetid contamination.[5]

The press played up the sermon. One reporter called it the "severest indictment of this Tammany-debauched municipal government that has been made"; another said, "Dr. Parkhurst 'took on dreadful' last Sunday. With well feigned virtuous indignation he rhetorically assaulted the whole municipal outfit." But he was not without his critics: the New York *World* and Charles A. Dana's *Sun* attacked the preacher, the latter declaring he should be driven from the pulpit.[6]

The New York Times supported the city government and as a reply to Parkhurst printed an interview with District Attorney Nicoll, who said after reading an account of the sermon, "It is the coarsest and most vindictive utterance from the pulpit that I ever heard of. So far as it affects me, I am frank to say that I feel aggrieved, outraged, and insulted by the falsehoods and misrepresentations that he spoke concerning me." He added that shortly after the minister was made president of the SPC he had met with Parkhurst, who mentioned two cases he thought should be brought before a grand jury. The District Attorney asked for evidence, and an agent of the society verbally presented some but it was insufficient.[7]

Parkhurst and the attorney for the society, Frank Moss, presented complaints of violation of the excise law (selling liquor on Sunday), charged the city government with allowing such violations, and the next day the minister appeared before the grand jury. The jury, however, handed down a presentment saying that the charges had no basis in fact and expressed its disapproval of Parkhurst. The judge congratulated the jury: "It is indeed gratifying to find that after your investigation there was nothing but rumor, nothing but hearsay to base any accusation upon."[8]

The rejection only strengthened Parkhurst's determination to obtain evidence of his charges. So together with a young man of his congregation, John Langdon Erving, and a detective, he visited the gambling dens, the saloons, and the houses of prostitution. He went disguised in a dirty shirt, loudly checked black and white trousers, a double reefer jacket, old red tie, and a battered slouch hat with his long curly hair smeared with soap.[9] A month later (March 13) he came into his pulpit which was piled high with affidavits. Before a capacity congregation, with 2000 more trying to get in, he preached on the text, "The wicked walk on every side when the vilest men are exalted." He then pointed out that he had a list of saloons which were open last Sunday in violation of the Sunday closing law, names and addresses of gambling houses in the neighborhood where there were more young men than he had ever seen in church, a list of thirty houses of prostitution — and since he had visited one of them, he knew how easy it was to get in and what they were like. Although his abiding aim was to help the young men of his congregation, he was under no illusion: "There is little advantage in preaching the Gospel to a young fellow on Sunday if he is going to be sitting on the edge of a Tammany-maintained hell the rest of the week." He concluded:

In a closing word, voicing the righteous indignation of the pure and honest citizenship of this tyrannized municipality, let me in a representative way say to Tammany: For four weeks you have been wincing under the sting of a general indictment, and have been calling for particulars. This morning I have given you particulars, two hundred and eighty-four of them. Now, what are you going to do with them?[10]

Parkhurst appeared before the Excise Board presenting evidence against saloon keepers accusing them of selling liquor on Sunday and permitting gambling on their premises. He listed the establishments and stated that "all these men are strong adherents of Tammany Hall." With Charles W. Gardner, a detective employed by the SPC, he appeared before the March grand jury testifying against saloon keepers and keepers of disorderly houses. He presented evidence he had personally gathered against four women charged with keeping brothels. They were arrested, soon released and returned to their work. The March grand jury did, however, hand down a general presentment against the Police Department and officials of the police courts. The presentment said that the police were good at preventing "gross crime" but "winked at disorderly houses, gambling places and excise law breakers." The *Times* called the report the "talk of the town," and added: "Although of a very general character, the allegations made were so sweeping as to call forth expressions of surprise on all sides, despite the fact that these allegations simply voiced what had long been the well-settled convictions in the minds of all men who know the light and dark phases of the city life."[11]

Parkhurst made his first court appearance in April at the trial of Hattie Adams, alleged keeper of a disorderly house three blocks north of the church. He testified that in disguise, without his clerical clothes, he had visited the house with a young man from his congregation. He told how Mrs. Adams had met them at the door and ushered them into a parlor where they were entertained by some girls who undressed and danced the can-can for them. When asked if he had been personally solicited he said he had been.[12]

As he appeared in court, he was subjected to considerable abuse. He was made fun of by Adams' "girls" when he entered the court room; they laughed at his white cravat, his sideburns and his dark hair slightly tinged with gray which fell almost to his shoulders. Her lawyer called him "a liar and poltroon" and impugned and ridiculed his motives, saying that his remaining through the orgies made him a part of the crime. Adams was finally convicted and sentenced to nine months on Blackwells Island. Parkhurst explained that he had nothing against her or women like her but was attacking the governmental officials for not enforcing the laws. He added that police could not enforce laws impartially except on the ruins of Tammany.[13] The campaign ended that spring with a mass meeting of business and professional men on May 26 at Cooper Union. They declared their support of the Parkhurst campaign.[14]

When he returned from his summer vacation in Europe, the city administration declared war on him. Superintendent of Police Thomas F. Byrnes called a press conference. He stated that he had never before criticized Parkhurst out of respect for his cloth and that he had "hoped he was a Christian gentleman and that his conscience would smote him and arrest his actions." He protested that the minister's persecution of the police grew out of a divorce suit of a woman in his congregation who was bitter because the police had done nothing about the "evil resort" where her husband maintained a woman. Parkhurst recognized the divorce case but said it had nothing to do with his campaign; he wrote "grilling letters" to Byrnes, supplied newspapers with material, and addressed many meetings.

Byrnes responded that he had closed 440 houses of ill fame during his seven months in office and that Parkhurst's crusade was a complete failure. It had not resulted in the arrest of a single policeman for taking bribes. The *Times* defended Byrnes and said he was the best superintendent of police in a generation and that Parkhurst had not succeeded in arousing public opinion.[15] Lincoln Steffens had been assigned by the editor of *The Evening Post* to cover police headquarters. He said that Parkhurst had been represented by some of the press as "a wild man, ridiculous, sensational, unscrupulous" but when he called on him he found him quiet, earnest, and determined to clean up the city by the election of good officials. They worked together exchanging information.[16]

The "fighting doctor" as he came to be called, had begun his campaign with accusations against individuals — saloon keepers who broke the law by keeping their saloons open on Sunday and madams of disorderly houses. In 1893 he switched from the exposé of individual violators to an attack on prominent government officials, and appeared as witness before grand juries accusing police captains and inspectors of neglect of duty and of blackmail. He also charged that many judges had bought their jobs and that there was a "judicial ring" intent on protecting police officers. The police retaliated by charging the detective, Charles W. Gardner, who had accompanied Parkhurst "traversing the avenues of our municipal hell," with extorting money from the keepers of houses of prostitution. He was found guilty of blackmail in a police court but the sentence was overturned by an appeals court. He did not, however, return to the Society for the Prevention of Crime.[17]

In 1894 Parkhurst turned his crusade into a political campaign to defeat Tammany. He had formed the City Vigilance League, of which he became president. Members in each election district were urged to keep watch on saloons open on Sunday, gambling dens, and disorderly houses. He suggested large maps be made showing such places in relation to schools and churches and that the names of the owners of the property be published. The object was to see that the laws were enforced. He suggested candidates for office might be asked — "How many dives are you running now?" He urged them to support honest candidates and forget their party allegiance.

He carried on a vigorous speaking campaign, addressing two or three meetings a week in churches, halls, and club rooms, from Harlem to the lower East Side. The theme was the same: "There is not a single department of our city government that is not steeped in corruption. . . . There is hardly a nerve, or muscle, or sinew or drop of blood that is not tainted with the loathsome dirty paws of the Tiger." He called on the people to sink political differences and combine for a clean municipal government.[18]

In January 1894, the legislature, responding to pressure from the Chamber of Commerce, had established the Lexow Committee to investigate police corruption in New York City. The resolution had been sponsored by Thomas C. Platt, and the committee was headed by Senator Clarence Lexow. Initially it seemed more inclined to concentrate on investigating the SPC than the Police Department. But with pressure from Parkhurst and the Society, John W. Goff was named as counsel to the committee, and William Travers Jerome and Frank Moss were made assistants.[19]

A committee of seventy, of which J. Crosby Brown, member of the Madison Square Presbyterian Church, was an influential member, selected as mayoral candidate, William J. Strong, wealthy drygoods merchant and independent Republican. The Democrats nominated Hugh J. Grant, who had been mayor when Parkhurst began his attack on the city government.[20]

A less-publicized issue in the campaign was the crusade for an amendment to the state constitution to provide woman suffrage. Many prominent clergymen had endorsed the movement but Parkhurst had not signed any of the petitions being circulated. A reporter cornered him for his opinion. He replied that he thought woman's place was in the home and that her greatest obligation was to her children. He stressed the femininity of women; they should be educated but not in a college with a curriculum similar to that in men's colleges. He preached a sermon on the subject, using as his text, *Genesis*, I:27, "Male and female created he them." Mrs. Parkhurst, however, was active in the Woman's Municipal League and urged women to use their influence to defeat Tammany.[21]

Strong was elected mayor by a plurality of 50,000. The Parkhursts celebrated by hanging three United States flags outside their home at 133 East 35th Street. The minister declared he was now going to confine his work more to the church. In two years he had received an international reputation as a civic reformer. At the beginning his methods had aroused opposition even among clergymen, but after the election's success he was praised. The New York Presbytery in January 1895, passed resolutions expressing "Presbytery's sympathy with the earnest struggle for the moral reform of the city which has been so ably headed by Dr. Parkhurst." There was one negative vote.[22]

Puck cartoon endorsing Charles Parkhurst's campaign; his findings contributed to the appointment of the Lexow Commission and Tammany Hall's temporary downfall.

The City Vigilance League gave a big dinner in his honor on November 27, 1894, at Jaegers (Madison Avenue at 59th Street) attended by five hundred "substantial looking men." One of the speakers was the Episcopal Bishop Henry Codman Potter, who claimed some credit for bringing Parkhurst to New York City; he had recommended him to one of the deacons of the Madison Square Presbyterian Church. A testimonial fund was raised to be used to make permanent provision for pure city government; the City Vigilance League was to be the agent. The *Times* pointed out that absent from the dinner were Governor-elect Morton, Senator Lexow and other friends of Thomas C. Platt. The Republican boss had been incensed when Parkhurst in one sermon had compared him with the head of Tammany, Richard Croker. Platt had immediately withdrawn from the Madison Square Church and had "hired" a pew at the Marble Collegiate Church (29th Street and Fifth Avenue), whose minister, Dr. Burrell, declared at a dinner that it made his blood boil to have his friend, Platt, referred to as a boss like Richard Croker.[23]

Parkhurst did not withdraw from the fight and declared that the Tammany tiger was not dead yet—had just had its tail badly twisted. The Lexow Committee had exposed a great deal of corruption but did not go as far as the reformers had hoped. It especially praised Superintendent of Police Byrnes. The report was said to be largely the work of Boss Platt. Parkhurst wrote Lexow accusing Platt of treachery and of being a boss. Lexow in the senate attacked Parkhurst and said that Platt was "not in it as a boss with Parkhurst." He added: "This man Parkhurst appears to consider himself the uncrowned king of New York."

The Lexow committee brought in bills to establish a bi-partisan committee to supervise the police of New York City and one for the reorganization of the Police Department. Parkhurst opposed the bi-partisan committee. He hoped to exterminate partisanship in municipal government. He favored a strong police commissioner. At a banquet in his honor in January 1895, Parkhurst spoke on "Byrnes, Platt and Strong." He denounced the first two and praised Strong. He said, "I say tonight I would rather fight five Crokers than one Tom Platt. This city has more to fear at this time from the unofficial, selfish and partisan influence of that man, than it has to fear from Tammany. We have got to stand by our Mayor at this juncture."[24]

In May, 1895, Mayor Strong selected Theodore Roosevelt to head the Police Board. The legislature had passed a law providing for a four-man, bi-partisan police commission in New York City. It was given authority over examinations and appointments but not the power of removal. The law did make retirement automatic on application after twenty-five years, thus enabling many police officers who had lost their reputation in the Lexow investigation to retire. One of those who took that route was Superintendent of Police, Thomas F. Byrnes. Shortly after Roosevelt took office he wrote his sister that he had "the most important and the most corrupt department in New York" on his hands. He was worried about how much power he would have because the legislature had failed to pass the police reorganization bill. He was also afraid that reformers like Parkhurst would expect too much from him. Roosevelt had attended Sunday School at the Madison Square Presbyterian Church but had never met Parkhurst. The family had moved from East 20th Street before Parkhurst became the pastor. He did give the minister much credit for both the Lexow investigation and the election of a fusion mayor. Shortly after the election when he had recommended Joseph Murray as a member of the board of excise, he had asked Parkhurst to support him in the enforcement of the excise law.[25]

One of Roosevelt's chief problems was the elimination of blackmail especially in connection with the enforcement of the state law requiring saloons (12–15,000 in the city) to close on Sunday, which was the most profitable day for saloon keepers. The policemen carried on a spasmodic enforcement of the law, which made blackmailing easy. The most powerful saloon keepers and the brewers who owned many saloons were controlled by the politicians, and they manipulated the police who in turn blackmailed other saloon keepers. The public also was divided on the issue of Sunday closing; the Germans especially objected as they had been accustomed to congregating at beer gardens on the Sabbath. Parkhurst had no sympathy: "If the same privileges were given to New York saloons that are accorded the German beer garden this city would be the most wicked spot on earth." Roosevelt thought the law was too strict but was intent on enforcing it. He declared there would be no favoritism in the enforcement. There were ways, however, to observe the law—by serving food with a drink even if the food was only a token. Roosevelt criticized the weak party platforms on the excise law adopted by both parties in the election in the fall of 1895. He noted that Parkhurst was back in the fight for a strong plank.[26]

Roosevelt tried to curb prostitution by treating the men caught in a raid in the same way the women were treated. He prosecuted the keepers of the brothels and publicized the names of the owners of property used for immoral purposes (a suggestion of the Rev. Charles Stelzle of the Labor Temple). He also got night courts set up with special commissioners to deal with such cases. Parkhurst continued from time to time to send to the Police Department lists of questionable places about which he thought the police should take action.[27] However, his period of great influence in civic affairs had passed. In 1897 he admitted that it was "exceedingly difficult" to keep his "thoughts and hands" off city politics since he had such a thorough understanding of the "intricacies of Municipal machinery." By 1907 he told a reporter of the *Times* that the subject of the police had become "stale and distasteful." He resigned as president of the Society for the Prevention of Crime the following year.[28]

II

For two years Parkhurst had spent much time as a crusader against crime in New York City. He says in his autobiography that there had been no opposition in his church. In the foreword to the autobiography James R. Day, ex-chancellor of Syracuse University, said:

> Through storm and calm his enemies never flattered themselves with the thought that they could substitute for him another occupant of his pulpit. They brought to bear upon him every force possible but every year saw him victorious over his foes and gathering to himself increasing power.[29]

The church and the mission work continued, and he was kept busy with its problems. His church was packed each Sunday when he preached, and his sermons were always reported in Monday's paper.

As a result of the economic panic of 1893, Madison Square Church began to experience some financial stringency. In an effort to combat yearly deficits, the assessment on pews was raised to 18% and subscription papers circulated. Early in 1900 a few men met at the home of D. Willis James to discuss the advisability of raising an endowment fund. A letter went out to parishioners and friends of the church stating that "if it (the church) is to remain in its present location, or in a location not far removed therefrom, and is to continue to be a power for the promotion of the Christian religion in that Section of the City, it must be endowed in at least the sum of $200,000." The trustees took official action on January 16, 1901, and by May, 1902, $160,833.33 had been raised. James gave $50,000, John Crosby Brown, $15,000 and William E. Dodge, Jr., $10,000. The principal was to be kept inviolable and, if the church were dissolved or moved from south of 42nd Street, the money was to be given to the Presbyterian Hospital. By 1910 the endowment was over $300,000 with two-thirds of it invested in bonds of the Northern Pacific-Great Northern Railroad and bonds of the City of Cleveland.[30]

By the end of the nineteenth century businesses were coming into the area, and in 1891 the Metropolitan Life Insurance Company erected a tower on land adjoining the church, thus encroaching on its light and air. There were also complaints that occupants of the insurance company building threw papers and partly eaten fruit from their windows which landed on the church roof and often blocked the gutters. Before long the Insurance Company wished to expand and approached Parkhurst and the trustees of the church. The minister was rather reluctant to change the site of the church as he liked the idea that the strangers in the hotels across the Square, when they looked out their windows, saw "the spire of the Madison Square Presbyterian Church standing, like the finger of God, pointing to heaven." An officer of the Insurance Company said that the church "looked like a mousetrap" surrounded as it was by tall buildings. He suggested the church move across the street to the northeast corner of 24th Street. There was a drawback to that particular property, however. In drawing up a will for the owner, Mrs. Catherine Wolf, her lawyer, John E. Parsons, included a restriction that the property could not be sold unless the occupant, her daughter, Mrs. Bishop, remarried. The owner (Mrs. Wolf) died, and the lawyer married Mrs. Bishop. So one Sunday Parkhurst announced from the pulpit: "The Lord took Mrs. Wolf, and Parsons took Mrs. Bishop. So we are able to procure a new site for our church."[31] A corporate meeting held February 2, 1903, with about seventy persons present approved the agreement with the Metropolitan Life Insurance Company whereby the church would receive the property on the northeast corner of Madison and 24th Street (74 feet on Madison and 150 feet on 24th Street) plus $325,000 in cash.[32]

McKim, Mead and White contracted for the design and construction of the church and parish house for $286,375. The prevailing Gothic style was rejected as Medieval and Roman Catholic, having "nothing to do with the simple forms of early Christian religion, or with that of the Reformation, or with the style of architecture which prevailed in our own country when it had its birth as a nation." Instead the front of the new church,

150

The Madison Square Church, built in 1906

facing Madison Square, consisted of a portico of six columns thirty feet high with Corinthian capitals. The church was cruciform in shape, and the arms of the cross projected just a little beyond the square mass. The building was topped by a dome surmounted by a golden lantern. So that the church would not be overshadowed by the building surrounding it, much color was used. It was built of buff brick and glazed terra cotta on a base of white marble; the columns were of pale green, while the dome was tiled with an alternating pattern of green and yellow.

The interior, largely the responsibility of Louis Tiffany, who was a member of the building committee, was Byzantine in style, similar to Santa Sophia in Constantinople. It was richly decorated with gold and mosaics. Over the chancel were the Ten Commandments done in Tiffany glass. Back of the pulpit was a "jewel of a window", a gift from the congregation to Parkhurst on his twenty-fifth anniversary. The memorial windows, done by Tiffany, consisted of three large medallions surrounded by smaller ones. The pews (146 on the ground floor and 56 in the gallery) were of a soft silvery gray wood, Quaker oak. It was "one of the most beautiful of all the city's edifices for religious purposes."[33]

The new church was dedicated on October 14, 1906, Dr. Parkhurst paid tribute to the architect, Stanford White, who had been killed on June 25 by Henry Thaw in the rooftop theatre of Madison Square Garden, a building he had designed. The special dedicatory service was held in the evening. Elder John Crosby Brown presided (D. Willis James had refused to do so). Addresses were delivered by Dr. George Alexander, representing the Presbytery, Dr. David H. Green, Bishop Coadjutor of the New York Diocese, the Rev. William Adams Brown of Union Theological Seminary, who was the grandson of the first pastor of the Madison Square Church. Dr. W. H. Baunce, president of Brown University, spoke of Dr. Parkhurst's "vigorous Christianity."[34]

The services at the new church were expanded. The Rev. George P. Montgomery was engaged as assistant minister. There was a robed choir of about twenty-five members under the direction of Dr. Parkhurst's brother. There was a new organ, one of the largest in the country. At the evening service there was a processional and recessional and a harpist as well as the organist. For twenty-seven weeks of the year special services were held during the noon hour for the people working in the neighborhood. The communion service was held in the afternoon although some had wanted it changed to the morning. At each end of the communion table there were chairs for the six senior elders. The deacons passed the elements through the aisles. From 1902 on there was discussion from time to time of changing from the common goblet to the individual glasses but there was opposition, and it was not until 1914 that the change was made.[35]

Demographic changes on the East Side led the Madison Square Church to make changes in their mission work. In 1911 they decided they could no longer continue their contributions to the Adams Memorial Church. They suggested that the Church Extension Committee of the New York Presbytery take it over. A gift of $100,000 from Mrs. D. Willis James enabled the committee to purchase the property from the Madison Square Church for $60,000. The rest of Mrs. James' gift was to be used for an endowment to carry on the work there.[36]

The work at Madison Square Church House flourished. The report of 1914–1915 described its Gospel work as including: 1) free Gospel services every evening; 2) open house all day every day; 3) special services in Italian and Spanish; 4) home visitations; 5) clubs and Bible classes for all ages. When asked why they had no Sunday School, the director replied that the "immigrant from Southern Europe was crowding out the English speaking population" so the smaller Bible classes were more effective in reaching such people. The Boys' Club had become so large that a house was rented at 209 E. 31st Street for its activities. It was a four story building with facilities for meetings and games, and a basketball court in the rear yard. The only regret was that there were not as many Boys' Clubs as there were saloons.[37]

The earlier work of the church had been with the Germans but the Germans had moved further north and had been replaced by Italians and the Spanish. The question of these groups becoming members of the Madison Square Church was raised but it was decided it would be better for them to unite with some church where the service was in their own language. In 1916 an Italian church was organized at the Church House with the Rev. Mr. Giardini as pastor. One deacon of Madison Square Church was assigned to the Italian branch.[38] They held their communion service in the sanctuary of the church. The Spanish worshipped in the parish house on Sunday afternoons and Thursday evenings under the auspices of the New York City Mission and Tract Society, with Samuel F. Gordiano as their pastor. When the church changed to individual communion cups, the old communion service was given to the Spanish group.[39]

III

The solid supporters of the church had steadily moved north so that by 1918 Parkhurst placed the "center of gravity" of his parishioners between Fortieth and Fiftieth streets. The region around Madison Square was becoming commercial. The Metropolitan Life Insurance Company had bought the land behind the church and had built a fourteen story printing plant there. The church officers protested but the insurance company insisted progress could not be stopped and suggested the west wall of the new building have a glazed brick finish as a background for the church. Before long the "green and gold temple" was surrounded by skyscrapers. Metropolitan was desirous of purchasing back the property on which the church stood. Because of declining membership and decreased revenue, the officers of the church considered leaving the Madison Square area.[40]

The leader in the proposed change was Arthur Curtiss James, son of D. Willis, who had died on September 13, 1907. The younger James was active in the church: elected a deacon in 1893 and an elder in 1908.

In January, 1918, Parkhurst and twenty-one officers of the church met at James' home, 39 East 69th Street, to discuss Madison Square Church's future. The choices considered were: 1) continue at the present site but change the type of service to appeal to a different group; 2) merge with Brick Presbyterian Church at Fifth Avenue and 37th Street; 3) unite with the First

Presbyterian Church at Fifth Avenue and 12th Street; 4) consult with other churches. A committee of nine headed by Elder James was selected to consider the proposals.

They met on January 24, 1918. Although there was considerable sentiment for joining with Brick Church, it was deemed important to have a strong downtown church, and they considered an alliance with First and University Place churches which were already involved in discussions of a union. Confidential overtures were made to Duffield of First Church and Alexander of University Place. Both proved sympathetic to the idea of establishing a strong downtown Presbyterian church. A committee of nine representing the three churches was then selected; the pastor and two laymen from each, and they met at the home of Robert W. de Forest, 7 Washington Square North. By unanimous agreement it was decided to consolidate the three Presbyterian churches. First Church seemed to be the logical location, for new zoning regulations had made that area a permanent residential area, while the area from 14th to 34th Streets had very few residences or hotels. All the pastors were to resign to become pastors emeriti. Thus, the new church would be free to choose the pastor.[41]

The question was presented by Alexander to the session of University Place Presbyterian Church on February 5. He pointed out that the matter of consolidation with First Church had been discussed from time to time over forty years. Each church of the three had a cash endownment of more than $300,000, and the property of Madison Square church was estimated to be worth one million dollars. University Place church, he said, had the largest and most active congregation. Each church would, therefore, make its contribution to the union. The three had had corporate meetings: First and Madison Square were unanimous in their approval, while there was a "substantial unanimity" in the University Place church.[42]

The new church, to be called *The First Presbyterian Church in the City of New York, Founded in 1716–Old First, University Place–and Madison Square Foundation,* was approved by the Presbytery on April 8, and the order coordinating the three was signed by the supreme court on May 6, 1918.[43] On May 31 the three ministers and five men from each church met in the chapel of First Church to make arrangements for the transition. Madison Square church had already discontinued services (May 26), and First Church did so on June 2. Summer services for the three congregations were to be held at University Place, and Sunday evening services were to be held on the lawn of Old First with tent set up when the weather was inclement. The Sunday Schools of First and University Place were combined and met at University Place while Old First was being renovated to be ready in the fall for the new First Presbyterian church.[44]

154

Parkhurst wrote in his autobiography:

The three congregations entered into the arrangement with varying degrees of cordiality, the three pastors interesting themselves in promoting the plan with their respective congregations; it being considered that by combining the three congregations and pooling their respective assets (of which Madison Square furnished nearly one million) there would be established an institution so securely planted as to be proof against the effect of shifting populations and all other adverse influences that might assert themselves for generations to come, becoming thus a monument of Presbyterianism as Old Trinity has been monumental of Episcopalianism.[45]

[1]Parkhurst, *My Forty Years, p. 107.*

[2]M.S. Session Minutes, II:264 (Jan. 3, 1881).

[3]Harry Emerson Fosdick, *The Living of these Days: an Autobiography* (New York, 1956), pp. 71–2. Permission to quote from Harper and Row.

[4]Parkhurst, *My Forty Years*, p. 106.

[5]*Ibid.*, 109–16; Lloyd Morris, *Incredible New York* (New York, 1951), 215–6.

[6]Parkhurst, *My Forty Years*, pp. 117–8; New York *World*, Feb. 15, 1892, 4:5; M. R. Werner, *It Happened in New York* (New York, 1957), 36.

[7]*The New York Times*, Feb. 16, 1892, 8:3.

[8]*Ibid.*, Mar. 1, 10:2, Mar. 2, 1892, 8:2.

[9]New York *World*, Mar. 14, 1892, 8:1–4; Morris, *Incredible New York*, p. 217; Werner, *It Happened in New York*, p. 48.

[10]New York *World*, Mar. 14, 1892, 2:1–3; Parkhurst, *My Forty Years*, pp. 126–134.

[11]*The New York Times*, Mar. 15, 8:1, Mar. 18, 10:2, Mar. 20, 10:5, Mar. 31, 8:3, Apr. 3, 1892, 16:4.

[12]*Ibid.*, Apr. 7, 1892, 3:1.

[13]*Ibid.*, May 5, 9:1, May 7, 8:1, May 8, 9:7, May 13, 1892, 9:4, 1:5.

[14]*Ibid.*, May 27, 1892, 1:7.

[15]*Ibid.*, Dec. 7, 1:7, 4:2 (ed.), Dec. 9, 8:1, Dec. 10, 1892, 4:5.

[16]Lincoln Steffens, *The Autobiography of Lincoln Steffens* (2 vols., New York, 1931), I:197–8, 215–6.

[17]*The New York Times*, Dec. 6, 9:3, Dec. 7, 4:2, Dec. 9, 1892, 8:2, Jan. 8, 1:6, Feb. 1, 8:1, Feb. 8, 9:4, Feb. 9, 1:7, Feb. 10, 1:7, Feb. 10, 4:4, Feb. 15, 8:1, Nov. 17, 4:5, Dec. 28, 1893, 8:4, Dec. 12, 1894, 9:4; Werner, *It Happened in New York*, pp. 57–9.

[18]*The New York Times*, Mar. 27, 1893, Apr. 21, 5:5, Sept. 15, 4:7, Sept. 18, 5:4, Nov. 25, 1894, 7:1.

[19]Alexander Flick, ed. *History of the State of New York* (10 vols., New York, 1933–1937), VII:177–9; Werner, *It Happened in New York*, pp. 59–60.

[20]*The New York Times*, Oct. 24, 1:7, Oct. 26, 3:1, Oct. 31, 1894, 5:2; Werner, *It Happened in New York*, p. 90; Charles H. Parkhurst, *Our Fight with Tammany* (New York, 1895), 256–66; Gustavus Myers, *History of Tammany Hall* (New York, 1917), 333–4.

[21]*The New York Times*, Apr. 21, 1894, 4:3, Oct. 27, 1895, 5:3.

[22]*Ibid.*, Apr. 11, 9:1, Apr. 12, 2:4, Apr. 18, 1892, 1:5, Apr. 12, 9:3, Nov. 7, 1:7, Nov. 8, 1894, 9:5, Jan. 15, 1895, 1:5.

[23]Lothrop Stoddard, *Master of Manhattan. The Life of Richard Croker* (New York, 1931), 103, 146; *The New York Times*, Nov. 15, 9:2, Nov. 28, 8:1, Nov. 29, 9:5, Dec. 31, 1894, 7:1.

[24] *The New York Times*, Dec. 18, 1894, 8:3, Jan. 15, 1:5, Jan. 19, 5:2, Jan. 22, 8:1, Jan. 31, 1895, 1:3; Werner, *It Happened In New York*, p. 113.

[25]Theodore Roosevelt to Charles Parkhurst, Mar. 8, 1895, in *Letters of Theodore Roosevelt* ed. by Elting Morison et al. (8 vols., Cambridge, Mass., 1951–1954), I:430; to Lucius Burrie Swift, Apr. 27, 1895, I:447; to Anna Roosevelt, June 1, 1895, I:459.

[26]Roosevelt, *Autobiography*, ch. VI; Roosevelt to Anna, June 30, 1895, in Morison, ed., I:464, to H. C. Lodge, Sept. 1895, I:478; *The New York Times*, Nov. 28, 1894, 9:7.

[27]*The New York Times*, Oct. 25, 1:7, Oct. 31, 1906, 5:1.

[28]*Ibid.*, Sept. 28, 1907, 9:5; Parkhurst to Dr. Clarence Beebe, Mar. 3, 1897, in file of correspondence, church archives.

[29]Parkhurst, *My Forty Years*, v.

[30]M.S. Trustee Minutes, Jan. 18, 1899, Jan. 16, 1901, May 23, 1902, Dec. 19, 1910. Madison Square Church, file on endowments.

[31]"It Happened only Yesterday," publication of Metropolitan Life Insurance Company, based on interview with Frederich Hudson Ecker; J. H. Tibbit to W. E. Stiger, Oct. 10, 1903, in Madison Square file of correspondence, church archives.

[32]M.S. Trustee Minutes, Jan. 8, 23, Feb. 2, 5, 1903.

[33]*Ibid.*, Feb. 7, 1905. Inventory in Madison Square File; *The New York Times*, Oct. 14, 1906, 9:1.

[34]M.S. Session Minutes, IV:49, 51 (Mar. 30, May 16, 1906); *The New York Times*, Oct. 15, 1906, 9:3.

[35]M.S. Session Minutes, IV:57, 67 (May 3, Nov. 2, 1906), 87 (Jan. 3, 1909), 123, 126–7, 129 (Mar. 10, May 1, Oct. 29, 1912); M.S. Deacons Minutes, I, May 3, 1908, Jan. 3, 1909, May 7, 1911, Mar. 10, May 6, Nov. 4, 1912.

[36]M.S. Session Minutes, IV:113–4 (Nov. 1, 1911), 123 (Mar. 10, 1912); M.S. Trustee Minutes, Dec. 15, 1911, Jan. 5, 1912.

[37]*Madison Square Presbyterian Church Year Book*, 1914–1915, pp. 11–28, 31–33.

[38]M.S. Session Minutes, IV:88–9, 91 (Apr. 8, 30, 1909), 146 (Feb. 12, 1916).

[39]*Ibid.*, 110–11, 114 (Mar. 26, May 3, Nov. 1, 1911), 138 (Oct. 28, 1914), M.S. Trustee Minutes, Jan. 10, 1912.

[40]Parkhurst, *My Forty Years*, p. 67.

[41]*Year Book*, 1919, pp. 1–13; M.S. Session Minutes, IV, 69 (Sept. 24, 1907), 83 (Oct. 30, 1908), 188–92 (Feb. 27, 1918).

[42]U.P. Session Minutes, IV:386 (Feb. 5, 10, 1918), M.S. Session Minutes, 177–83 (Feb. 6, 10, 1918).

[43]M.S. Session Minutes, IV:196 (May 6, 1918).

[44]U.P. Session Minutes, IV:391 (May 8, 1918); Minutes of the Consolidated Churches, I:4.

[45]Parkhurst, *My Forty Years*, p. 68.

CHAPTER EIGHT

Harry Emerson Fosdick and First Church

The newly formed church ("The First Presbyterian Church in the City of New York, Founded 1716—Old First, University Place, Madison Square Foundation") had its first worship service on November 3, 1918, and the New York *Herald* reported: "The lower part of Fifth Avenue looked like the good old days yesterday because it was crowded on both sides before and after church services. This was due to the reopening of the historic First Presbyterian Church." The church was crowded with 1,188 present. The three pastors in their Geneva gowns were in the pulpit. Dr. Duffield presided, Dr. Alexander read the Scriptures, and Dr. Parkhurst preached. He said that the old Madison Square Church was dead, the Old First Church was dead, and the old University Place Church was dead. "There were three parents in this case, and they all died in giving birth to this church—the New First Presbyterian Church." The retiring pastor of Old First boasted: "The First Church at last has come into its own. It is now to be the Presbyterian Cathedral of New York City." The article noted that the president of the board of trustees, Arthur Curtiss James, had arrived in good time and sat in the middle aisle and expressed himself greatly pleased with the attendance and the service.[1]

The committee appointed to select a minister for the new church reported to the congregation of their failure to secure their first choice, Dr. John Timothy Stone of the Fourth Presbyterian Church in Chicago. They also told those at the meeting in the lecture room at West 11th Street on January 8, 1919, that Harry Emerson Fosdick had declined their invitation. He had preached several times at First Church (and his sermons had been enthusiastically received) but he did not feel he wanted to leave his teaching post at Union Theological Seminary to take on the heavy administrative responsibilities that would be entailed with the

Rev. Harry Emerson Fosdick, Associate and preaching Minister of the Consolidated First Presbyterian Church 1919–1924, whose liberal interpretation of the Bible aroused fundamentalist Presbyterians.

newly consolidated congregation. The committee then suggested another course of action: "It ... became apparent to your Committee that the qualifications which they sought in Pastor, Preacher, and Executive in charge of Church activities, were not likely to be found in any single person, and that the ideal of our church organization was to obtain these qualifications in different persons under the leadership of a Pastor."[2]

A novel and creative proposal was made: George Alexander to be the pastor with Fosdick as an Associate Minister to carry regular responsibility for preaching at the morning services, along with another associate minister, Thomas Guthrie Speers, to preach at evening services and to carry many of the administrative duties of the parish. The three accepted the invitation although Alexander had hoped to continue in retirement, being seventy-four years old at the time and having been a minister for almost fifty years. (It was said that Duffield wanted the position, being the youngest of the three retirees—63 years old.) Speers had recently returned from duty as an Army chaplain in France—he was 28 years old.

Others on the church staff included: Frederick P. Mudge, who had been assistant at Old First, was retained to work with the young people; Florence Weiss, Alexander's secretary for 12 years at University Place, was given oversight of the details of administration; Anne P. Swann was the social worker; David J. Beaver the gymnasium instructor; and Alice Salt was the church visitor. The music remained under the direction of William C. Carl of Old First, who had a quartette and choir of twenty-four. It was an effective team.[3]

158

The arrangement's most radical aspect was that of inviting Fosdick, an ordained Baptist minister, to occupy permanently the pulpit of a Presbyterian church. He was surprised at the invitation, warning that he would not make "the creedal subscription necessary to be a Presbyterian clergyman, and had no desire . . . to change affiliation from a comparatively free to a very stiff denominational system of ecclesiastical control." Although when the committee had originally approached him he had told them he did not feel "qualified to fill the position of Pastor and organizer of church activities . . . he was quite ready to enter the service of the church as permanent Preacher." The proposal of shared responsibilities was something for which he had seen a need. When he served as student assistant at the Madison Avenue Baptist church, 1901–1902, he noted that the church "as a whole was run on an inadequate plan—one minister, with a few assistants for minor tasks, very little going on throughout the week except the Wednesday evening prayer meeting, and everything centered and focused in the two sermons on Sunday." He characterized such an approach as representing "Protestantism's sorry failure in dealing with the metropolitan problem, carrying over into the thick of a great city a church organization and program fitted to a primitive rural area."[4] The union of three congregations "having different traditions, with individual members holding widely divergent theological views" was in itself efficacious, and then to invite a Baptist to become a member of its ministerial staff was a great advance in interdenominational cooperation.

Arthur Curtiss James, trustee, benefactor, and prime-mover for the consolidation in 1918.

The installation service for the new collegiate ministerial group was held on Wednesday, January 29, 1919, with Fosdick preaching the sermon. The presbytery had unanimously approved the arrangement and even invited him to sit with them "as a corresponding member" whenever convenient. Fosdick anticipated many years of service, combining the two careers he most enjoyed, preaching and teaching. He said of his associates, "Dr. George Alexander was one of the most admirable and lovable men I ever knew and my relationships with him were completely satisfying. Along with Guthrie Speers, our colleague, we made a harmonious team."[5]

The church was jammed with every pew rented. Fosdick's early sermons were in no way controversial; he did not discuss complex theological questions. His emphasis was always on Jesus Christ. He felt religion had become involved in too many entanglements, that Christianity was simply Christ. Although some people preferred elaborate theological excursions, as Fosdick viewed matters, the important thing was the life of Christ as a way of life. He emphasized an individual's relation to God and Christ.

As an encouragement to those made uneasy by challenges to tradition and orthodoxy, Fosdick stressed the changes in attitudes experienced by the Christian community through the centuries of its history as it grew in enlightenment and understanding. He gave as example attitudes toward human slavery that had moved from tolerance and acceptance to abhorrence and rejection. Sin for him was "simply living in the present age upon the ideals and standards of an age gone by." There was need for words of faith relevant to the stresses and anxieties in human lives in their present situation. He reported that a sermon on "Forgiveness of Sins" had been responsible for the saving of at least one life that he knew of because the one saved had later told him what happened.

A man in such total despair that he spent his last dollar in a drugstore for a poison he intended to take, passed First Church and was intrigued by the crowds that entered the sanctuary. He joined them, heard Fosdick talk of forgiveness, and poured the poison down the sewer manhole when he left. Fosdick said that the sermon was not addressed to the person with "no uneasy stirrings of conscience about his attitude toward anything or his relationship with anybody." He pointed out that it was not easy to forgive if sin really mattered to a person—that even Jesus found it hard to forgive. Sin always hurt other people which made it especially difficult to forgive. He concluded by urging individuals to get rid of the unforgiven sin. "Whatever theology you hold, it is the way of the Cross—penitence, confession, restitution, pardon," he said, that mattered. Throughout his sermons the focus remained on Jesus—his personality; with that in focus, no elaborate theology was needed.[6] A later pastor of First Church wrote of Fosdick in those years:

160

His theology found in the Christian faith basis for the liberal persuasion that progress is made in history, human nature is essentially good and responsive to education, the Kingdom of God is a possibility for earth. He was optimistic. In much of this there was naivete and many of his answers were simplistic. But the assurance that human beings were not powerless, that things could be improved by rational, sensible people operating in good faith and with good will struck a responsive chord with the large numbers who came to hear his sermons. Confidence drawn from the Christian faith as he interpreted it provided strong support for many living in a time of major and dramatic change.[7]

In the initial year at First Church Fosdick's sermons dealt extensively, and at times it seemed exclusively, with World War I. He had advocated American participation in the war as early as 1914, and in sermons referred to the great debt owed the men who fought, who sacrificed so much for their country. He spoke of "fair faced Christian lads, trained in our churches" eager to surpass the Germans in the use of weapons of war, even poison gas, in order to defeat them and thereby destroy the fiendish Prussian philosophy. He recognized the brutality of war but said this was a war of the people, and war drew them out of themselves; the people, he said, had come out of the war "with a new conviction of the eternal Righteousness and Justice."

Gradually the tone of the sermons changed as he began to underscore the needs of reconstruction and particularly the necessity for a League of Nations to avert another war. He persistently urged the United States to support and become a member of the League.[8] When the nation rejected the League and retreated into isolationism, Fosdick became an ardent pacifist, a position he held to for the rest of his life.

II

By the spring of 1919 First Church proved to be too small for the crowds that wished to attend services. All the pews had been rented; the rates were from $45 to $200 while sittings rented for $10 a year. It was decided to extend the church to the west by adding an additional bay to be used as a choir loft. The Skinner organ of the Madison Square church was also installed in the addition, and the gallery where the choir had been was then available for additional seatings. In addition, the south wall was cut through to the chapel and so supplied seats for two hundred who could both see and hear the preacher. New lights were installed and a stone walk built along the north side of the church.[9]

The reredos, painted by Taber Sears in 1917 and dedicated on April 28, 1918, was moved to the new west wall and repainted. It was a gift of the members and friends of Old First "as a visible and abiding witness to their recognition of the goodness of God during the two centuries of the Church's history." There were over one hundred contributors. It had as its theme the *Te Deum Laudamus,* an ancient canticle of the Christian church. Above the reredos was a blue stained glass rose window given by Mr. and Mrs. Robert W. de Forest.[10]

III

Fosdick had expressed the fear that "with all possible good intention on my part, I might become in some ways a source of discord and difficulty." He says in his autobiography: "On both sides of my family I have a strong tradition of nonconformity." A Fosdick ancestor had come over from England in the 1630's at the time of the Puritan "rebellion" against Archbishop Laud. He was later in trouble in Puritan Massachusetts, excommunicated from the church, and fined for reading heretical Anabaptist books. Other ancestors were Quakers and Baptists, one of whom, a minister, had been excommunicated for not believing in hell. The pursuit of religious freedom prompted another of his forebears to move from Massachusetts to Rhode Island, and his maternal grandmother had been an early advocate of woman's rights. Fosdick, himself, at the age of seven had insisted on being baptized in the Baptist Church and was zealous in his religious activities ("The fundamentalists in later years have hated me plentifully but I started as one of them.") but like many college students when first exposed to philosophical and scientific learning, he rejected the church completely. The rejection was short-lived and by his senior year in college (Colgate, in Hamilton, New York) he had decided to become a minister, "to make a contribution to the spiritual life of my generation."[11]

He continued at Colgate for one year in the Divinity School and then transferred to Union Theological Seminary. When he graduated he was ordained by the Baptists on November 18, 1903. He was pastor of the Baptist Church at Montclair, New Jersey, for eleven years,[12] and in 1915 became Morris K. Jesup Professor of Practical Theology at Union (he had taught there part time since 1908). Under the auspices of the YMCA he had been itinerant preacher during the war to the troops in England, Scotland and France, visiting the front trenches.

He enjoyed teaching and having the opportunity to preach in a variety of pulpits on Sundays. But when the invitation came from First Church Fosdick realized that he looked forward again to having his own congregation "with an opportunity for consecutive ministry and the chance to combine the two vocations I had always cared for most, teaching and preaching." The arrangement at First Church worked well. He noted that the six years there were

162

"among the happiest in my life." He added, "The spirit of the church was liberal . . . I had a free pulpit and was conscious of no restraint."[13]

This tranquility ended when on a Sunday in May, 1922, he preached a sermon, "Shall the Fundamentalists Win?" challenging a movement with numerous adherents in most of the Protestant denominations, but perhaps most especially in the Presbyterian and Baptist churches.

Fundamentalism was a reaction to the promulgation of Charles Darwin's theory of the evolutionary development of the earth's life. It was equally a reaction to exponents of Biblical criticism who viewed the Bible as a document compiled over several centuries and reflecting a changing understanding of God. Some theologians sought to reconcile theories of evolution with the accounts of creation in *Genesis* by interpreting the Biblical *days* as geologic *ages*. Others chose to find the Bible as a religious guide never intended to be taken as a historical or scientific treatise. Still others avoided the subject by preaching only on the political and social problems of the time. Fosdick, however, felt that the newer knowledge in no way inhibited the vitality and reality of the Christian faith's truth to meet the needs of people and society. In his view it was not a matter of either/or. It was possible to accept the newer scientific discoveries and still possess a living relationship to the God and Father of Jesus Christ.[14]

Three prominent Presbyterian clergymen were charged with heresy in the late nineteenth century. One, the Rev. Dr. Charles A. Briggs, Old Testament scholar at Union Theological Seminary, had been vigorously defended by Parkhurst, and a special collection had been taken up in the Madison Square Presbyterian Church for his defense; when he was tried for heresy in the Presbytery of New York, he was acquitted. The General Assembly in 1892 made official the Hodge-Warfield (two Princeton professors) doctrine that the "inspired word as it came from God . . . is without error." The next year's Assembly suspended Briggs for his heretical beliefs. Parkhurst had attacked the narrowness of the Presbyterian Church and the persecution of Professor Briggs. He pointed out that the eleven apostles had only one thing in common and that was "their faith in God and their living belief in his Son." He especially criticized the Princeton Theological Seminary, the center of the conservative theology, and declared: "If the Apostleship had not started before Princeton did, there would have been no show for the apostleship." In spite of the General Assembly ruling the Union Theological Seminary refused to remove Briggs from his professorship and severed its connection with the Presbyterian Church.[15]

The Fundamentalists defended their views by means of an intensive, well financed campaign, and in 1910 began publication of pamphlets, *The Fundamentals: A Testimony to the Trust,* of which more than three million were distributed. The "Five Points" in their program were: (1) infallibility of the Bible; (2) Christ's virgin birth; (3) his substitutionary atonement; (4) his physical resurrection; (5) his second coming. The General Assembly in 1910 issued a declaration proclaiming these five points as "essential and necessary" doctrines of the church. In 1916 the General Assembly required ministerial candidates to subscribe to this declaration. The entrance of the United States into the war suspended the campaign of the fundamentalists but there was a renewal of effort after the war.

The anxieties of the post-war years strengthened their cause. The war dealt a blow to the optimism and belief in the inevitability of progress fostered by theories of evolution. The decline in Puritan morality in the younger generation worried many, and not a minor contributor was the fact that many of the Biblically critical scholars were Germans. Many people felt that the whole social structure would fall if the Bible or the Christian religion were questioned. They were alarmed at the spread of modernism (as the non-fundamentalism was labeled) and associated it with the sinister evolution theory and the evil of communism.[16]

Fosdick was considered by many, a modernist. His sermons at the First Presbyterian Church, however, had been conservative and noncontroversial. He was an advocate of the Interchurch Movement promoted by the Board of Foreign Missions of the Presbyterian Church, U.S. (Southern), in December, 1918. The northern Presbyterian General Assembly had cooperated with thirteen other churches, representing 25,000,000 Christians, in an attempt to raise a billion dollars for a united missionary effort. It was looked upon as the "religious counterpart to the League of Nations." The fundamentalists opposed such interdenominational cooperation, and both the Northern Presbyterian and Baptist churches withdrew from the effort in 1920. They also opposed the Presbyterian New Era movement which was "an evangelical campaign in the missions." When Fosdick visited China and Japan in the summer of 1921 and addressed several missionary conferences, he was disturbed by the divisions among missionaries. Instead of cooperating in the mission field the fundamentalists concentrated on attacking their liberal brethren. This experience may have influenced him in his choice of title for his sermon—which rather than the contents was a gauntlet thrown down to the fundamentalists.[17]

"Shall the Fundamentalists Win?" he asked the congregation on that Sunday morning. He began by saying that everyone must have heard of the fundamentalists whose intent seemed to be "to drive out of the evangelical churches men and women of liberal opinions." Knowledge had expanded so rapidly in the recent years that it was impossible to exclude religion from that knowledge. He listed the "Five Points" and observed that liberals did not protest the holding of these opinions but did rebel "against their being considered the fundamentals of Christianity." He discussed three of the five: the virgin birth of Christ, the inerrancy of the Scriptures, and the second coming of Christ. He explained possible differing points of view on each, saying, for example, that for one group the virgin birth was an historical fact while others pointed out that "virgin birth as an explanation of great personality is one of the familiar ways in which the ancient world was accustomed to account for unusual superiority." He did not say that he rejected the first interpretation but he was accused of denouncing the virgin birth. As to the Scriptures he said one interpretation was that the original documents of the Scriptures "were inerrantly dictated by God to men . . . that everything there—scientific opinions, medical theories, historical judgments, as well as spiritual insight—(is) infallible". On the other hand, he went on, "There are multitudes of Christians, . . . who think, and rejoice as they think, of the Bible as the record of the progressive unfolding of the character of God to his people."

He concluded: "These two groups exist in the Christian churches, and the question raised by the Fundamentalists is: shall one of them drive the other out?" He did not feel that was necessary. He pled for "tolerance and Christian liberty."

His plea for tolerance probably would not have succeeded but his sermon might have attracted less attention had not Ivy Lee, a public relations agent for the Rockefellers, had it printed and widely distributed. Fosdick learned of this shortly before the distribution but did not oppose it, and although it was retitled, "The New Knowledge and the Christian Faith", only a few minor changes were made in the text.[18]

IV

Clarence Edward Macartney, Presbyterian pastor in Philadelphia, responded to Fosdick's sermon with a pamphlet, "Shall Unbelief Win?" A correspondence between the two began and in a long letter Fosdick argued that Macartney had missed the sermon's basic point—it was a plea for tolerance, not an attack. He proposed they sit down together and have "a heart to heart talk."

At a meeting of the Philadelphia Presbytery, on October 2, Macartney presented a paper "calling attention of the New York Presbytery to the unsound teachings being promulgated from the pulpit of the First Presbyterian Church of that city, and asking that presbytery to take some steps to correct this in the general interest of the church." At an adjourned meeting, on October 16, a vigorous debate took place primarily between alumni of Union Theological Seminary and Princeton Seminary. By a vote of 93 to 72 it was decided that rather than send a letter to the New York Presbytery it was better to overture the next General Assembly, pointing out that there had been "a public proclamation of the Word which appears to be in open denial of the essential doctrines of the Presbyterian Church in the U.S.A." in the First Presbyterian Church of New York City. It was also noted that these teachings had received wide distribution. The Philadelphia Presbytery asked the General Assembly to direct the Presbytery of New York "to take such action as will require the preaching and teaching in the First Presbyterian Church of New York City to conform to the system of doctrine taught in the Confession of Faith." Nine other presbyteries approved the overture.[19]

The General Assembly, meeting in Indianapolis on May 17, 1923, began with a contest for the position of moderator. William Jennings Bryan (three times a Democratic presidential candidate) was defeated as was his proposal that no institution permitting the study of evolution in its curriculum receive money from the Presbyterian Education Fund.

The Philadelphia overture was referred to the Judiciary Committee of the General Assembly which recommended that no action be taken by the General Assembly since the New York Presbytery was considering the issue. There was one dissenting vote in the committee by the Rev. A. Gordon MacLennan (of John Wanamaker's church in Philadelphia), who then introduced a deliverance directing the New York Presbytery "to take such action . . . as will require the preaching and teaching in the First Presbyterian Church of New York to conform to the system of doctrines taught in the Confession of Faith" and to remind the Presbytery of the "Five Points" adopted by a vote of 439 to 359. William Jennings Bryan's advocacy of the minority report was a factor in its passage, for the "silver tongued orator" still had the ability to sway audiences. Sixty-six of the Assembly's commissioners declared the subject beyond the authority of the General Assembly and drew up a pamphlet, "An Affirmation Designed to Safeguard the Unity and Liberty of the Presbyterian Church in the United States of America" (known as the Auburn Affirmation). It argued that the resolution of the 1916 General Assembly requiring ministers to support the "Five Points" was illegal.[20]

Dr. Fosdick presented his resignation to the session, on May 24, 1923, immediately after General Assembly action. The session refused to accept it.[21]

An investigatory committee of the New York Presbytery, headed by Edgar Whitaker Work, pastor of the Fourth Presbyterian Church, held its first conference with Dr. Alexander and the session of First Church on Tuesday afternoon, November 13. Several questions were listed for consideration: 1) what method was used in the selection of Fosdick as preacher and why was he selected?; 2) what was the general character of his preaching and was it in any way subversive of the Confession of Faith; and what was the attitude of the congregation, especially those reared in the Old Presbyterian faith toward it?; 3) what were the circumstances leading to the deliverance of the sermon, "Shall the Fundamentalists Win?", and what was the reaction to it?; 4) what effect had Fosdick's preaching had on the members of the church and the growth of the organization?

The conference was held at 7 West 11th Street with the two pastors (Alexander and Speers), thirteen elders, Dr. Duffield, moderator of the Presbytery, and four members of the committee present. Alexander and some of the elders explained in detail the arrangements made for Fosdick to become "associate minister," explaining that he had no responsibilities as a pastor, an "ecclesiastical term and the recognition of ecclesiastical vows." The arrangement had been approved by the New York Presbytery and had not been challenged either by the Synod or General Assembly so it was assumed to be satisfactory.[22]

The discussion of the controversial sermon was postponed until the next meeting, November 22. The elders commended the motive which led to the preaching of the sermon, the plea for tolerance. They regretted the challenging character of the title and especially the widespread distribution of the sermon by a person unknown to them. They stated that the "sermon in question was exceptional. The preaching in the First Church", they went on,

> is ordinarily uncontroversial, but searching, inspiring and full of the spirit of the Gospel. It is devoid of sensationalism and deals almost exclusively with the great themes of evangelical religion,—the Reality of God, the Deity of Christ, His Incarnation, Sinlessness and Vicarious Sacrifice, His Resurrection from the Dead, and His Indwelling in Believers; the Sinfulness of Sin, the Call to Repentance, the Necessity for a New Birth, and the Beauty of the New Life in the Spirit.[23]

The chairman of the committee asked formal statements from the session and Dr. Fosdick to be a part of a report to Presbytery and to the General Assembly. He was not satisfied with the session statement; it was merely a copy of the minutes and minutes were too bare, cold and formal. He approved of the statement prepared by Dr. Alexander and urged him to have the session adopt one along those lines "making it a warm and persuasive document." Dr. Work had put himself into the position of defender of First Church rather than an investigator. The new statement met his approval. Dr. Fosdick, in his reply, said he was committed to the side called "liberal" but he regarded himself as "an evangelical Christian." "I believe in Christ, his deity, his sacrificial saviorhood, his resurrected and triumphant life, his rightful Lordship, and the indispensableness of his message to mankind. In the Indwelling Spirit, I believe, the forgiveness of sins, the redeemed and victorious life, the triumph of righteousness on earth, and the life everlasting." He concluded: "The joy of my ministry is now, as it always has been, to lead men into vital relationship with Jesus Christ, to bring them under the spell of his Mastership, and to inspire them to make him and all that he stands for dominant in the life of the world."[24]

The committee reported to the Presbytery on January 14, 1924, affirming full confidence in both the elders and the ministers who testified that the preaching was evangelical "in meaning and force." The committee "was deeply impressed by what we have learned of the effect of the public proclamation of the Word in the First Church. Few such challenging voices have ever been heard in this city in defense of religion.... If his voice should for any reason fall silent, the Committee believes that it would be an incalculable loss and calamity to the church of God in this city." They added that the ministry in the Presbyterian church recognized the obligation of ordination vows, and, therefore, "it is our belief that a minister from another denomination, occupying one of our pulpits, should voluntarily bear responsibilities and obligations which, although not based upon the force of ordination vows, are nevertheless real and cogent in the circumstances." The Presbytery accepted the committee's report but twenty-two ministers and elders who opposed it sent a complaint to the General Assembly that met in May, 1924.[25]

The decision of the Assembly's Permanent Judicial Committee was that the relationship of Fosdick to the First Presbyterian Church was "wholly without precedent," and if he wished to remain in a Presbyterian pulpit he should become a Presbyterian, subject to the jurisdiction and authority of that church. The report was accepted without debate. Each side hailed the decision as a victory for its position. The action had moved the issue from one of heresy to one of denominational membership.

The Assembly had been largely under the control of fundamentalists: Macartney was elected moderator, and he appointed Bryan to the post of vice-moderator. William P. Merrill, pastor of New York's Brick Church, was excluded from the Board of Foreign Missions, a position he had held for twelve years. On the other hand, the report on Fosdick was considered a moderate one, and non-fundamentalists were encouraged when the Assembly rejected as unconstitutional such doctrinal tests for minister and elders as acceptance of the "Five Points."[26]

Fosdick was lecturing in England when the action of the General Assembly was cabled to him with a plea that he not make any decision until he heard the full details. Alexander wrote him at length and said: "You have the unprecedented distinction of receiving an invitation from the Supreme Court of the Presbyterian Church to enter its communion and with no ulterior purpose to drive you out." Fosdick replied that he could not accept the invitation. It was not that he objected to changing denominations but he was averse to the kind of creedal subscription required by the Presbyterian Church. He honored the Westminster Confession "as a great historic document," but not as binding in the present. He also noted that if he became a Presbyterian he would be subject to the jurisdiction of its governmental bodies and as soon as he uttered a view some might judge to be too liberal, he would be brought up on charges of heresy. He concluded that fundamentalism in the church was not dead.[27]

In accordance with the ruling of the General Assembly the New York Presbytery on September 1 invited Dr. Fosdick to enter the Presbyterian ministry. The invitation was very cordial and considered an "unusual honor." Many leaders in the church, notably Henry Sloane Coffin, pastor of the Madison Avenue Presbyterian Church and later president of Union Theological Seminary, urged him to accept. On the other hand, Dr. Parkhurst did not see how he could join the Presbyterians. The session urged Fosdick to remain and said they would not receive his resignation. However, he was unconvinced, and submitted his resignation on September 7,1924. At a meeting of the congregation of First Church, on October 22, 1924, the following resolution was passed:

> That we the officers and members of the Church and congregation express to Dr. Fosdick and make known to the Presbyterian Church at large our unreserved confidence in him, our warm affection for him, our faith in his spiritual leadership and our belief in his teachings. We further wish to make unequivocal and emphatic expression of our desire that he should remain with this church in the relationship which has not only been so profitable and precious to us as individuals but which has notably illustrated in practice that interdenominational spirit which is seeking an organic unity in the evangelical churches....
>
> We affirm our loyalty to the Presbyterian Church, our accord with its faith and order, and our enthusiastic support of its world-wide work....We respect the historic position of the First Presbyterian Church and would resist any attempt to wrench it from its ancient moorings.

Fosdick's resignation was accepted but the session invited him to preach at First Church whenever he was free.[28]

V

The congregation was in a difficult position. It was the only downtown Presbyterian Church in a district with a population made up of many nationalities and young people of modest means. It was proud of the interdenominational character of its ministry. Its preaching minister had great appeal to youth and drew large crowds. The membership had increased to 1,883, and all pews had been rented. The budget for benevolences of the church had risen to $163,898. Yet on the other hand, the congregation did not want to sever the Presbyterian affiliation it had held for over two hundred years. By inviting Fosdick to preach when he could, they thought they could have it both ways. That was not to be. Fosdick refused and asked that a date be set for the termination of his connection with the church.[29]

He officiated at the Communion service at 4 p.m. on February 1, 1925, and a month later delivered his last sermon at the First Church. The New York Presbytery had fixed the terminal date as March 1, 1925. The congregation began to gather two hours before the service and stood in the rain until the doors were opened. There was pew room for 1,088 and over 700 more were seated in the two chapels or stood; more than 500 were turned away.

Dr. Fosdick preached on Acts 18:18, the sermon Paul delivered when he said good-by to the church at Corinth which was as near a settled pastorate as the itinerant Apostle ever had. He reminded the congregation that the early years of the Christian church were troublesome times and many of those first Christians had demanded conformity to Jewish law and that some had called Paul a "determined heretic" when he advocated an inclusive church, free of the "paraphernalia of legalism." Fosdick referred to other "respectable heretics" such as John Knox and John Calvin and told how six years earlier First Church had tried an adventurous experiment—an interdenominational ministry. The church had aimed for an inclusive church and had stood for tolerance and for the "social application of the principles of Jesus Christ." He had been happy at First Church and although there had been stormy times outside there had been none at home within the church. He made it clear he would not return to the pulpit of First Church. He urged the congregation to stand by the church and not to worry about him. It was a very emotional time. After the benediction he was surrounded as he tried to descend from the pulpit. Finally lines were formed so everyone could shake his hand. It was fully an hour before the congregation let him leave the church.[30]

The session prepared a memorial to be presented to the 137th General Assembly meeting in May, 1925. It pointed out that the First Presbyterian Church had a complete Presbyterian organization with a session consisting of two ministers and twenty elders which had "at all times accepted full responsibility for its pulpit administration, its worship and service." Yet it had been attacked by a neighboring presbytery and been publicly denounced as "disloyal and rebellious." It went on, "It seemed to the session that the attempt on the part of people, remote and ill informed with regard to the actual situation, to break up a relation so happy and fruitful was unwarranted, and that it was prejudicial to the highest interests of the Presbyterian Church to show inhospitality toward a minister who more than any other man of his time has acquired the art of making the great doctrines of the ancient creeds intelligible and winsome not only to the youth but to many of mature life." It concluded: "We respectfully ask this General Assembly, by some appropriate action to vindicate the loyalty and good faith of a church which for more than two centuries has been a mother of churches and a staunch supporter of the principles at the heart of our communion."[31]

Arthur Curtiss James attempted without success to persuade William Jennings Bryan to moderate his opposition to Fosdick, and as a member of the General Council of the Presbyterian Church, Bryan had considerable influence. Alexander felt that it was his harangues and the columns in "The Presbyterian" which had brought about the dissension in the church and declared that if Bryan's party was strong enough to cast out those who disagreed with him then he would be willing to accept exclusion.[32] By the time the General Assembly met, however, Bryan was involved in the famous Scopes trial in which the validity of a Tennessee law prohibiting the teaching of the theory of evolution in the schools was being tested. His fundamentalist beliefs were ridiculed by Clarence Darrow, defense attorney for the young teacher (Bryan died shortly after the trial ended, July 26).

There seemed to be a greater spirit of tolerance at the 1925 General Assembly. The Judicial Committee dismissed the case of *Buchanan et al vs. The Presbytery of New York* in which the Presbytery had been criticized for allowing First Church to retain Fosdick as preacher for some months after he had refused to accept the creed of the Presbyterian Church. The question had become a moot one—Fosdick had left First Church before the meeting of the General Assembly. The complaint had been filed to prevent his return to the pulpit but he had already declared that he would not. The Commission did note, however, "that the date fixed was not as early as it should have been to comply properly with the decree of the court." The General Assembly accepted this report and the Fosdick case was ended.[33]

[1] New York *Herald,* Nov. 4, 1918, 4:2.

[2] Minutes of the Session of the Consolidated Churches (hereafter cited as ·Consolidated Churches Session Minutes), I:26 (Dec. 23, 1918), 30 (Jan. 21, 1919).

[3] *Ibid.,* I:7,20 (Aug. 1, Nov. 21, 1918), 63–4 (Sept. 25, 1919).

[4] Fosdick, *Autobiography,* p. 79. Permission to quote from Harper and Row.

[5] *Ibid.,* p.133.

[6] Fosdick Papers, church archives, contain many of his sermons. *The Church Tower* was established in 1923 to print the sermons of Dr. Fosdick. See, e.g. "What is Christianity," in *The Church Tower,* December, 1923, pp. 5–12.

[7] John B. Macnab, "Fosdick at First Church," in *Journal of Presbyterian History,* v. 52, no. 1, p. 1.

[8] Fosdick Papers, sermon of March 23, 1919. For his change of attitude toward the war see his sermons on Armistice Day in 1923 and on Sept. 13, 1925; Fosdick, *Autobiography,* pp. 120–1.

[9] Consolidated Churches Session Minutes, I:58 (Sept. 21, 1919).

[10] First Church Session Minutes, IV:156 (Mar. 21, 1917), 201 (May 22, 1918); Consolidated Churches Session Minutes, I:75, 80 (Jan. 4, Apr. 18, 1922). Mr. de Forest was president of the Metropolitan Museum of Art and founder of the American Wing.

[11] Consolidated Churches Session Minutes, I:32 (letter of Fosdick to Jesse F. Forbes, Jan. 15, 1917); Fosdick, *Autobiography,* pp.15, chs. 1—3.

[12] Fosdick, *Autobiography,* pp. 74—81.

[13] *Ibid.,* pp. 112, 122—3, 133—4.

[14] Winthrop Hudson, *Religion in America* (New York, 1965), 266—8; Fosdick, *An Autobiography,* p. 93.

[15] Loetscher, *Brief History of Presbyterians,* pp. 85—7; M.S. Session Minutes, III:166, 177 (Feb. 1, Dec. 6, 1893); *The New York Times,* May 25, 8:1, May 27, 1891, 5:3. Two of the founders of Union Seminary were the Rev. Mr. Adams of Madison Square and Charles Butler of Mercer.

[16] Sweet, *Story of Religion in America,* p. 407; Ahlstrom, *Religious History of the American People,* pp. 813—5; Norman F. Furness, *The Fundamentalist Controversy, 1918—1931* (New Haven, 1954), 10—23, 130—1

[17] Ahlstrom, *Religious History of the American People,* p. 897; Furness, *Fundamentalist Controvrsy,* pp. 131—2; Fosdick, *Autobioggraphy,* p. 135; *The New York Times, Jan. 31, 1919,* 10:8.

[18] Fosdick, *Autobiography,* pp. 143—6; "Shall the Fundamentalists Win?," in Fosdick file, church archives.

[19] Furness, *Fundamentalist Controversy,* pp. 132—3; Fosdick to C. E. Macartney, Oct. 13, 1922 (copy), Macartney to Fosdick, Oct. 15, 1922 (copy), *The Presbyterian,* Oct. 26, 1922, in Fosdick file; *The New York Times,* Oct. 18, 1922, I:6.

[20] Furness, *Fundamentalist Controversy,* pp. 133—4; *The First Presbyterian Church and Dr. Fosdick,* pp. 8—9.

[21] Consolidated Churches Session Minutes, I:241 (May 24), 243—4 (copy of letter of Fosdick to Henry N. Tifft, May 24, 1923), 244—5 (Tifft to Fosdick, June 1), 253 (Fosdick to Tifft, Sept. 27, 1923).

[22] Consolidated Churches Session Minutes, I:252, 259 (Sept. 27, Nov. 13, 1923); *First Presbyterian Church and Dr. Fosdick,* pp. 13—5; Minutes of the Committee of Presbytery, Nov. 12, 1923, Fosdick file.

[23] Consolidated Churches Session Minutes, I:262 (Nov. 22, 1922); Minutes of the Committee of Presbytery, Nov. 22 (1923).

[24] *First Presbyterian Church and Dr. Fosdick,* pp. 18—21; Edgar Work to Dr. Alexander, Dec. 4, 13, 29, 1923, Fosdick to Work, Dec. 28, 1923, in Fosdick file.

[25] *First Presbyterian Church and Dr. Fosdick,* pp. 21—31.

[26] *Ibid.,* 33—4; Furness, *Fundamentalist Controversy,* pp. 133—4.

[27] Consolidated Churches Session Minutes, II:317 (Alexander to Fosdick, Sept. 1, 1924, 319 (Fosdick to Work, Sept. 5, 1924); *First Presbyterian Church and Dr. Fosdick,* pp. 38—42.

[28] Consolidated Churches Session Minutes, II:325 (Fosdick to Tifft, Sept. 7, 1924), II:302—3, 326—9, (Sept. 25, Oct. 24, 1924), 363—5 (May 6, 1925); *First Presbyterian Church and Dr. Fosdick,* pp. 44—49; Fosdick, *Autobiography,* p. 166.

[29] *First Presbyterian Church and Dr. Fosdick,* pp. 51—5.

[30] Consolidated Churches Session Minutes, II:352 (Feb. 1, 1925); Fosdick, *Autobiography,* pp. 175—6; *The New York Times,* Mar. 2, 1925, p. 5.

[31] Consolidated Churches Session Minutes, II:364—6 (May 6, 1925).

[32] James to Alexander, March 30, 1925, Alexander to James, Apr. 3, 1925 (copy) in Alexander correspondence, church archives.

[33] Benjamin M. Gemmell, "The Judicial Decision of the General Assembly of 1925, " in *Princeton Theological Review,* July, 1925, p. 354.

CHAPTER NINE

The Aftermath Years

"A quarter of a century ago we faced empty pews, a depleted exchequer, an organization paralyzed, a congregation devitalized. The historic glory of this ancient institution seemed sinking to its setting"; such was Howard Duffield's introduction to an appraisal of the First Presbyterian Church he made in 1924. He rejoiced that the present was a sharp contrast—a constantly growing membership that had reached 1,880, the church open each day of the year, activities every night in facilities that had become too small to house them all. The retired former pastor was enthusiastic and with justification. He, perhaps more than either Alexander or Parkhurst, knew the trials of the past and could appreciate the bounty of the present.[1]

Fosdick's departure hit the church hard, and the *Yearbook* of 1925 noted: "The past year has brought to the First Presbyterian Church undesired notoriety, as well as disappointment and grief.... The spiritual vigor of the Church has been tested by adverse winds that ruffled its peace and blighted its cherished hopes." Instead of seeking an immediate replacement, a series of visiting preachers were invited to occupy the pulpit, with Speers, and less frequently, Alexander, also preaching. For the most part, however, Speers continued to conduct the evening services each week and to take responsibility for the administration of the program and the pastoral activities. Soon after Fosdick's departure the Rev. Robert Blackshear was called as assistant minister, "chosen especially with reference to the work of religious education." This meant Speers no longer had to oversee that part of the church program.[2]

The weekly pulpit occupants covered a broad spectrum of the church's life. Some were missionaries on leave; others were seminary and college teachers, while still others were ministers of leading congregations in other parts of the nation. At least once each month one of the First Church ministers preached at the morning worship so that the church membership continued to experience the benefit of the presence and leading in this vital area of the congregation's life. It was, a time of healing and worked its purpose, due in large measure to the unusual capacities of both Alexander and Speers as conciliators. In the late spring of 1926, somewhat more than a year after Fosdick's departure, the *Yearbook* noted: "During the past year the First Church has been like a craft voyaging under jury rig. The storm has subsided, the wreckage has been cleared away, observations taken, and the future course laid out."[3]

In order to give the church total freedom in choosing a future course, Alexander and Speers both submitted their resignations to a congregational meeting on April 21, 1926. It was voted unanimously not to accept them but instead to appoint a committee "to seek, with the approval and concurrence of the other ministers, another collegiate pastor who shall share both the preaching and the other ministerial work of the church." There were nine on the committee, one third of whom were women. The chairman was Arthur Curtiss James, and one of the members was Mrs. John H. Finley, whose husband was an elder and an editor of *The New York Times*.[4]

It would be more than a year before the committee was ready to recommend a candidate. In the meantime First Church was faced with a constantly changing neighborhood. In 1923 it had been noted that:

In the Greenwich Village section old residences are being divided up into small apartments.... Families of moderate means are pinched out and the space occupied by unattached individuals, sometimes in groups of two and threes, chiefly young men or women, engaged in business or professional pursuits.... Such conditions suggest a possible change of emphasis in some of our church activities.

The following year church members were reminded that such change was a

beckoning opportunity. The section between 14th Street and Washington Square is undergoing a swift transformation.... population is crowding out business and steadily enlarging the residential area. The character of the buildings now going up [multi-story apartment houses] gives assurance that for a generation to come the Washington Square district will furnish homes for three times as many people as it sheltered in its palmiest days.

In an effort to make contact with the new residents in the neighborhood, First Church in 1925 joined with other churches in the area (Grace, Ascension and Judson) in a program of visitation. Their hope was to encourage church attendance and participation in all the churches.[9]

The areas surrounding the various missions of First Church were also undergoing changes in constituency as the urban population shifted:

Julius Moldenhawer, First Church Pastor 1927–1948, whose scholarly competence led First Church "through difficult days of transition and trial."

In all these fields the Nordic type is fast disappearing. The Mediterranean type is almost exclusively in evidence about Bethlehem Chapel, the Semitic at Emmanuel, while the Church House and Boys' Club have to deal with a strange medley of races and languages and religions. Methods of approach that are promising in one of these centers may be futile in the others.[5]

In the late spring of 1927 the committee seeking the third collegiate minister reported their choice, the Rev. Julius Valdemar Moldenhawer (1877–1948), who had been pastor of the Westminster Presbyterian Church in Albany, New York, for twenty years. A classmate of Henry Sloane Coffin's at Union Theological Seminary, Moldenhawer's entire ministry had been in upstate New York where he was a recognized leader among Presbyterians. He had been among those who had preached on occasion at First Church following Fosdick's departure.[6] "At a meeting held April 20th, a hearty and unanimous call was extended to him.... His reputation as a scholar and a preacher, as well as his many engaging qualities, encourage the expectation that his ministry in the First Church will be most inspiring and fruitful." He was installed on October 19, 1927, with Coffin, who had become president of Union the previous year, preaching the sermon. The collegiate ministry was once again a threesome, and "the feeling of uncertainty with regard to the future course of the Church, which has somewhat retarded its progress for the past two years, is now happily relieved."[7]

There were soon to be new disruptions, however. Early in 1928, after three years at First Church, Robert Blackshear accepted "a call to the pastorate of the Northminster Church of this City." Shortly after, in the spring of the same year,

.... came the more serious announcement that the Brown Memorial Church of Baltimore had finally convinced Thomas Guthrie Speers that its call for his pastoral service was a compelling one....therefore, the First Church must release him after nine years of devoted and eminently successful ministry. It is a happy circumstance that his unsettlement did not occur until after Dr. Moldenhawer had more than half a year in which to familiarize himself with the situation and to become entrenched in the confidence and affection of the people. Through those months there has not been a shadow of misunderstanding or disharmony. Regret for the departed will not halt endeavors to fill the vacancies which their going has made.

Two years earlier Speers had married Elizabeth Thacher, of Tenafly, New Jersey, much to the distress of several hopeful, unmarried women in the church.[8]

The Rev. Phillips Packer Elliott was called as the new associate minister. After his graduation from Union, he had spent a year studying at Oxford University as the seminary's traveling fellow, its highest scholastic honor. Following this, Elliott had done student work for the YMCA in New England. He was highly recommended by President Coffin. Married with one child, the Elliotts moved into the Speers' apartment at 31 West 12th Street which adjoined that of George Alexander. The installation of the new minister took place on April 2, 1929, with Howard Duffield presiding as the Presbytery's moderator. The Rev. Dr. Carl H. Elliott (a Presbyterian minister and the son of a Presbyterian minister) came from Oregon to deliver the charge to his son at the service. The church once more had a full collegium of three.[9]

In the same year First Church enrolled its ministers in the new pension plan adopted by the General Assembly, considered to be one of the best at a time when pension programs, except for civil servants, were a rarity. Will Hays, former Postmaster General, had been instrumental in its adoption. The church's contribution amounted to 7½ percent and the minister's share was 2½ percent of his annual salary.[10]

The new collegium was to prove of short duration as a working team. Shortly after his 86th birthday in 1929, George Alexander had sought once more to resign, and once more he had been asked not to. The session did, however, release him from his pastoral duties after January 1, 1930. His health failing, he died in December of that year "only two months after our celebration of his eighty-seventh birthday.... Those who had known him long felt the loss of him as the passing of something central to their very world. And those whose acquaintance with him was of the very briefest had already learned to rejoice in the wonderful blessing of his presence."

A memorial service for him was held on March 1, 1931. Those who spoke represented the wide range of his various activities: e.g. Robert E. Speer told of his forty-six years of service on the Board of Foreign Missions, many of those as its president; an alumnus of New York University pointed to his service since 1887 on the Council (vice-president from 1898–1909 and then president until his death). He had been on the board of directors of Princeton Theological Seminary for forty-six years and on the boards of trustees of Union College and Mackenzie College in Brazil. He was a beloved pastor, had never married, and had devoted himself to a host of religious and educational activities.[11]

Two years later another of the three ministers who had brought about the consolidation of the churches would be dead. Charles Parkhurst had gone to live with a grand-nephew in New Jersey after the death of his second wife in 1931. (A friend of his first wife, he had married her in 1927 after his first wife had died.) Parkhurst had not been well and had an attendant to care for him. But while the attendant was asleep in the next room, the ninety-one year old minister had fallen to his death from a porch roof outside his bedroom—he had walked in his sleep—on September 8, 1933. Howard Duffield, the surviving member of the trio, was the youngest of the three when he died at eighty-five some eight years later, January 5, 1941, after a long illness. Over three hundred attended his funeral service in First Church, conducted by Moldenhawer and the Rev. Donald B. Aldrich, rector of the neighboring Episcopal Church of the Ascension. Duffield had been a frequent worshipper at that church.[12]

II

Moldenhawer and Elliott had come to a church with many organizations and responsibilities, some of which each of the three churches had been involved in prior to the consolidation and others that had developed since the union. From the outset there had been some apprehension that the community concerns and organizational programs might overshadow more essential spiritual matters. In 1924 the congregation had been assured: "The officers of the Church are not oblivious to the peril that so extensive a program of service to the community as our Church has undertaken may obscure its spiritual mission and defeat the purpose for which its exists." Some years later it was again noted that there were "five distinct centers" in which First Church members were directly and personally involved—the church and activities on Fifth Avenue, the Madison Square Church House, the Madison Square Boys Club, the Emmanuel Mission, and the Bethlehem Chapel—and "in no two of them are the same conditions encountered or the same methods employed. In all [however] the one dominant purpose is to make Christ manifest and to persuade people to trust and follow Him."[13]

The church house at 12 West 12th Street was expanded when in 1926 Arthur Curtiss James made a gift of the adjoining house at 14 West 12th. (He had acquired it when the Salmagundi Club moved to Fifth Avenue in 1917.) The houses were twin buildings, designed by Alexander Jackson Davis. The church offices were then moved to the new building from 47 University Place and that property sold. The large chapel and other activities rooms on 11th Street continued to receive heavy use.[14]   Two services were held each Sunday. In 1928 the average attendance was 446 in the morning and 200 in the evening. Communion services were held four or five times a year at four in the afternoon (after 1931 they were sometimes held after the morning or evening service) and for several years daily services were held at noon in the winter months. The Wednesday evening prayer meetings continued to be a strong factor in church worship.[15]

J. V. Moldenhawer was a highly competent scholar and teacher in the fields of English literature and the classics of Christian devotional writings in addition to his skill in Biblical and theological disciplines. Not long after beginning his pastorate at First Church he instituted a series of lectures and readings from Shakespeare and other classical writings in which he had versed himself. He conducted this initially in his study on Tuesday evenings. He had hardly begun when the number of those who attended made it necessary to move to a more sizable room until only the large chapel in the 11th Street building was sufficient to accommodate the number of students. One who came to these Shakespeare studies in 1933 wrote: "These lectures though primarily for our own church have attracted individuals from churches and literary groups throughout the city and suburbs." Some of the reason for this popularity can be gathered from the same participant's appraisal and appreciation of the teacher's skill:

> Under Dr. Moldenhawer's tutorship, his vivid portrayal of characters and scenes; his scholarly criticism; his profound understanding, and vital presentation of the elements of pathos, of comedy and of tragedy; and last but not least his excellent reading of classic lines, the plays of Shakespeare came to have new and more significant meaning, and brought deeper and finer appreciation of some of the more basic and eternal elements and circumstances of life.[16]

Equally notable were his lectures on Wednesday evenings during Lent when he dealt with subjects such as, "Classics of Religious Literature"—St. Augustine's, *Confessions; The Little Flowers of St. Francis;* Thomas à Kempis', *Of the Imitation of Christ;* John Bunyan's, *The Pilgrim's Progress;* William Law's, *A Serious Call to a Devout and Holy Life,* etc. On other occasions he lectured with similar erudition on the *Old Testament Prophets,* on one or all of the four Gospels, the letters of Paul, or the Psalms. He was also fond of Lewis Carroll's, *Alice in Wonderland,* A. A. Milne's, *Winnie the*

Pooh, and the fairy tales of Hans Christian Andersen, of which he did his own translation.[17]

During the years of his sojourn at First Church, J. V. Moldenhawer published two books: *Fairest Lord Jesus* (1937), a volume of sermons, and *The Voice of Books* (1940), a series of essays, many of which were given as lectures to ministers at Union Theological Seminary. His first book included "a preface on the Rediscovery of Orthodoxy," a perceptive examination of theological currents of the first decades of the 20th century. He had written it originally for the journal, "Religion in Life." His interests were wide and his explorations deep in many of the liberal arts. Probably not since Samuel Miller, some 125 years earlier, had First Church's pulpit been occupied by a scholar of such capacity. Indeed, Moldenhawer's interests were even more comprehensive than those of his earlier predecessor.

The music of First Church was renowned, and more than one tenth of the annual budget went for its support. Although the choir was composed of professional singers, William Carl insisted on four rehearsals a week. One member of the choir was Milton Cross, a ballad singer on the Westinghouse radio program, later well known to Saturday afternoon opera audiences. Once a month on Sunday evenings Carl put on a special musical program, usually a major oratorio. The Motet choir was a model for church choirs and was famous throughout the city. In 1933 a new Skinner organ was located in the chancel.[18]

The Sunday Church School was of medium size: 160 pupils and teachers in 1928, as compared to Madison Square Church House's 298 and Emmanuel's 350 in the same year. Christian education for children was, however, a primary focus, with a budget for materials and supplies that amounted to more than $1,000 a year. When Blackshear left in 1928, Josephine M. Bingham was brought in to be the Director of Religious Education, a position she held until 1947. She had been superintendent of the High School department of the church school from 1922–1926 and was thus familiar with the church's program.

The entire school attended church services in a body each week, remaining for some twenty-five minutes. A Permanent Committee on Education to coordinate the various branches of educational work of the church was set up in 1927; two of its members were nominated by the women's organizations.[19]

The Industrial School (carried over from the Madison Square Church) became in 1927 the Saturday Morning School. It was a program of handicraft, dramatic and play activities for children from kindergarten through high school and was in reality an extension of the Sunday School: ".....more intensive work was done in training in worship and dramatization of Bible stories....a Christmas box sent to a family in trouble, gifts bought and delivered to sick members, and last but not least—the *Junior Tower*....This paper, which is in every respect the children's own, was the crowning visible achievement of the year." Mere busyness was not the primary purpose of the program:

> As for the invisible—those intangible accomplishments in character which are the highest aim of the school—we have room for a glimpse into the heart of one little Junior girl, who writes for the Junior Tower, "I have learned a great many things in our school. I have learned to be friendly, kind, and true to everybody. I hope you have learned as much as I did."

The number enrolled in 1927 totaled 150 of which 54 were American whites, 3 American blacks, 25 Italian, 18 Irish, and a scattering of other ethnic groups.

In 1928 the church established a Weekday Nursery-Kindergarten for children in the neighborhood. Tuition was charged and in a subsequent year a first grade was added. It had a small enrollment—about a dozen pupils—and was abandoned in 1932 when the economic pressures of the depression years took their toll.[20]

There were other organizations in the church for all ages. The Woman's Association (founded in 1919) consisted of the Woman's Missionary Society, College and Professional Women's Club, Sewing Club, McAll Association, several Greek letter societies, and a girl scout troop. The boys also had a scout troop of which only twenty percent of the boys came from Protestant families. The groups changed names from time to time although the activities remained largely the same.

One of the most active organizations was the Young Peoples' Society (later called the Sunday Evening Society) that attracted the younger business and professional people moving into the neighborhood. There were about 150 active members who met on Sunday and Tuesday evenings; the latter was an informal social gathering with square dancing being particularly popular. In the summer they went on picnics and hikes. Many marriages resulted from these gatherings and even when they left New York City or the Village they often brought their children back to First Church to be baptized.[21]

In 1923 a group of men had organized what they called the Committee of 99 which "pledged united efforts to further the welfare of the church." Beginning in December, 1923, this group began publication of *The Church Tower* primarily to make available a Fosdick sermon each month, and also to give news of activities of the church and chapels. They gave up the preparation of the *Tower* in 1930 and the church staff took it over. Shortly afterwards they changed the name to the Men's Association. There were also many "hobbies clubs," e.g. the Glee Club, Tap Dancing (taught by a young assistant minister, Martin Hardin), Dramatics, Art and Sculpture, Craft class, etc.[22]

In February, 1920, a community lunch program in the University Place Church lecture rooms was launched. Meals were served to young men and women working in the neighborhood. The lunches cost about 33¢ a person and over 600 were served every day. This ended, however, when the University Place property was sold in 1925: the church leaders felt they should not hold on to such valuable property and keep it off the tax rolls.[23]

The church had two vacation homes. One had been presented to University Place Church in 1898 by Miss Sarah Tibbal in memory of her brother. She had been unable to take vacations when she was young, so wanted other young women to enjoy a vacation. The house was at Ocean Grove, New Jersey, and women could go there for a very reasonable sum. This vacation home was sold in 1929 and some of the money from the Tibbal fund was given to Florence Weiss to provide vacations for women at other locations.

The second was Fredericka House, given in 1926 by Florence L. Schepp in memory of her grandmother, Fredericka Bauer Schepp. It was used as a summer camp for needy girls (aged 5–12) of New York City. The property was vested in a Connecticut corporation managed by a board of trustees (in 1952 two trustees and one elder of First Church were on the board). Located at Sandy Hook, Connecticut, it consisted of a white clapboard, two story main house with eleven rooms, and a barn which had been converted into auxiliary sleeping quarters. There was a little theatre and facilities for arts and crafts, and a small artificial lake. It operated each summer to capacity. Over 150 children from First Church, Bethlehem, Emmanuel and Madison Square Church House enjoyed a vacation there each year.[24]

III

The benevolence budget amounted to about two-thirds of the total budget. The major benevolences were those sponsored by the General Assembly: Ministerial Relief, Education, Church Extension, Publications and Sunday School, and Missions. Many of the organizations for which funds were collected in First Church had been on the list for one hundred years or so, e.g. the Bible Society, American Tract Society, and Temperance and Seamen's groups. Since the Civil War the church had contributed to the Freedman's Bureau and from time to time to educational institutions of the Blacks, such as Howard University and Hampton Institute. In 1931 a special collection was taken up to help restore the Norman tower of the church in Dalmeny, Scotland, which had helped out the Wall Street Church in 1724.[25]

First Church was particularly interested in the missions in Cuba and China. They sent not only money but a communion service used by the Madison Square Church to the First Presbyterian Church in Havana. They also took responsibility for missionaries in China at Yuan Kiang, Hwai Yuan and Nanking. The names of these missionaries were listed in the church calendars.[26]

The Chinese mission work in the city also received support. Begun in 1868 at the Five Points House of Industry, in 1879 the Presbyterian Board of Foreign Missions assumed direction of the work. In 1885 the Rev. Huie Kim had arrived to be a missionary among the Chinese, and in 1910 the First Chinese Presbyterian Church was organized at 22 East 31st Street; Mr. Huie remained as pastor until 1925. The thirtieth anniversary of the Chinese Church was celebrated in First Church in December, 1940.[27]

First Church gave sanctuary to a group of Waldensians who sought a place to worship in 1921. The Waldensians were a small group of Protestants who had struggled in Italy for centuries against the dominant Roman Catholicism of that country. Groups of them had migrated to America over the years (some were supposed to have settled in Staten Island as early as 1657) and by 1910 there were a goodly number of them in the city. They worshipped in various churches and in 1921 organized the American Waldensian Church. They asked Alexander for permission to worship in the chapel at First Church, conducting services in French three times and in Italian, once, each month. The session also gave them a yearly grant. They worshipped in the chapel until 1939 although the church discontinued money support in 1931. They were allowed to hold an annual bazaar to raise funds, however.[28]

The American Waldensian Aid Society had been organized in 1906 to raise money for the work in Italy. On March 18, 1945, a special service of intercession for the Waldensian Church in Italy was held in conjunction with the American Waldensian Society in First Church with Moldenhawer giving the address. He pointed out that the Waldensians had never become Fascists and had helped the allied cause and been active in the resistance movement.[29]

The primary focus for First Church benevolence continued to be missions and chapels established by University Place and Madison Square churches. Dr. Fosdick said:

> Moreover, the new combined church took over four pieces of social service, including the Madison Square Boys' Club and the Bethlehem Chapel, inherited from previous congregations, so that seven days a week, at the home church and its branches, our ministry went on. I was proud of the spirit and program of the church and threw myself into my share of it with a full heart.

Special committees were established to oversee each of these activities: a committee of ten (including Parkhurst) had responsibility for the gospel work at Madison Square Church House; another group had oversight of a committee on chapels to oversee the Girls' Club, Young People's Auxiliary, and the Helping Hand Society at the same site; a committee of eleven (including Speers) was in charge of the Boys' Club; and another committee of eleven was responsible for the Bethlehem Chapel and Memorial House. The aim was to give larger autonomy to the chapels and missions.[30]

Through the generosity of Emily Wheeler a new, fireproof, concrete building for the Bethlehem Mission was completed in the fall of 1919 at the cost of $110,000. The pastor from 1918 to 1922 was Ernest Louis Walz, and he was succeeded by the Rev. Theodore Cuyler Speers, Guthrie's younger brother. Responsibility for work with the Italians belonged to the Rev. Thomas Barbieri; he was also pastor of the new Chiesa del Vangelo (Church of the Gospel) organized by the Italian community and received into the Presbytery in 1918 in affiliation with First Church. It had 145 communicants in 1925.

In those years Italians composed about 85% of the population of this most congested area southwest of Washington Square; 14,000 people lived within a two block radius of Bethlehem Chapel and its religious activities were extensive: Sunday School at 9:30 a.m. with 142 enrolled; English services with 122 communicants at 8:00 p.m. on Sunday; prayer meeting on Thursday and Christian Endeavor on Wednesday. Services in Italian were held at 5:00 p.m. each Sunday, prayer meeting on Friday evenig and Bible class on Tuesday. There were also many secular activities with a day nursery, kindergarten and afternoon playground program for children, mothers' meeting on Wednesday, Industrial School on Saturday, story hour on Friday and a dozen clubs meeting at odd times. Theodore Speers pointed out that most people lived in very crowded tenements, and, therefore, club rooms at the chapel were of great importance. He also stated that Bleecker Street on which Bethlehem Chapel was located was the main business artery of the Italian center, and he hoped to make services attractive to passersby.

Speers resigned in 1928 to accept a call to the First Presbyterian Church in Utica, New York. Barbieri also left shortly afterwards. It was decided to combine the Italian and English congregations to bring about closer ties between the two groups, and the Rev. Matthew C. Cavell from the First Presbyterian Church of Marlboro-on-Hudson was put in charge of the work.[31]

The area changed rapidly as was so often true in New York City. With the widening of the Holland Tunnel, the coming in of small factories and the demolition of tenements, many Italian families moved to the suburbs. This meant there was less need for the missions. The New York City Mission in 1915, over the opposition of George Alexander, had built a church on Charlton Street to serve the Italians. In 1931 Charlton Street Church, the Church of the Gospel and Bethlehem Chapel combined to form the Bethlehem Memorial Presbyterian Church. First Church leased the building at 34–40 Charlton Street for one dollar a year and assumed the cost of its maintenance. Emily Wheeler in 1931 left $30,000 in trust to First Church for the work with Italians.

The Bethlehem Memorial
Presbyterian Church,
in its Charlton Street location, 1934

The buildings at 196–198 Bleecker were leased to the Little Red School House which purchased them in 1937 for $55,000.

The work at Bethlehem went well for a while. The Sunday School had about one hundred enrolled; daily vacation school in the summer enrolled 106 children. Sunday morning service was in English and the evening service in Italian. The two congregations numbered about 150. The Rev. Gaetano Lisi was the pastor, and the church had its own elders and deacons. In 1941 the City Mission sold the property on Charlton Street, leaving the Bethlehem congregation without a home. After an unsuccessful attempt to work with the Judson Memorial, Bethlehem transferred its work to the Spring Street Presbyterian Church in 1942. Joint services did not work well so the Bethlehem congregation met separately at a different hour with the Rev. Sylvan S. Poet as pastor.[32]

Emmanuel Mission on the lower East Side (737 East 6th Street) had been constituted as the Emmanuel Presbyterian Church by Presbytery in 1918 but remained as affiliate of First Church. That year University Place Church had reported that it had a membership of 1,528 and a Sunday School enrollment of 1,210. The pastor from 1912–1923 was the Rev. George E. Sehlbrede. His pet project was the class for unfortunate men from the Bowery. They met in a downstairs room in the chapel, nicknamed the "Four o'clock Room," every Sunday afternoon for a gospel service, sandwiches and coffee. A banquet was given to the men on New Year's Day. This was financed by Leopold Schepp and after his death in 1926 by his daughter. He had been one of the first, if not the first, scholar at the old Dry Dock Street Mission, and after becoming a wealthy man had established the Leopold Schepp Foundation with gifts of over two and a half million dollars to be used for the benefit of boys and girls.[33]

Demographic changes in the city meant troublesome times also for the Emmanuel Chapel. The population in that area from 1910 to 1940 decreased from 339,000 to 125,000, and most of the people in the area were non-Protestants. Few attended the worship services, and the Sunday School which once had been the largest in the city, had fallen by the 1930's to less than 500, still sizable enough. In 1939 the Daily Vacation Bible School was established; of those who attended 18% were Jewish, 21% - Roman Catholic, 23% - Greek Catholic, and 38% were Protestant. The facilities of the chapel were popular with the children of the neighborhood especially the gymnasium which was used for basketball, wrestling and boxing. Most of the activities revolved around clubs, the most effective method for teaching dress and manners. A new group of Russians began worshipping with the Protestants in the chapel. They had their own Sunday School but in spite of the differences in ceremonies the two groups worshipped together, and the Russians elected one elder and one deacon. Most responsible for incorporating the Russian group was Donald J. Walton, pastor from 1937–1943.[34]

With the coming of World War II in the 1940's the population in the neighborhood changed rapidly, and families with children moved away. The New York City Mission which had furnished workers especially for the Russian program withdrew their workers. In 1942 First Church session debated whether or not it was worthwhile to continue the work at Emmanuel where membership had declined to 150. They reduced their contribution to $1,000 (it cost at least $15,000 to keep the chapel operating).

Home of Dry Dock Mission (left) 118 Avenue D. 1852-1874
and The Emmanuel Presbyterian Church (right) on East Sixth Street, 1952.

In 1944 the problem of juvenile delinquency was worrying the police, and the aid of the churches was sought. Each precinct organized a Neighborhood Council. The police in the 11th precinct requested the use of the Emmanuel gymnasium for their athletic program for several evenings a week. The response was so good that they requested the use for another evening for girls. Emmanuel took new hope when in 1945 two housing projects (Jacob Riis and Lillian Wald) were built in the area. There was a whole new population and among the residents were many Protestants.[35]

Madison Square Church House on Third Avenue had a very active program—sixty to seventy different activities. The minister of First Church was a member of the Board of Directors "as the official channel of communication between it in all its work and the Session." Two-thirds of its budget was contributed by First Church. This area also changed drastically. When the work there was started, there were many English-speaking people in the area but by the 1930's there were over forty different languages or dialects spoken. The church house tried to meet the needs of many of them. There were services in English, Italian, Armenian, Slovakian and Russian. A union communion service there must have been similar to the first Pentecost service, for here also people of many different languages appeared to hear the service in their own tongues. The minister for forty years, Lee W. Beattie, died in February, 1937, and in 1938 Clarence E. Boyer, minister for nine years at Broughton Memorial Presbyterian Church in Bloomfield, New Jersey, took over. He had been a member and student assistant at First Church from 1926–1928.[36]

In 1944 the work at the Adams Memorial Church was combined with that at Madison Square Church House. This was approved by the Presbytery in April. It was called the Adams-Parkhurst Church which made an active membership of four hundred and thirty. The Rev. Harold S. Rambo, pastor of Adams Memorial, was installed as co-director of Madison Square Church House, and Clarence Boyer became collegiate pastor of Adams-Parkhurst. Morning services were held at Adams-Parkhurst and evening services at Madison Square. The Sunday School was divided between the two buildings by grades[37], with club and other activities held at the Madison Square Church House. One of the most vital of these was the Children's Health Station, established in 1923, managed by the New York Diet Kitchen Association. There was a nurse in charge all of the time and a doctors' clinic two days a week. There was a graduate dietitian to instruct mothers on the proper feeding of children. In 1944 a Kiddie Kanteen was set up to care for children whose mothers were working; there were usually fifty children present.[38] In 1946 the Adams property at 432 Third Avenue was sold and the last service held there in October, 1946. Madison Square Church House was remodeled: pews were installed, with stained glass windows and a Hammond organ added. They had their own church organization with elders but continued to receive financial aid from First Church.[39]

One of the best known and most useful organizations started by the Madison Square Church and assumed by First Church was the Boys' Club. It was the second oldest boys' club in the city. It had been organized in 1885 by Arthur Curtiss James and William M. Kingsley and other young men of Madison Square Church, and was first housed in that church. In 1902 when the Madison Square Church House was built the Boys' Club was given rooms in the basement. Then in 1912 it needed more rooms and obtained a separate house at 209 E. 31st Street, and in 1916 moved to larger quarters at 102 Lexington Avenue. At that time Albert B. Hines became director. After the union of the three churches a committee consisting of Parkhurst, Fosdick and Elders Munn and Humphrey conferred with the trustees of the Boys' Club to consider the "present plight" and secure a suitable home. First Church loaned them $25,000 and $5,000 for maintenance, and with the aid of the Rotary Club of New York City a campaign was put on to raise funds. Three houses (312–314–316) on Thirtieth Street were obtained. The title to the property was in First Church and would revert to the church if the Boys' Club ever went out of existence. It was agreed that two-thirds of the Board of Trustees should be members of First Church.[40]

At the time of its incorporation in 1920 the aims of the Boys' Club were listed as: "The physical and social guidance of boys and young men in order to fit them to become worthy members of the community and good American citizens." The district covered was from Broadway to the East River and 23rd Street to 42nd Street. It was nonsectarian and not only Protestant boys in the district but also Catholic and Jewish boys found its activities congenial. There was a modern gymnasium at the rear of the houses, a game room, radio room, a press room where boys learned the printing trade, a kitchen with cooking classes, and a library which was particularly popular. In the assembly room they held classes in dramatics, concerts and showed motion pictures. Much of the work was done by volunteers. One of the buildings had three floors of living quarters for working boys without homes; they paid a small sum for room and board. The plan had been to limit the membership of the club to 500 but by 1931 it had risen to nearly 1,200 and over 400 attended its summer camp at Clear Pool—437 acres with a lake near Carmel, New York.

The club was of particular value during the depression when so many youths were unemployed. In their report to First Church in 1930 they pointed out:

> The Boys' Club is considered by students of sociology and criminology to be the most efficient organization in existence to combat crime,

because its program is particularly suited to reach the under-privileged boys living in congested districts where most of our crime starts.

The crime problem is a boy problem because criminals are made from boys; and this is supported by statistics which show that 80% of criminals are under 25 years of age, 44% under 20, and 60% of all hold-ups are committed by boys between 16 and 18 years of age.

With these facts in mind, the Madison Square Boys' Club takes pride in the fact that for three months in 1930 in a congested district which would naturally produce criminals, we had no boys on probation.

In November, 1937 there was a celebration to honor Albert Hines' twenty-five years of service as director. The occasion was broadcast on a nation wide hook-up; one of the speakers was President Herbert Hoover, honorary chairman of the board of the Boys' Club of America.[41]

In 1938 the will of Charles Hayden provided $450,000 for a new club building on East 29th Street. The will also asked elimination of the provision that two-thirds of the trustees be members of First Church, and that the club be managed by fifteen directors. This was done. The new building was opened in May, 1940; it was a four story building with swimming pool, auditorium, two gymnasiums, and a marionette theatre.[42]

IV

With the onset of the depression in 1930 the church was called to respond to new situations of need. That year a special offering was taken for an unemployment fund "in view of the exceptional situation now prevailing." Loans were made from its funds, and promissory notes given in return although there was little expectation of repayment. The next year the church gave support to the Welfare Council which set up a Central City Registration Bureau for homeless men. The national Presbyterian Church established an Emergency Relief Fund which First Church supported. The Federation of Churches opened a restaurant at Broadway and 27th Street for unemployed white collar workers. Books of tickets enabling one to obtain lunch for 10−15¢ were provided at the church office.[43] Presbyterians, in conjunction with the Y.M.C.A., established a Presbyterian Employment Service to counsel, guide and find employment for "worthy members of our Presbyterian fellowship." First Church contributed $100 a year to the service. No fee was charged to those using the service. Available jobs were listed in *The Church Tower*. Albert Flanagan, an elder in First Church, ran the new service, and one who obtained a job through the service went on to become an executive in one of the large oil companies.[44]

As the depression deepened the church felt the pinch of

declining income. Return from endowments held up fairly well; the funds were invested primarily in railroad and utility bonds. Pew rents declined substantially and as early as 1927 there had been attempts to eliminate them entirely in the hope of making the services more popular. The amount raised by pledges in 1930 was still $111,000 but by 1935 the amount had dropped to $51,000. In the same period the membership also declined from 1,650 to 1,118.[45]

It is not surprising that in 1932 the church began making drastic cuts in practically every category in the budget. The salaries of those who received more than $1,000 were reduced; the pensions of the pastors emeriti were lowered. When Phillips P. Elliott left in the same year to become minister of the First Presbyterian Church in Brooklyn, he was replaced by a student assistant. The rent of Moldenhawer's apartment was reduced by $1,400. Moldenhawer observed to the members of the church in the *Yearbook:*

> Everyone knows that we have entered the year April 1932-March, 1933 under the pressure of still further reduction in our income. The corresponding reduction in all projected outlay has been adjusted as fairly as possible. The diminution of salaries and wages has not only been cheerfully accepted, but was actually initiated at the suggestion of those directly concerned....We begin to surmise that God actually can get his tasks done with less intermediation of funds if He can. depend upon men and women. The cash substitute for personal service may well be going out of fashion.

In the same communication he spoke warmly of Elliott's "four years of excellent service....His contribution to our corporate life has been rich and varied. He has been tireless and resourceful and devoted."[46] With the death of Dr. Carl in December, 1936, the new organist, Willard Nevins, was appointed at a lower salary, and volunteers replaced paid voices in the choir. Nevins had been associated with Carl in the Guilmant Organ School and wrote a weekly column, the "Choir Loft," in The New York *World Telegram.* Many in the church congregation thought First Church should give up its support of the Madison Square Church House ($9,420), and the Boys' Club ($8,000) but that was not done although the sums given the auxiliary bodies were reduced.[47]

In 1941 the finances were reorganized and consolidated into three accounts: General Endowment Fund, made up of the endowments brought into the union by the three churches in 1918; the Consolidated Benevolences Fund, made up of many funds which had been given primarily for the use of the several missions; and a third account consisting of the real estate, mortgages, etc. In the same year the church began to receive money from the James Trust, originally set up in 1930 under the will of D. Willis James and continued by his son, Arthur Curtiss James who died in 1941. Each year the church received twenty to thirty thousand from the James Foundation. In 1943 the return from the endowment amounted to $67,000, and the members (825 in number) were asked to subscribe $26,000.[48]

V

Women began to play a more prominent role in the church's leadership in the 1930's. They were primarily responsible for initiating a campaign that produced the $200,000 needed to build the Alexander chapel. Following his death, women of the church proposed making one of the rooms in the 11th Street wing a small chapel as a memorial to George Alexander. (This was in addition to the memorial plaque placed on the north wall of the sanctuary.) The chapel was completed in 1937 and was designed to reflect the Scottish roots of which he was so proud. Its entrance gates included symbols of the thistle, heather and ivy; and the three stained glass windows at the east end depicted the cathedral on the Isle of Iona, the Ionic cross of St. Martin against the bleak Hebridean landscape, and, in the center, a young Crusader setting forth from his Scottish homeland. A commemorative tablet was embedded in the floor of the chapel's aisle. This chapel soon proved to be ideally suited for small weddings and funeral services. It was a thoughtful tribute that expressed the deep affection they felt for him.[49]

In 1930 two women were elected to the board of deacons, the pioneering move in the New York Presbytery. The General Assembly in 1915 had changed its constitution to permit it. The issue had been brought up in First Church in 1924, when the number of deacons was increased to twenty-one, but no action was taken until December, 1929, when the congregation unanimously agreed to their election.

In 1930 the session called upon the New York Presbytery to overture the General Assembly: "Proposed action in the Presbyterian Church, U.S.A. with respect to the Eligibility of Women for Ordination in the Ministry and in the Eldership." The General Assembly, that year, voted to permit women to become ruling elders. It was not until 27 years later, however, that First Church elected its first women elders.

During the 1930's the young people at the church were influenced by the peace movement, a reflection of the national sentiment that was still in strong reaction against World War I. The Young People's Society passed the following resolution in 1935:

> I have quietly considered what I would do if my nation should be drawn into war. I am not taking a pledge, because I do not know what I would do when the heat of the war mood is upon the country. But in a mood of calm consideration, I do today declare that I believe war to be socially destructive, economically unsound, and irreconcilable with the way of Christ.
>
> I therefore set down my name to be kept in the records of the

church so that if war should come it will be for me a reminder of my better judgment and for those who held to this conviction in time of war an encouraging declaration that I believe them to be right. I desire with my whole heart that I shall be among those who keep to this belief.

The following year the church held a special armistice day service on behalf of the peace movement.[51]

But events in Europe steadily made the future of peace increasingly dubious, and a wave of patriotism began growing in the country. These activities were discussed in the official minutes of the boards of the church. In 1938 the session passed a resolution that the American flag be displayed in the chancel. In 1940 after war had erupted abroad there were special contributions for war purposes: for the Red Cross war relief and war refugee fund, to the YMCA for prisoners of war. The Presbyterian church established a million dollar War Time Service Fund to meet the needs of Christian services for soldiers, sailors and defense workers, and drives were carried on in the church for funds. (The church allotment was about $4,000). The Red Cross appeal for blood donors was carried in the church calendar.[52]

First Church's early recognition of the dimension of Europe's catastrophe came primarily because Val Moldenhawer saw it and addressed himself to it from the pulpit. The nation's mood remained strongly isolationist: America was never again to permit itself to be drawn into the conflicts on the other side of the Atlantic. But he felt differently, and of all the so-called "Avenue" church preachers, he was alone in arguing that Christian moral responsibility made pacifism and isolationism impossible. Although he had been brought to the United States at a young age, he had been born in Finland of Danish parents. These ties of family made him particularly alert to the spread of Nazi conquest, and a special service was held in September, 1940, to mark the anniversary of the accession of Christian X to the throne of Denmark. In November of the same year the title of his sermon was, "Prayer for Britain," in which he took note of the fact that President Roosevelt had called on the churches to pray for peace. He said: "We all pray for peace. I do not pray for peace at any price. I never have." He would pray instead, he said, for a British victory, for Britain and France "were standing for something of inestimable value, not only to them, not only to us but to the whole human race." He declared that a prayer for Britain meant a prayer for all oppressed peoples including the subjected people of Germany. He concluded: "What a frightful thing it would be if the authority of the crosses of St. Andrew and St. George were replaced by the kind of authority symbolized by the Swastika, Hammer and Sickle and the Sun Flag."[53]

The bombing of Pearl Harbor and the U.S. declaration of war against Japan and Germany brought many changes in church activities. The second Sunday service was held in the afternoon rather than in the evening and because of the required dimout no lights were lit on the outside of the church. The Sunday Evening Society held special functions for the servicemen and women who came to the city, and received a grant from the church to take those who attended the morning service to dinner afterwards. From 1943 to 1945 over 1,200 guests were served. One of the members of the Society undertook to write the parents of those who were shipped out before having an opportunity to write home. An honor roll of men and women from the church who were in service was published in *The Church Tower*. Some $150,000 in securities in the endowment fund were sold and invested in war bonds at a loss of income of $4,000. Certificates of honor were given to the Boy and Girl Scout troops for their work in selling the fourth issue of war bonds. Red Cross work once a week was carried on in the church house and it was used by the Office of Civilian Defense for a day nursery.[54]

Throughout the war Moldenhawer insisted that America could not withdraw from its international obligations. The nation had to put aside "the whole dogma of nonresistance." It was his opinion that the United States ought to have used force when Japan first went into Manchuria, should not have shirked its obligations at Munich and should have protected Ethiopia against Mussolini. He declared that war had been forced on the allies and us. We had been in great danger. There was no doubt as to the pastor's position on the war.

In December, 1943, a special thanksgiving service was held for the missionaries (approximately seventy) who had just returned from East Asia where they had been interned as war prisoners. The church was used by the National Council of America for a United Nations celebration, July 5, 1944, and the following March a notice in the church calendar requested special prayers for the convening of the San Francisco conference where the United Nations charter was to be framed. On V-J Day Sunday (August 19, 1945) Moldenhawer celebrated a victory over our enemies "a victory surely given by Him....We do not dare think about another war," he said. "The weapon which brought the defeat of Japan is so overwhelming that we must all be peace seeking." On July 6, 1947, he was made a Knight of the Order of Danneborg by King Frederick IX of Denmark.[55]

In the middle of the war the session appointed a special committee on Advanced Program for First Church. Its report was adopted unanimously June 24, 1943. It suggested that the trustees of the James Foundation be kept informed of the program with former Governor Charles S. Whitman (trustee since 1936) acting as liaison officer since he was a member of the special committee and his law firm was counsel for the James interests. The committee recommended first that an additional student assistant be obtained to work with the young people; that from

The First Presbyterian Church
on Fifth Avenue and Twelfth Street
as it appeared in 1921.

The George Alexander Chapel
in First Church, dedicated in
1937 to the memory of a venerable,
beloved Presbyterian leader

time to time a special eminent preacher be invited to fill the pulpit. The committee also recommended that the activities of Madison Square Church House be increased and that aid be given to the Chinese Presbyterian Church, to the St. Augustine Church in the South Bronx, to the Labor Temple and to Mr. Waddell's mission in Brazil.[56]

The Rev. Wilbert B. Smith, Jr. who had been the assistant minister for four years was called into the service of the Army and Navy YMCA. He was replaced by a much older man and long-time friend of Val Moldenhawer, the Rev. Dr. Paul D. Moody, for twenty-nine years president of Middlebury College. He had also served as a chaplain and director general of the Committee on Army and Navy Chaplains, 1940–1941.[57]

VII

Shortly after the end of the war First Church marked the centennial of its move to the Fifth Avenue location. A large committee, headed by Elder Border Bowman was selected in October, 1945. The celebration began on Sunday, January 6, 1946, and the pastor preached on "Faith of our Fathers Living Still." Among the observations he made was the fact that in the one hundred years since its move, the church had passed through two "most searching trials of its fidelity to the Christian Faith, and that by God's grace the same Church has emerged with its Faith not only undamaged, but renewed and beautiful". The reference was to the two major debates of the late nineteenth century: Darwin and the relationship of his theories of evolution to the Biblical account of God's creation, and the critical study of the Scriptures. But Faith and the Gospels continued and the crises passed. At the evening service on the same day former ministers at First Church preached: Phillips Packer Elliott (1928–1932), Thomas Guthrie Speers (1919–1928), and Harry Emerson Fosdick (1919–1924).

A series of special events followed throughout the remainder of the month: a large dinner at the University Club with Governor Whitman as toastmaster (among the many church leaders who spoke was Theodore Cuyler Speers, pastor of New York's Central Presbyterian Church and moderator of the Presbytery); "an old fashioned prayer service"; a Centennial Communion Service; a Sunday School pageant that depicted scenes of church life in the 1860's; a homecoming night; an historical address by church historian, Arthur W. Courtney, and a pageant presented by the church young people, directed by Thora Moldenhawer (one of four Moldenhawer daughters). This pageant was narrated by the former student assistant minister, John O. Mellin, newly graduated from Union Theological Seminary and ordained by the Presbytery of Pittsburgh. On January 1st he had begun his new responsibilities as First Church's Assistant Minister.[58]

Although it was not realized at the time, the centennial celebra-

194

tion would be the last large major program Julius Valdemar Moldenhawer would initiate and lead as First Church's pastor. His health had been failing in the recent years and he was soon to be plagued by repeated illness that would increasingly interfere with his capacity to preach regularly. His final sermon, for which he got out of a sickbed against the advice of others, was preached on Easter Sunday, March 28, 1948. He died three days later.

In the more than twenty years he served the First Church, Val Moldenhawer had faithfully led the congregation through difficult days of transition and trial. He had come to a church not yet recovered from the Fosdick trauma, and had wondered to a friend at the time, "Am I the lamb for this burnt offering?" His faith and courage had steadied the church. During his ministry the congregation would be welded into that single, strong community envisioned by those remarkable people who had proposed the plan of union thirty years earlier. It was a task made even more difficult by the severe economic crisis of the society in the 1930's and the nation's subsequent involvement in yet another world war.

[1]Howard Duffield, "First Church," in *The Church Tower*, July, 1924, p. 21.

[2]*Year Book of the First Presbyterian Church, New York, 1924*—25 (hereafter cited as YBFPC), pp. 13—16; Consolidated Churches Session Minutes, II:357 (Apr. 2, 1925).

[3]*The First Presbyterian Church Programs*, 1925—26, 1926—27; *YBFPC*, 1925—26, p. 13.

[4]Consolidated Churches Trustee Minutes, II, May 11, 1927.

[5]*YBFPC*, 1923—24, pp. 14—15; 1924—25, p. 16; Consolidated Churches Session Minutes, II:385 (Nov. 27, 1925).

[6]Consolidated Churches Session Minutes, II:441 (Apr. 20, 1927). His salary was $8,000 and an apartment at 43 Fifth Avenue which rented for $5,000 a year.

[7]*YBFPC*, 1926—27, pp. 15—16.

[8]*Ibid.* 1927—1928, pp. 17—18; Consolidated Churches Session Minutes, II: 401, 403—4, 409 (Mar. 23, 25, May 13, 1926), 476 (May 4, 1928).

[9]Consolidated Churches Session Minutes, II:483 (Aug. 13, 1928), 496—7 (Jan. 16, 1929); Consolidated Churches Trustee Minutes, II, Sept. 8, 1928; Henry Sloane Coffin to Arthur Curtiss James, June 13, 1928, and John P. Munn to James, July 23, 1928, in Misc. correspondence, church archives.

[10]Consolidated Churches Trustee Minutes, II: Sept. 8, 1926; III, July 9, 1942; *The Church Tower*, July 1927, p. 27.

[11]Consolidated Churches Session Minutes, II: 495 (Dec. 30, 1928), 496—7 (Jan. 16, 1929), 549 (Jan. 31, 1931), 551—6 (copy of memorial); *YBFPC*, 1930—31, p. 6.

[12]Consolidated Churches Session Minutes, III:285 (Feb. 2, 1941); *The Church Tower*, Nov. 1933, pp. 69—70, January 1941; *New York Evening Post*, Sept. 8, 1933, 1:6,7. contains a Nast cartoon showing Parkhurst as David beating Goliath (Tammany); *The New York Times*, Jan. 6, 15:3—4, Jan. 9, 1941, 21:4.

[13]YBFPC, 1923—24, p. 16; 1927—28, p. 19.

[14]Consolidated Churches Session Minutes, II:410 (May 13, 1926); *The Church Tower,* Jan. 1950, p. 8; *The New York Times,* Feb. 8, 1958.

[15]Consolidated Churches Session Minutes, II: 551, 565, 570 (Jan. 21, May 28, Sept. 24, 1931), III: 2, 66 (Sept. 22, Nov. 23, 1933).

[16]*The Church Tower,* Apr. 1, 1928, p. 1; Feb. 1933, p. 28.

[17]*Ibid.,* Feb. 1933, p. 18.

[18]Consolidated Churches Session Minutes, II: 575−6 (Nov. 24, 1931), 588 (Mar. 17, 1932); Trustee Minutes, II, Feb. 7, 1929; *The Church Tower,* Aug. 1926, p. 19.

[19]Consolidated Churches Session Minutes, I: 183 (Jan. 26, 1922), 241 (May 24, 1923), 295 (May 22, 1924), II:386 (Nov. 27, 1925), 461 (Dec. 6, 1927), 550 (Jan. 21, 1931); *The Church Tower,* III, June 1926, p. 18.

[20]*The Church Tower,* April 1, 1927, p. 1; *YBFPC,* 1926−27, p. 64.

[21]*The Church Tower,* Dec. 1923, pp. 1, 30−31, June, 1926, pp. 9−10; Consolidated Churches Session Minutes, III:41 (Jan. 23, 1934).

[22]*The Church Tower,* Dec. 1923, p. 1, May 1924, p. 20; Consolidated Churches Session Minutes, II:343 (Dec. 26, 1924), 514 (Sept. 25, 1929), 540 (Sept. 25, 1930).

[23]*The Church Tower,* May, 1924, p. 24.

[24]*Ibid.,* July, 1926, p. 17; Consolidated Churches Trustee Minutes, II, Jan. 9, 1927, Aug. 14, 1929, Feb. 2, 1933; Session Minutes, II: 418 (Sept. 23, 1926), III:70 (Nov. 22, 1934).

[25]Consolidated Churches Session Minutes, I:192 (Mar. 23, 1922), 222,352 (Jan. 25, Sept. 27, 1923), III:251 (Mar. 28, 1940; *The Church Tower,* May 15, 1931.

[26]Consolidated Churches Session Minutes, I:276 (Jan. 24, 1924), II: 395 (Nov. 27, 1925), 592 (May 26, 1932.)

[27]*Ibid.,* II:396 (Jan. 28, 1926), III:216, 224 (May 25, Sept. 21, 1939; Savage, *Presbyterian Churches in New York City,* p. 134.

[28]George B. Watts, *The Waldenses in the New World* (Durham, No. Ca., 1941), ch. 1, pp. 163−7, 190−1; Consolidated Churches Session Minutes, I:166 (Sept. 22, 1921), 176 (Jan. 4, 1922), II:507 (May 23, 1929), 536 (May 22, 1930), 571 (Sept. 24, 1931), III:73 (Nov. 29, 1934).

[29]American Waldensian Aid Society, "The Amazing Waldensians."; *The Church Tower,* March, 1945. Another service to "Commemorate The One Hundredth Anniversary of the Granting of Religious Liberty to the Waldensian Church in Italy," was held on Feb. 22, 1948.

[30]Consolidated Churches Session Minutes, I: 93−4, 103 (Apr. 2, May 27, 1920; *The First Presbyterian Church and Dr. Fosdick,* pp. 6−7; Fosdick, *An Autobiography,* p. 134.

[31]Consolidated Churches Session Minutes, I: 64 (Sept. 25, 1919), 192 (Mar. 23, 1922), 480, 484 (June 3, Aug. 13, 1924), II:468 (Jan. 24, 1929); *The Church Tower,* Feb. 1924, p. 28, May, 1925, pp. 17−18, Oct. 1926, p. 17.

[32]Miller, *People are the City,* pp. 115, 166; Consolidated Churches Session Minutes, II:544 (Nov. 26, 1930), 549, 556 (Jan. 21, Mar. 26, 1931), III:140 (Jan. 29, 1937), 236 (Dec. 3, 1939); 303 (May 28, 1941), 333 (Mar. 31, 1942), IV: 384, 405 (May 27, Nov. 23, 1943); Trustee Minutes, II: Apr. 2, 1931, III, Jan. 6, 27, 1937.

[33]*YBFPC,* 1925−26, p. 15; *Dry Dock Mission, Emmanuel Chapel and Emmanuel Presbyterian Church. One Hundredth Anniversary, 1952.* pp. 47ff.

[34]Consolidated Churches Session Minutes, III:120 (May 28, 1936), 162 (Nov. 24, 1937), 207, 225−6 (Mar. 23, Sept. 21, 1939), IV:365 (Dec. 30, 1942).

[35]*Ibid.,* IV; 365 (Dec. 30, 1942), 378 (Mar. 28, 1943), 414 (Feb. 6, 1944), 479 (Sept. 27, 1945), 493 (Jan. 24, 1946).

[36]*Ibid.,* II:466 (Feb. 1, 1928), 481 (Dec. 17, 1931); *The Church Tower,* March, 1924, p. 15, Dec. 15, 1926, March 1934, p. 15, Feb. 1937, p. 31, March 1937, p. 43.

[37]Savage, *Presbyterian Churches in New York City,* p. 109; Consolidated Churches Session Minutes, IV: 419, 426, 433 (Mar. 9, 23, June 7, 1944); *The Church Tower,* March, 1925, pp. 16ff.

[38]Consolidated Churches Session Minutes, IV: 440 (Oct. 29, 1944), 470 (May 24, 1945); *The Church Tower,* Feb. 1949, p. 19.

[39]Consolidated Churches Session Minutes, IV: 528 (Sept. 26, 1946); *The Church Tower,* Feb. 1949, p. 19.

[40]Consolidated Churches Session Minutes, I:67,73 (Nov. 28, 1919); Trustee Minutes, II, April 15, 1922.

[41]*The Church Tower,* Dec. 1937, pp. 7–8; Albert B. Hines, "Getting the Boy," in *The Church Tower,* January, 1924; *YBFPC,* 1930–31, p. 99.

[42]Consolidated Churches Trustee Minutes, III, May 4, 1938.

[43]Consolidated Churches Session Minutes, II:547 (Dec. 7, 1930), 565 (May 28, 1931), 595 (May 26, 1932).

[44]*Ibid.,* III:174 (Mar. 24, 1938), 224 (Sept. 21, 1939).

[45]*Ibid.,* II:499 (Jan. 24, 1929), 544 (Nov. 26, 1930), III: 239, 246 (Jan. 25, Mar. 25, 1940); Trustee Minutes, III, April 29, 1937.

[46]*YBFPC,* 1931–32, p. 6.

[47]Consolidated Churches Session Minutes, II:599 (June 16, 1932), III:133–4 (Nov. 25, 1936), 141 (Jan. 29, 1937); Trustee Minutes, II, May 5, July 13, 1932, May 3, 1934, III, Jan. 6, 1937.

[48]Consolidated Churches Trustee Minutes, IV, Apr. 29, Dec. 12, 1941; Session Minutes, IV, 358 (Nov. 24, 1942).

[49]Consolidated Churches Trustee Minutes, III: Aug. 17, Dec. 10, 1937; *The Alexander Memorial Chapel Service of Dedication.* New York, 1938.

[50]Consolidated Churches Trustee Minutes, III, April 29, Aug. 17, 1937, May 4, 1938; Session Minutes, I:286 (Apr. 2, 1924), II:522 (Dec. 19, 1929), 525, 528 (Jan. 22, Feb. 19, 1930).

[51]Consolidated Churches Session Minutes, III:102 (Nov. 21, 1940).

[52]*Ibid.,* III:262–3 (Sept. 26, 1940); Trustee Minutes, III, Oct. 26, 1938. Madison Square Church in 1861 (Trustee Minutes, Apr. 30, 1961) stated that if no expense were involved a United States flag could be put in the church.

[53]Consolidated Churches Session Minutes, III:263 (Sept. 26, 1940); a similar service was held in 1937 (III:147); *The Church Tower,* Nov. 1940, p. 89.

[54]Consolidated Churches Trustee Minutes, III, Jan. 20, Oct. 22, 1942, III, Dec. 6, 1943; Session Minutes, III:325, 329 (Jan. 22, Feb. 1, 1942), IV: 353 (Sept. 24, 1942), 417–8, 429 (Mar. 25, May, 25, 1944), 454 (Feb. 4, 1945).

[55]Consolidated Churches Session Minutes, IV:408 (Dec. 1943) 622 (Mar. 28, 1945); *The Church Tower,* October, 1945, p. 85; December 1942, p. 5, May, 1948, p. 59.

[56]Consolidated Churches Session Minutes, IV:391–2 (June 24, 1943).

[57]*Ibid.,* III:348 (June 18, 1942); Trustee Minutes, IV, July 9, 1942.

[58]*The Church Tower,* Nov. 1945, Jan. 6, 1946; *The Services in Celebration of the Two Hundredth Anniversary of the Founding of the Old First Presbyterian Church in the City of New York,* December 1916.

CHAPTER TEN

Church as Community Center

Through one of those odd turns in events Moldenhawer's illness became a needed interim between his pastorate and that of his successor. It served to prepare the people of First Church for the fact of change. As he became increasingly less able to preach, teach and carry on other responsibilities, the church adjusted to the inevitability of new leadership. It was in reality not unlike that needed hiatus between Fosdick's departure and Moldenhawer's own beginning at First Church.

The interim began officially on January 1, 1947, when Val Moldenhawer was granted a leave of absence for reasons of health. To his young assistant, Jack Mellin, fell the primary responsibility for the pastoral duties and the preaching at the evening services. (Paul Moody had resigned to take effect, May, 1946).[1] On Sunday mornings Joseph R. Sizoo, the president of New Brunswick Seminary, did most of the preaching, with Moldenhawer returning to the pulpit from time to time as his health permitted. Sizoo had been pastor at the St. Nicholas Collegiate Church on Fifth Avenue until the Consistory of the Dutch Reformed Churches in New York agreed to sell its property and disband the congregation. It had been Moldenhawer's hope that Sizoo might be his successor at First Church, bringing with him a remnant of the St. Nicholas congregation.[2]

On the advice of the Presbytery's stated clerk, Theodore F. Savage, Mellin was called and installed as Associate Minister in October 1947. This meant he was eligible to be the moderator of the session, and it could function in Moldenhawer's absence, something which had not been possible prior to the installation. It also meant, whether directly intended or not, that the church once more had a collegiate ministry.[3]

When J. V. Moldenhawer died some six months later, a committee was elected to begin the search for a new pastor. Of course while the committee went about its work Mellin, aided since January 1948 by Clarence Boyer, and members of the staff (including two particularly outstanding student assistants from Union—William C. Schram and Arthur Hall) continued to carry on the program. Among other things a successful effort was mounted on behalf of the Presbyterian Restoration Fund, a $27,000,000 project "to rebuild and to rehabilitate its war devastated work abroad and to meet very vital demands which the war created here at home." First Church's share was $86,000, a tremendous sum the officers thought; they offered to raise $10,000. Mellin, Florence Weiss and a committee acquired the total sum in pledges by December, 1947. Their efforts had a big boost when the Crusaders, the high school group, invited to their beef stew supper, the railroad and real estate financier, Harry Harkness Flagler, an elder, 1946–1949. He was so pleased to be included that he immediately wrote a check for $25,000 for the fund (when he died in 1952 he left First Church $10,000).[4]

After more than a year the pulpit committee had still not found an acceptable candidate. In the meantime increasing numbers in the congregation felt that the church already had its candidate at hand in the associate minister. He had proven his capacity to be the pastor virtually for three years and should be called despite the fact that he was not quite 28 years old. His age was not a problem for the growing group of members being drawn from the Metropolitan Life's new housing projects—Peter Cooper Village and Stuyvesant Town. Many of them were Mellin's contemporaries in age since returning veterans of World War II had preference in the projects. Many of the other members were older, however, and not so sure. As they saw it, First Church had "a magnificent past and an uncertain future," and to reassure them the committee suggested calling an older assistant. The hesitant ones were not in a majority, and on June 8, 1949, the call was extended and accepted. Since he had been installed already, according to the church policy then in effect, no new service was necessary.[5]

To replace Clarence E. Boyer, who had moved to Emmanuel Church, Harry W. Foot was called from a similar post in Brown Memorial Church in Baltimore to be assistant minister. He left in 1952 to be executive secretary for the General Assembly's meeting in New York. He was followed by Harold L. Ogden, a former Marine Corps chaplain, who after two years accepted a call to become pastor of the Westminster Church in Albany, New York.[6]

With three assistants in six years, First Church was gaining a reputation as a revolving door, and the program would soon suffer from repeated starts and stops. The time seemed right for Mellin to promote an idea he had held for some years, predating the days when First Church was looking for someone to succeed J. V. Moldenhawer—a collegiate ministry of contemporaries.

He had discussed his hope at length and over a period of years with his friend and Union classmate, John Brown Macnab, who was serving a growing church in suburban Long Island at Oceanside. Macnab was skeptical that First Church could be persuaded to take a chance on the proposal when both members of the collegium were of an equally young age, and for him the matter was academic for he was totally involved where he was. Mellin did not share the skepticism and believed that, on the contrary, only where there was a similarity of age could there be a genuine and real collegiate ministry. As the discussions were renewed periodically the two men began to develop a somewhat clearer picture of how a shared ministry might be handled with a minimum of conflict. Certain essentials surfaced in the discussions: there had to be a similarity of theological orientation and focus; there had to be a common understanding of the church's nature and responsibility in the life of its members and the social community; the collegium had to permit each participant to practice a total ministry of preaching, teaching, pastoral work and administration, with a division of responsibilities geared to take advantage when possible of particular talents, interests or abilities of each partner. Heavy emphasis was placed on the need for communication and exchange between members of the team. This latter was one of the primary benefits of a partnership that gave colleagues the opportunity to discuss, to argue, to be guided by each other's thoughts and insights. It was also deemed vital to the success of such a venture that any proposal for change in congregational activity be supported by each and that whatever discussion or debate was needed be had before its presentation to a larger audience. On the whole the proposal was meant to be primarily informal and one that would lend itself to change and modification as events dictated.

In the fall of 1954 Macnab felt he was ready to put their ideas to the test if Mellin felt able to persuade First Church leaders to go along. Some of them were dubious and would have been more comfortable had the plan not called for an associate relationship of the two men. This meant congregational and presbytery approval and installation and had a permanency about it that assistantships did not. This latter, however, was not the collegium that Mellin envisioned. Differences were not major and were soon resolved. A congregational meeting issued a call to John Brown Macnab in December, and the latest, albeit significantly different, of its collegiate ministries began at First Church in February, 1955.[7]

Other changes in the church's staff personnel were soon to come. Alice Salt, who had been for thirty-seven years the church visitor, had died in 1945, and she had been replaced by Thora Moldenhawer, who served until her death in 1958. Josephine

200

Bingham retired as Director of Religious Education early in 1948, and Florence Weiss retired as church administrator in June of the same year. Both had completed long years of service to First Church. Florence Weiss had spent a total of forty-one years in service to the University Place and First churches. She was a venerated and beloved member of the community and when she retired so did her position. Eight years later, Willard Irving Nevins was to retire, for reasons of health, as the organist and choir director of the church.[8]

For some years following Jo Bingham's retirement, the assistant minister assumed direction and oversight of the Christian education program. By the mid-1950's, however, the Sunday church school had grown in numbers (primarily due to the influx of young families from Stuyvesant Town and Peter Cooper Village), and the church felt in need of a Director of Christian Education. Mildred A. Neumeister was called to the position in 1957. She was an established, experienced authority in the field, widely recognized for her ability as a church educator. A native New Yorker, born not far from the church, she was a Commissioned Church Worker in the Presbyterian Church, a designation established before women were admitted to its ordained ministry, but for which the requirements were nearly equal to those of ordination.

The budget for the educational program was increased to $5,000. The church school enrollment was somewhat over 200 pupils representing 153 families of which 82 were members of First Church. There were 50 volunteer teachers, and Mildred Neumeister held training sessions for them and also organized parent discussion groups. Under her direction the educational program became a model for other churches, and she was in demand as a teacher at summer leadership schools as well as a participant in educational programs at Union and Biblical seminaries.[9]

There was also a renewed interest and emphasis on Christian education for adults of the church. In place of the familiar lectures by invited dignitaries and authorities, the Lenten season of 1955 introduced small, informal discussion groups that came together each week to exchange views on a particular book of significance to Christians. These were led by the pastors and occasionally by members of the congregation. The groups were not unlike those of the "Great Books Foundation" that had been initiated out at the University of Chicago. The emphasis, of course, was not the same. By 1958, the evening worship service was abandoned in favor of groups reading and discussing works by theologians Reinhold Niebuhr and Paul Tillich as well as others. The focus of study and discussion was frequently a Biblical book such as the *Psalms, Job,* one of the gospels or epistles of the New Testament. Much of the approach was experimental but it allowed examination of a variety of subjects—drama, novels, politics—from the perspective of the Christian faith. At the time,

First Church was one of a few churches developing a pattern of adult education that would in time become common and familiar in many churches. It was also developing a pattern that it would continue to follow in the decades ahead.[10]

Another recognized leader was added to the First Church staff when John Huston became the organist and choir director at the beginning of 1957. Only the third person to fill that post, he came to a church where music played a large role, with over ten percent of the budget spent on the choir. He was the organist at Holy Trinity Episcopal Church in Brooklyn at the time he was invited to succeed Willard Nevins. He was also on the faculty of the School of Sacred Music at Union Seminary, a position he continued to fill even with his new responsibilities. Later he was made the organist at Temple Emanu-El in addition to his work at First Church, and he would continue to fill both positions until his sudden death in April, 1975. He supervised the construction of a new organ built by the Austin Company for the church in 1964, and maintained a choir and musical program known for its excellence throughout the nation.[11]

By 1957, First Church had secured a professional staff that would remain and work together for several years to come. They were aided by Mary Gravestock, the church's receptionist, who was senior in service to them all, having begun her career at the church in 1943. She would remain the constant nonprofessional amid several changes by others of the office and custodial groups. Her contribution to the work of the church was invaluable for in her post she was often the first to be aware of needs in the parish, did not hesitate to alert others to them, and regularly acted as friendly counselor to the lost and lonely who wandered in from the street or who called on the telephone. Mary Gravestock was often described as the church's "other minister," and she earned that affectionate designation with thirty-four years of faithful service.[12]

Educational activities were hardly the entire program of the church, and the 1950's saw a variety of groups that made the church something of a center for the social life of many of the members. All male members were encouraged to become a part of the Men's Council, a movement gaining popularity in other Presbyterian churches in various parts of the country. Despite continued attempts, however, this movement gained little support in First Church. The groups for women, on the other hand, flourished, and organizations for them (the Missionary Society, the Tuesday and Thursday Sewing Groups, the College Club later to become the Business and Professional Women's Club, the Women's Guild, the Mother's Guild) all united in 1958 as the Federation of Women's Organizations to cooperate "in spiritual fellowship with a program of education, services, prayer and giving." This body was represented in the New York Presbyterial and affiliated with the Manhattan United Church Women.[13]

202

Women were elected ruling elders for the first time in 1958, when the membership of the session was increased from twelve to fifteen. The three who were chosen were all active in the church's life. Rosalie Hooper had been a missionary with her husband in the Philippines and had served on several deputations to survey the work Presbyterians were involved in there. She was president of the Women's Missionary Society. Helen E. Irvine was secretary of educational and medical work of the Presbyterian Church's Board of National Missions, a teacher in the Sunday church school and prominent in the Business and Professional Women's Club. The third new elder, Margaret Martin, was also active in the same group, involved in a neighborhood political club's work and an expediter with the National Foundation for Infantile Paralysis. She was later (in 1967) to be the first woman elected to the church's board of trustees. This belated inclusion of women on the session was puzzling in light of the support for their ordination as elders that had been demonstrated many years earlier. Thereafter, however, they would play a part at least of equal importance to that of men in First Church leadership.[14]

The role played by the First Church ministers' wives would also change. Each departed from the traditional pattern of alter ego frequently expected of women in their position.

Gloria Rivers Mellin had married her minister husband while she was still a senior at Smith College, and spent the first year of their marriage as a commuter between New York and Northampton. Later, along with her involvement in First Church's life, she became a prime mover in the formation of the Association for Mentally Ill Children and remained an important contributor to its work. Once her four sons were sufficiently along in school, she received a master's degree in education from New York University and became a teacher in the New York public school system. She continued as an active participant in the church's program but in a manner closer to that of any responsible communicant.

Mary Crutchfield Macnab had received her master's degree in sacred music from Union Theological Seminary before being married to her classmate husband. Soon after going with him to the First Presbyterian Church in Oceanside, she was hired as organist and choir director of that church. Some of the members resisted the idea of paying a minister's wife anything beyond her husband's salary, although the amount was hardly more than a token gesture. She insisted, however, that since she was to fill a position for which she was professionally trained, she was entitled to separate compensation. The church officers agreed, and she developed a total music program for that congregation. By the time the Macnabs came to First Church two, and soon three, young daughters had first call on her time, and her musical activities were limited to volunteer work with the church school, the local public school and as an emergency substitute at the organ for John Huston. Later, when the children were more independent, she was hired by the Brearley School to provide the music for the dance department, and then accepted appointment as Assistant Organist and church school choir director at First Church. Her participation too was more nearly that of other members.

The Sunday Evening Society continued to be a vital part of the First Church program. Sunday evenings were devoted to supper and discussion, and Tuesdays were for folk and social dancing. A Couples Club was well-established and dinner meetings held each month, and the former Crusaders group was replaced by two flourishing programs for junior high and senior high students that met each week on Friday evenings. There were Girl Scouts and Brownies, Cub Scouts and Boy Scouts, and a group that worked in ceramics, as well as another group that engaged in woodworking in the church's maintenance shop.[15]

II

By 1955, it had become evident that the physical plant of First Church was inadequate to the needs of its program activities. The two brownstone houses on Twelfth Street, site of most of the organizational meetings, were inefficient and in a progressively deteriorating condition. Many, indeed, were convinced that they were dangerous as places of public assembly, and only the tolerance of the civil authorities permitted the church to continue using them.

Early in the year the session and trustees of the church began discussion and investigation of extensive renovation or replacement of the properties on Twelfth Street, and the latter was deemed the more expedient of the two. There were those, however, who had strong feelings that preservation and renovation were preferable. Despite objections, plans for construction of a new church house were made.

Overtures to the James Foundation for funds met with a negative response. The decision to proceed remained firm, and in the spring of 1956 the congregation embarked on an ambitious campaign to secure pledges of support totaling $250,000 payable over three years. It was an effort that involved the total church and successfully reached its goal. The James Foundation agreed to match the building fund with a nearly equal amount of $200,000.

A building committee composed of members of the session, deacons, trustees and the Women's Association was headed by Lester F. Allen, a younger elder who lived in Stuyvesant Town. The pastors and the director of Christian education served as *ex officio* members.

The first task was the choice of an architect, and after several interviews it was decided to retain Edgar A. Tafel, whose office and home was on East Eleventh Street within sight of the church.

John O. Mellin, and
John B. Macnab, present
first laying of the corner
stone for the new church
house, 1958.

Some members were apprehensive because he had been a pupil of
the renowned Frank Lloyd Wright, whose designs were considered too modern and unconventional. Tafel accepted the challenge of designing a building that would be functional and
efficient but at the same time harmonize with the design of the
19th century church structure that it would abut. He placed a
parapet on top of the building, a balcony facing Fifth Avenue, a
pseudo-balcony above it and on the Twelfth Street exposure, all
of which featured a quatrefoil design that was the same as that
used on the church building. (The quatrefoil is an old Christian
symbol signifying the four Gospels.) The exterior of the new
building was done in Roman brick, colored to match the
brownstone of the church. The two buildings blended amazingly
well, and the church house won an architectural award from the
Fifth Avenue Association in 1960, the same year in which the
Guggenheim Museum on upper Fifth Avenue and designed by
Frank Lloyd Wright won a similar award. Teacher and pupil
shared high honors. On an open stair leading to the second floor
inside the building a seven foot Celtic cross dominated the
landing. This cross was designed and carved by Conwell Savage,
an elder of First Church, a member of the building committee
who was also chairman of the board of directors of the Village Art
Center. It was made of chestnut wood with grapes and wheat
depicted in the circle braid and symbolizing the communion
elements of bread and wine.[16]

The building venture was an unusual undertaking for a church
in a downtown urban location. Even though the immediate
neighborhood was primarily residential, the population was constantly changing. Therefore, the committee tried to avoid the
danger of designing a building only in terms of present needs and
that might be made useless by future changes in the neighbor-

The prize-winning Church House
of First Church,
completed in 1960.

The First Presbyterian Church
as it presently appears.

hood's composition. Classrooms were made large, and all furnishings were selected with an eye to flexibility. For example, instead of building permanent closets for coats and supplies, movable cabinets were substituted and racks for coats were made to be easily removed from the walls. Even the blackboards were made so that they could be changed easily if such was indicated at some later time. Mildred Neumeister's long experience in other building projects in which she had been involved proved to be particularly valuable. No classroom was designed for one particular age. The result was a building that was featured in counsel the United Presbyterian Church offered to those constructing educational facilities in other parts of the nation, even in non-urban areas.

Late in 1957, after various changes and reductions to stay within a budget of nearly one million dollars, the contract for construction was awarded to Cuzzi Brothers and Singer, Inc. The Twelfth Street buildings were vacated (a manse to house the Mellins was purchased at 55 West Ninth Street), and all the activities of the church were transferred to the Eleventh Street wing. During the two years that construction went on, the church operated from those limited quarters. By means of advance planning and careful scheduling the full program continued with a minimum of conflict.[17]

When the pledges to the first building fund were paid in 1959, a second campaign was conducted. The results were almost as rewarding as in the first effort, and again the James Foundation gave a matching grant. When the new building was ready for occupancy in January 1960, the committee could take pride that they had been able to stay within the budget, and the church would not be saddled with a mortgage on the property. About ten percent of the cost had come from the endowment surplus thus leaving the principal intact. The church treasurer, Elder A. T. Hanes, suggested to trustee Robert C. Shriver that as an encouragement to prospective members a sign be placed on the exterior of the new building: "There is no mortgage on this building." Both men had played major roles in the project from its inception, and Shriver was particularly active in the relations with the James Foundation.

When the church activities moved out of the 11th Street building, those facilities were made available to the Presbytery of New York to be used as executive offices. In exchange for their use First Church was credited with a benevolence contribution to the Presbytery in lieu of any cash rent payment. Under the arrangement the church retained use of the Alexander chapel and a basement room. As the work of the Presbytery expanded and the number of staff increased, all other parts of the 11th Street building were soon used for that purpose. It was noted that when that building had been constructed in 1893, it had been hoped that the Presbytery would regularly meet there. That was still not the case nearly seventy years later, but occupancy in 1960 was a partial fulfillment of that hope.[18]

III

Not only did the new church house supply room for all First Church activities, it also contained features that allowed for an expansion and change of that program. The large kitchen and assembly room in the basement made dinners for a sizable group possible, and in the first year the practice of presenting the budget needs of the church at a dinner began. Even the larger room was not sufficient to seat all who came, so identical gatherings were held on two nights. This proved to be the most effective and congenial way to inform members of the financial needs, and it was continued without interruption in the years after. Instead of having to go to a hotel for larger dinners, as had been the case previously, the church community was able to gather in the new church house.

Because the new parlor and assembly room were airconditioned the summer as well as the winter months could be used for programs. Bible and other study groups met during the week even in the hottest months of the year, and although New Yorkers were prone to leave the city on summer weekends, many were anxious to take advantage of the study program offered in the summer evenings.

The summer groups also provided seminary students an opportunity to gain experience in teaching and pastoral responsibilities. Each year, beginning in 1960, the church engaged a seminarian to work at the church during the time that the pastors were on vacation, and to be the "minister in residence", leading worship in the morning (guest preachers were invited to give the sermon), leading the adult studies in the evening and during the week, visiting the sick and supervising the church's staff. Because of the wide range of experiences offered by the church there was little difficulty attracting highly qualified people, many of whom worked under Macnab's supervision (he was a Pastoral Associate in Union Seminary's field education program) during the winter months.

Beginning in 1970 First Church joined with the neighboring Episcopalians of Ascension and Grace churches in united services, and after 1974, when the pastors began alternating vacation time, seminary students were no longer engaged.[19]

An outdoor playroof encouraged the expansion of the Nursing School program for young children into the summer months. Additional classrooms in the new building also meant that the school could accommodate a larger number of students. What had begun in 1952 with one class had grown by the 1960's into four classes in the morning and two in the afternoon. The entire fourth floor of the church house was used by this school during the week, and on Sundays those of a similar age in the Church School met in the same room.

From the outset the Nursery School had been used more by the community at-large than by First Church members although it had been hoped that it would serve to bring outsiders into the membership. This had not happened, and in 1960, with an enrollment of 92, only 19 were children of church members. Another 12 whose parents were not members attended the Sunday church school. Of the others 30 were Protestant; 11 were Roman Catholic; 11 were Jewish and the rest professed no religion.[20]

In the mid-'60's the school reached out in a special program to children from Emmanuel and Church of the Crossroads on the lower east side. They came by bus (as did many of the other students) each day to be part of a church-sponsored "head start" effort. $10,000 was provided in the benevolence budget for this purpose. Special help in English was given to those from Spanish speaking homes. The project continued until a new day care center was established at Emmanuel in the early 1970's.[21] Some of the pupils received scholarships to neighboring independent schools for their elementary education, and in the few instances where later progress was known, the benefits of the early start and training proved highly satisfactory.

First Church leaders had felt from the beginning that the classrooms in the new building should be used during the week as well as on Sunday. The possibility of a parochial school was considered briefly, but the uncertainties and problems of embarking on such a venture appeared more than could be handled. Moreover, the General Assembly had in 1957 adopted a policy of strong support by Presbyterians for public education, and it was felt that this emphasis could not be ignored even though the public schools of New York City were experiencing severe and growing problems.

In March of 1963 the session agreed to provide classroom space to a school for children with seriously disturbing emotional problems. The Manhattan School, as it was called, was the first project of the recently formed Association for Mentally Ill Children (AMIC). Several members of First Church had been instrumental in the founding of the Association, and it was natural that they turned to the church for help in establishing the educational program geared to meet the needs of children for whom the public educational system made no provision. Because of the special needs of the children, each teacher had only three pupils. Also since much of the curriculum was experimental and untried, it was decided to begin with a small number of children in the younger ages.

Students from the Association for Mentally Ill Children (AMIC). The school is housed at First Church.

Members of AMIC joined with others in obtaining state legislation which required the New York City Board of Education to assume responsibility for the education of these children. Bus transportation, school lunches and salaried teachers soon followed. AMIC took responsibility for the support of needed social workers, psychiatrists, psychologists and special teachers in dance, art and music. The church contributed the classroom space and the custodial maintenance. Three institutional groups had thus united in an effort to deal with the special needs of the children and their families, and it was not long before all available classrooms in the church house were in daily use. The school expanded rapidly, and similar programs patterned on the one at First Church were started in other public schools in various parts of the city. The church, however, remained the only one to house a public school (PS 203M) on its premises. A later tie was made to the psychiatric department of neighboring St. Vincent's Hospital, where the children could be tested and treated as was necessary. The church also aided with guidance and funds in the establishment of a summer camp program for AMIC youngsters in the Presbyterian camp at Holmes, New York. This added an additional month to the school year and hastened the progress and growth of the school enrollees.[22]

In addition to the schools, a variety of community groups used the facilities of the church house on a less regular basis. Among those that did were the local community planning board, neighborhood block associations, tenants' groups, a chapter of the NAACP, a St. George's Association group of public health employees, Alcoholics Anonymous, the Crossroads Chamber Orchestra, the Village Light Opera Group, to cite but a few. The church house lobby early became one of the election polling places for the neighborhood also.[23]

The church could not have supported financially the extensive facilities and program had it not been for its substantial endowment fund. By 1976, for example, the budget was more than double what it had been 20 years earlier, and exceeded $350,000. In each of those years the income from the endowment provided two-thirds of the necessary funds (approximately those needed to support the facilities and program at the church) while pledges and contributions from the membership supplied the remaining one-third of the total (approximately the money spent on benevolence causes).[24] In the latter years, however, it is to be noted that membership and number of pledges were well below what they had been 20 years previously. The largest single addition to the endowment was made by the James Foundation in 1964, about 2 million dollars. Under terms of Arthur Curtiss James' will, the Foundation's life was limited to 25 years, and at the end of that time the trustees were to distribute its assets as they saw fit. Although First Church had been one of the original beneficiaries named, the Foundation trustees were under no obligation to honor that designation in the distribution unless they concluded it was worthy of support. They did. The grant added about forty percent to the church endowment, and by September 30, 1972, its total value was $6,414,000.[25]

An investment committee of three elected by the church's trustees annually had oversight of the endowment, and in 1971 it was decided to instruct the account's custodian, the United States Trust Company, to transfer to the church operating budget a specific amount each month to meet budgetary needs. If the dividends and interest were not sufficient to meet the scheduled needs, the bank was permitted to invade the principal. This was not necessary, however, since careful budgeting kept expenditures within the limits of income, and if additional money was taken from the endowment income, a similar percentage was asked of the congregational contributors. With later declines in security values, the endowment fell below the five million dollar figure, invested in a ratio of approximately 50–50 between equities and debt.[26]

IV

Although, as already indicated, new building construction was not typical of a downtown city church, in the suburban areas surrounding American cities such was not the case. In fact, the 1950's produced more new church buildings than any previous decade of the nation's history. In connection with this expansion it was facetiously observed by some that congregational enthusiasm invariably peaked with the dedication of a new educational wing. There are indications that such may have been the case at First Church, although it was certainly not immediately evident.

The social turbulence of the 60's brought change to the congregational life. Two factors had heavy impact: the rapid deterioration of the public educational system in the city and the relentless increase in the cost of housing, particularly for the larger apartments that families with growing children required. More and more of these families concluded that the economic pressures of urban living were more than could be handled. One after another of the middle class group that had been so instrumental in the church's membership growth took up residence in a neighboring suburb. The number of teenagers in the church school, for example, declined significantly in the middle of the decade. Only those with young children (who could be accommodated in smaller apartments) seemed to remain, and it would soon be noted that fifty percent of the Sunday church school consisted of pupils under six years of age. As the economic pressures of inflation grew, increasing numbers of families had need for a second income, and wives returned to work. This affected the number of women who could take part in the traditional organizations of the church, and these steadily declined. The religious enthusiasm that had marked the 50's and swelled the membership rolls of churches eroded in the following decade, particularly when church leaders became more vocal and active in support of civil rights and opposition to use of military power. Among young adults, such as those who had earlier composed the Sunday Evening Society, there was at the same time a growing disenchantment and disdain for the traditions and institutions of the established society, and the church, along with marriage, was among those rejected.[27]

In many ways First Church itself reflected the lessening interest in the traditional patterns of church organizational life. In the 60's it became less self-centered and more concerned about the issues troubling the national conscience, and this emphasis is reflected in the session's minutes. This was a contrast to the minutes of earlier centuries which dealt almost exclusively with the problems of the worship service, selection of ministers, education of children, and made almost no mention of secular matters. Once in the past there had been a protest to the City Council about a proposed cabaret on 12th Street near the church. The protest was successful. On another occasion they took cognizance of complaints about the food in a nearby restaurant. These,[28] however, were isolated cases in the early years of the century. In the 1960's, however, members of the session attended meetings of the city's Board of Estimate to speak on various projects, notably the hospital budget and the Women's House of Detention in the Village. Representatives were sent to Washington to attend forums on housing and problems of the aging.[29] In fact the discussions at a session meeting were not so different from those at a Community Planning Board.

In 1963 the session reorganized its committees, and among those added was one on matters of church and society. It soon became one of the most active and took over some of the work previously in the province of the board of deacons. In 1970–1971 one of its special projects concerned welfare residents in old, dilapidated hotels in the area. One, the Jane West Hotel, housed about one hundred formerly homeless men. The committee made plans to establish a clinic and secure the services of a visiting nurse. The clinic had to be abandoned because the management of the hotel wanted $100 a month rent, but an examining room, medical supplies and visiting nurse were secured. The Broadway Central Hotel housed a large number of families on relief that included almost 300 children. In most cases they had been burned out of their homes. First Church set up an unofficial day care center for the children and equipped it with old furniture repaired in the church workshop. Money was collected to buy clothes, especially shoes; toys were obtained from toy manufacturing companies. Volunteers in the church prepared Christmas dinners for some of the families, and under growing pressure in

1972 these welfare hotels in the immediate neighborhood were closed.[30]

In the 1960's the church took cognizance of the protest movements although few in the church were activists in a direct way. Both the ministers, however, were considered liberal and were directly involved in efforts to elect the first black moderator of the General Assembly, the highest office in the church. In 1960 the New York Presbytery nominated Edler G. Hawkins, pastor of St. Augustine Presbyterian Church, for that position, and both First Church pastors were on the committee. Jack Mellin made the nominating speech at the General Assembly. It was unusual to have the nominating speech made by a member of the same presbytery which presented the name. No one from another presbytery was willing to do so, however. Contrary to predictions, Hawkins lost by only two votes, and he was quickly appointed vice-moderator, another unusual occurrence. He was again nominated by the Presbytery in 1964 and once more both pastors were involved, with John Macnab as the "campaign manager". This time he was elected by an overwhelming vote and became the first Black to hold such a high office in any of the Protestant churches. This was at the height of the civil rights efforts, and the crucial Civil Rights bill was pending in Congress. The ministers frequently brought up the issue of civil rights in their sermons. On Palm Sunday, 1968, a memorial service for Martin Luther King, sponsored by the New York Presbytery, was held in the sanctuary of the First Presbyterian Church.[31]

In the spring of 1968 a study group was formed in the church to discuss the report of the President's advisory committee on Civil Disorders. An appeal by Martin Luther King on behalf of the poor was climaxed by a march on Washington. The church sent a bus with members of the congregation to join this Poor People's march.

On October 15, 1969, there was a peace demonstration and the session agreed after much debate to open the church for prayer. Petitions were on hand in the narthex and at a table on the sidewalk in front of the church for people to express their opposition to the war in Vietnam. On examination it was discovered that only 75 of the 2,000 signatures were members of First Church. The petitions were sent to appropriate members of the state's congressional delegation.

The following month, November 2, 1969, the session considered the Vietnam moratorium proposal. When it was suggested that a meeting be held on the Vietnam war the session decided that the discussion be broadened to include the Christian faith and peace and war rather than concentrating solely on Vietnam. It also voted that elders who wished to organize a bus trip to Washington could use the church facilities but it would not be a session project. Two buses, funded by a trustee and elder, did go to Washington to protest the Vietnam war.[32]

Perhaps also indicative of the increased awareness of events beyond the immediate organizational activities of the church itself was the response to President John F. Kennedy's assassination on November 22, 1963. A memorial service was held on Monday, November 25th, and a near capacity crowd filled the church sanctuary. The details of the service were spread upon the minutes of the session and a copy, including the prayers and Bible readings used, was sent to the President's widow.[33] What makes the action noteworthy is its contrast to other such national tragedies: no mention was made in the session records of the assassinations of Presidents Lincoln, Garfield or McKinley, and there was no memorial service held when President Franklin D. Roosevelt died. That such a service was held in a Presbyterian church for the nation's first Roman Catholic President (to whose election many First Church members had been opposed on religious grounds) appears to indicate the increasing sensitivity of church leaders to issues of importance to the community beyond the particular congregation.

By the 1970's interest and activity on behalf of social issues had lessened, or at least taken less strident forms. Speaking of changes over the last twenty-five years, Mellin noted that first there was the "togetherness," then "activisms" but now the emphasis was on study groups and relevancy. He said: "Now the church discovers that action for action's sake is not enough and that we have to find out what our convictions are and how to communicate them."[34]

On the other hand it is possible that the social awareness revealed itself in other ways in the early 70's. One of the deacons suggested the church set up an advisory committee to assist members of the community on real estate matters and thus encourage people to move into the area. He even urged the church to guarantee mortgages and loans to people interested in buying property in the neighborhood. The church did that on a small scale in 1972. Tenants in two houses in the Village were attempting to form a cooperative and purchase their buildings from an owner who petitioned for permission to evict them to renovate the buildings. They could get some money for rehabilitation from the city and also a loan from the Bowery Savings Bank but they did not have enough money to purchase the house from the landlord. The boards of the church discussed the problem and finally decided to advance the money secured by a second mortgage and by a pledge of the shares of the vacant apartments. This was a neighborhood project for the benefit of Greenwich Village, for only one resident in the house was a member of First Church at the time. It was a successful venture not only for its social value but also because the mortgage was promptly paid in full in a short time.[35]

Much of the work of the church in the neighborhood became ecumenical in the 70's. An example of this was participation in the Caring Community of Greenwich Village. This was a cooperative

214

venture of churches, synagogues and social welfare agencies in the community to care for the needs of older people in the Village. It provided "meals on wheels" on Saturday as well as weekdays. Church people "manned" the Senior Service Center at 20 Washington Square North and provided a telephone alert for the home bound. The center provided a variety of classes and projects and served a hot meal at noon. The organization was closely related to the Village Nursing Home, the only one on the west side south of 42nd Street. There was also the Village Visiting Neighbors to which the church contributed money and personnel. Volunteers visited senior citizens, shopped for them, and acted as escorts.[36]

The unrest of the sixties led the church to become socially conscious about its assets. First the church decided that some of its money should be deposited in black-owned banks. The General Council of the General Assembly in 1969 wrote companies in which its funds were invested regarding their compliance with the Fair Employment Practices. The trustees of First Church discussed the question "to what degrees, if any, should social considerations be taken into account in shaping our investment program", and decided this was primarily a concern for the elders rather than for the trustees. Presbytery had formed a committee on Social Concerns and suggested that on voting the proxies of companies the shareholders' proposals should be considered, and the trustees referred proxies to the session for decision. The session in a proxy for Procter and Gamble, for example, decided to follow the recommendations of the management. The vote was 5 to 3 after extended debate. This did not seem to be a good method of handling the matter so the issue was turned over to a committee to review the proxies of the corporate stock of First Church and advise the appropriate action.[37]

V

The various missions affiliated with First Church were still an important part of its life in 1950, and about $31,000 of the annual budget was designated for their use. But change was on the way and twenty years later only Emmanuel Church would remain.

Bethlehem Memorial Church, whose steady decline in membership had been noted for some years, was dissolved by action of the Presbytery on June 7, 1959, and its assets and remaining membership were transferred to First Church. The Rev. Gaetano Lisi, who had been Bethlehem's pastor since 1923, conducted Italian language services in the Alexander Chapel each week for the few who still preferred it. Unfortunately he died suddenly in early 1960, and the Italian services were discontinued. Several of the Bethlehem members soon began to play an important part in First Church's life and some of them were elected to the session, deacons and trustees.[38]

The removal of the "El" from Third Avenue in the mid-50's brought rapid increase in the real estate values of the area. Much of the population served by the Madison Square Church House and the Adams-Parkhurst Church was forced to move as buildings were sold, demolished and replaced by high-rise, luxury apartments.

The Adams-Parkhurst Church, although independent, had kept in touch with First Church reporting their activities, and from time to time a member of the First Church session attended a session meeting of the former church. The Rev. Harold S. Rambo, the sole minister since 1948, reported that their average attendance was 175 (in 1954—249), that they had five departments in the Sunday School (150 students), and three choirs, many clubs and an evening service. At the latter they had a half hour of hymn singing which seemed to appeal. In 1953 the Rev. J. McGown became the new minister and began a special program to appeal to the Puerto Ricans in the congregation, and an attempt was made to add a Spanish-speaking person to the staff. He was succeeded in 1958 by the Rev. Robert J. Stone, who served as both pastor of the church and as director of the Madison Square Church House. Eileen Ward, having served for many years, retired as director and this made the double appointment a possibility. It also evidenced the diminishing role both institutions were called upon to play as the neighborhood changed. In December 1965 Adams-Parkhurst voted to merge with the Church of the Covenant on East 42nd Street.[39]

The need for the settlement house program of the Church House declined severely as those formerly served by such a program were forced to move from the area. The Church House was sold in 1964 and what remained of its program was moved to rented quarters in a housing project near by. This did not solve the problem, however, and in 1971 the organization was dissolved and its assets and liabilities transferred to First Church. The funds transferred ($605,000) were restricted to benevolence support.[40]

In 1963 the real property of the Fredericka House camp was sold after the state of Connecticut passed a law requiring that 75% of the children served by the camp be from that state if the property were to retain its tax exemption. The corporation that held title to the property and other assets remained, however, and income from the assets was used to send needy children to other camps, primarily those conducted by the Presbyterians.[41]

First Church continued to contribute to the work of the Madison Square Boys' Club ($7,000 in 1950), but the relationship became increasingly distant. The question of title to the Boys' Club property was raised in 1950, when a large gift ($500,000) was made to erect a branch club in Queens. The Boys' Club requested the Presbyterian Board of Trustees to cancel the article which gave First Church reversionary rights to the property if the Boys' Club was dissolved. The Board of Trustees on October 31,

1950, voted to recommend to the congregation that change but at the corporate meeting on January 17, 1951, the resolution was tabled by a vote of 64 to 30. Negotiations continued and finally although not without opposition a resolution permitting the changes in the By-Laws of the Boys' Club was approved at a congregational meeting on January 21, 1953. The original resolution had been changed so that if the Boys' Club were dissolved the property would be transferred to the Church or some society approved by the trustees of the Church. If transferred to the church the money would be used for furtherance of boys' work in the city. The church in 1954 contributed $3,000 to the Boys' Club, but soon after dropped it from the benevolence budget.[42]

Only at Emmanuel was the work to continue beyond the 1960's. Clarence Boyer replaced John McCarthy as pastor in mid-1949. In his first report to First Church he emphasized the interracial character of the work at Emmanuel with Black mothers helping in several classes in the church school and "the final successful mixing of the races in the gymnasium activities, a negro woman as treasurer of the Woman's Missionary Society, and the election of a negro Elder." In 1953 he listed the activities as follows: two missionary societies, 17 increase in church membership, 318 in Sunday School, 425 in Vacation Bible School, 194 in the Saturday School, 96 sent to camp, 52 cottage prayer meetings, 52 Bible study and prayer group meetings, 52 evening gospel hour meetings, 150 gym periods, 132 meetings of the Spanish congregation.[43]

Emmanuel wished to incorporate as a separate church, and First Church favored the move. In 1955 Emmanuel became a legal corporation under the Religious Corporation Law, and in 1960 the real property was transferred by First Church as a gift to Emmanuel.

Clarence Boyer retired in 1963 to be succeeded by Euton Williams, that church's first Black pastor. A new church building was needed, and Presbytery voted funds for it from its Presbyterian Progress Foundation. A large grant (of which First Church contributed the major portion) was made in 1970 to construct a Day Care Center and facilities for church programs and community projects. First Church continued support for the Emmanuel program through the Presbytery's mission committee and through the session's committee on Church and Society.[44]

VI

By the middle of the 1970's attitudes toward tradition and heritage began to move away from the rejection and dismissal of the previous decade to an appreciation and respect for moral values that had perhaps been too readily disregarded. The revelations of the Watergate scandal along with the bitterness and disillusionment of the prolonged involvement in the Vietnam

John O. Mellin and John B. Macnab, co-pastors of The First Presbyterian Church.

conflict became matters that weighed heavy on the nation's spirit. The celebration of the American Revolution's bicentennial gave an opportunity to renew a flagging national feeling.

First Church joined the national celebration with enthusiasm, boldly presenting itself to the public as "The Church of the Patriots," a reference to its many members who had been "zealously attached to the American cause" in 1776. Episcopal church neighbors, unmindful of the historical reference good-naturedly chided Presbyterian friends for what seemed an audacious claim. A committee, headed by elder John F. Wilson, planned and presented a series of activities throughout the year of celebration. Monthly lectures—each given, with one exception, by an informed member of the church community—covered such topics as: the geography of New York City in 1776; the role of the church and its members in the break with Britain; the part played by Black Americans in the revolt; the position of a Tory preacher, Jonathan Boucher; and an examination of some of the literature of the colonial period. The archives of the church, rich in materials of the period, were organized and exhibitions of records and pictures were arranged, including the colonial silver on permanent loan to the Metropolitan Museum of Art. An all-church dinner, a replicated worship of the period (with one major difference—it was only one hour long), a musical lecture, a colonial costume party with old-fashioned square dances, and in the spring a picnic on the church lawn followed by a pageant portraying a series of church events in the 1765–1783 years. One might say the celebration ended with a unique service on July 4—held at the very un-Presbyterian hour of 9 a.m. so that

218

members could take part in other community festivities of celebration.[45]

In January of the same year, Robert Baker became the fourth organist and choirmaster of the church. Undoubtedly one of the most renowned of church musicians, he was the former dean of Union Seminary's School of Sacred Music. He had moved from there when the seminary closed the school to become professor of organ at Yale University's Institute of Sacred Music, and when John Huston died suddenly in April 1975, Baker (a close personal friend of Huston's) had agreed to help the church in the emergency. When the session's committee insisted he consider making the arrangement a permanent one, he agreed and immediately began to recruit volunteers from the church membership to sing in the choir and to make the music more a part of the church activities than it had been historically. Because of his excellence as a musician, he had no difficulty attracting not only members but others from various parts of the city who wanted to sing and learn under his direction.[46]

What lies ahead for this oldest of Presbyterian congregations in New York City? Its material assets, both in terms of the physical plant and the endowment, are substantial. Prudent stewardship of these can supply needed resources in times ahead as they have in the past. Its location in a stable, middle-class community (on which it has always depended for its membership) also means a source of worshippers. It is the only integrated church of its tradition in a sizable area. The membership will in all probability continue to be highly transient, it being estimated that average membership is presently three years in length. This will continue to translate into perpetual change in leadership in session, deacons, trustees and more dependency on the professional staff than might be true in more stable situations. The choice of such staff will have a somewhat crucial influence on its life. The nature of its mission and ministry will change as it has for more than two and one half centuries when events in the society and world call for response. It has never strayed far from the traditional and classic interpretations of the Christian faith, and it has seldom expressed that faith except in traditional patterns. There is value to tradition, a value to be dispensed with at a certain peril, and most assuredly with caution.

The observation made earlier that First Church had "a magnificent past and an uncertain future," has continuing validity, as indeed it had at any number of places in the course of its long history. It can also be made with candor today, and by the grace of God it will be made many times in the future. Will it celebrate its tricentennial in 2016, or the bicentennial of its location on Fifth Avenue in 2046? These are questions for which there is no sure answer, nor should there be if those who compose its particular community of Christians abide in an Apostle's observation: "For here we have no lasting city, but seek the city which is to come."

[1]Session Minutes, IV, 495, 503, 514 (Jan. 24, Mar. 28, May 23, 1946, 544 (Jan. 23, 1947). Hereafter the words Consolidated Churches will be omitted.

[2]*Ibid.,* IV, 569 (May 29, 1947). Correspondence between Dr. Moldenhawer and Dr. Sizoo, pp. 572–3.

[3]*Ibid.,* IV, 575, 577 (June 25, July 16, 1947); Trustee Minutes, V, April 16, June 28, 1947. *The Church Tower,* October, 1947.

[4]Trustee Minutes, IV, Nov. 13, 1946, VII, June 24, 1952; *The Church Tower,* Nov. 1946, October, 1948, March, 1949.

[5]Session Minutes, IV, 629 (May 25, 26, 1948), 685, 693 (May 26, June 8, 1949).

[6]*Ibid.,* V, 2 (Sept. 22, 1949), 124 (Mar. 25, 1952), *The Church Tower,* May, 1952.

[7]Session Minutes, V, 256, 259 (Nov. 23, Dec. 1, 1954). 278 (March 1, 1955), Trustee Minutes, VIII (Nov. 1954); *The Church Tower,* Nov. 22, 1954. Feb. 1955. Mr. Macnab's recollections.

[8]Trustee Minutes, V, Feb. 21, June 28, 1947, VI, Jan. 21, Apr. 28, 1948; Session Minutes, IV, 483 (Nov. 2, 1945), 595 (Nov. 25, 1947).

[9]Session Minutes, V, 20 (Feb. 1, 1950), 123 (Nov. 25, 1952), 361 (Jan. 16, 1957), VI, 5 (Jan. 15, 1958), Trustee Minutes, X, Jan. 16, 1957; *The Church Tower,* July-August, 1970.

[10]Session Minutes, V, 395 (Jan. 21, 1958); VI, (Jan. 16, 23, 1963. Mr. Macnab's recollections.)

[11]Session Minutes, V, 349 (Dec. 9, 1956); Trustee Minutes, Jan. 16, 1957; *The Church Tower,* December, 1953, Summer, 1964.

[12]Trustee Minutes, V, Feb. 25, 1946, Nov. 13, 1946, VI, Mar. 1, 1949; *The Church Tower,* Feb. 1946, Jan., 1947, March, 1949; when she left a special celebration was held for her on March 29, 1977.

[13]*The Church Tower,* Oct. 1953; Session Minutes, V 81, (March 6, 1951). Now there exists only the Woman's Missionary Society which has changed its name to United Presbyterian Women. The Sewing Club, which from 1971–1976 made 1680 garments which were distributed through Presbytery to orphanages, disbanded in 1981.

[14]Session Minutes, IV, Jan. 27, 1949, V, Jan. 21, 1958; Trustee Minutes. XIII, Feb. 14, 1967.

[15]*The Church Tower,* Feb. 1946, Jan., 1947, March, 1949; Session Minutes, IV, 534 (Nov. 14, 1946).

[16]Session Minutes, V, Oct., 1955, Mar. 13, 1956, Jan. 21, 1958, VII, Feb. 3, 1965; Trustee Minutes, X, Nov. 6, 1957, Feb. 12, 1958, Jan. 13, Sept. 29, 1959, Jan. 20, 1960, XII, Feb. 14, 1967; *The Church Tower,* March, 1957, May, 1959, Jan. 1960; *The New York Times,* May 22, 1960.

[17]Trustee Minutes, X, Feb. 7, 1957. In 1971 a two family brownstone house at 13 Monroe Street, Brooklyn was purchased for $135,000 as a manse for Mr. Macnab (see Trustee Minutes, XII, June 8, 1971).

[18]*Minutes of the General Assembly of the United Presbyterian Church in U.S.A.,* Seventh Series, vol. X, 1976, Part II, 305–7; *The Church Tower,* June 1977.

[19]*The Church Tower,* July-August, 1970; Session Minutes, Apr. 2, October 2, 1974. In 1974 for the first time the summer pastor was a woman, Miss Deborah Kapp.

[20]Session Minutes, IV, Feb. 19, Mar. 30, 1946, May 22, 1947, V, Sept. 14, 23, 1952, Jan. 24, Mar. 13, 1956; Trustee Minutes, V, May 8, 1947, VII, Sept. 16, 1952, X, Jan. 16, 1957, Jan. 20, 1960.

[21]Session Minutes, VII, Jan. 26, Mar. 30, 1965; *The Church Tower,* Summer, 1960.

[22]Session Minutes, VI, Feb. 24, 1963; *The Church Tower,* March, 1964, Dec., 1971,

May 1972. The name of the association has been changed from Association for Mentally Ill Children and is now known simply as AMIC. Children are now described as having biologically determined developmental disabilities rather than mental illness.

[23]Trustee Minutes, X, Feb. 2, 1969; *The Church Tower,* Feb., Oct. 1974.

[24]Trustee Minutes, VII, Feb. 20, Sept. 12, Nov. 19, 1952, IX, May 10, 1954, XII, Oct. 29, 1964. Annual reports at corporate meetings.

[25]*Ibid.,* VII, Feb. 20, Sept. 12, Nov. 19, 1952, IX, May 10, 1954, XII, Oct.. 29, 1964.

[26]*Ibid.,* XII, Nov. 17, 1970, Apr. 5, 1971, Feb. 11, 1975.

[27]Session Minutes, V, Jan. 21, 1958, VII, Feb. 3, 1965; Trustee Minutes, X, Jan. 20, 1960, XII, Feb. 14, 1967.

[28]Session Minutes, II, May 26, 1927, III, May 27, 1937.

[29]*Ibid.,* IV, Jan. 21, Mar. 10, 1964, Mar. 30, 1971; Trustee Minutes, XII, Apr. 16, 1968.

[30]Session Minutes, VI, Feb. 24, 1963, Sept. 30, Dec. 2, 1970, Feb. 3, 1971; *The Church Tower,* Jan., Feb., April, 1971.

[31]*The New York Times,* Feb. 2, 18:2, May 19, 16:5, May 20, 20:4, 1960; May 22, 1:1, 20:2, 1964. Blacks have served on the session and on the board of trustees and as deacons at First Church since 1965.

[32]Session Minutes, VII, Nov. 23, 1967, Oct. 8, Nov. 23, Dec. 3, 1969.

[33]*Ibid.,* VI, 276. In the First Presbyterian Church the pulpit was decorated in mourning for President Zachary Taylor and at Madison Square Church for President Lincoln.

[34]*Ibid.,* Feb. 3, 1971.

[35]Trustee Minutes, XII, Apr. 16, 1967, May 4, 1971, Feb. 15, Apr. 11, Nov. 29, 1972.

[36]*The Church Tower,* Oct. 5, 1975, Dec. 14, 1975; *The New York Times,* Nov. 21, Dec. 13, 1977.

[37]Trustee Minutes, Dec. 7, 1970, Feb. 18, Apr. 5, 1971; Session Minutes, VII, Nov. 25, 1969, Jan. 29, Oct. 2, Nov. 26, 1974.

[38]Trustee Minutes, X, Feb. 17, 1956, Jan. 21, May 11, 1959; Session Minutes, V, Feb. 26, 1950, Nov. 20, 1951, VI, Jan. 13, 1959.

[39]Session Minutes, V, March 29, 1950, Jan. 24, May 20, 1952, Nov. 24, 1953, Apr. 7, 1954.

[40]*Ibid.,* VI, Nov. 24, 1964, VII, Sept. 28, Dec. 4, 1966; Trustee Minutes, XII, May 4, 1971, Oct. 3, Dec. 12, 1972.

[41]Trustee Minutes, X, Apr. 9, 1963, XII, Apr. 18, June 13, 1967; Session Minutes, VI, Sept. 19, 1961.

[42]Trustee Minutes, VII, Sept. 25, Oct. 31, 1950, Jan. 17, 1951, Nov. 25, 1952, Jan. 21, 1953; *The Church Tower,* Nov. 1952.

[43]Trustee Minutes, VI, 1949 report of Clarence Boyer; Session Minutes, IV, May 26, 1949, V, Nov. 22, 1949, March 6, 1951, Jan. 20, 1953.

[44]Trustee Minutes, VII, Apr. 24, 1950, June 6, 1951, X, Feb. 17, 1956, Oct. 30, 1957, Feb. 4, 1958, May 3, Oct. 26, 1960.

[45]Bicentennial Scrapbook, Presbyterian Church archives.

[46]Session Minutes, Dec. 3, 1975; *The Church Tower,* May, 1975.

Bibliography

CHURCH RECORDS

These records are in the archives of the First Presbyterian church in New York City, 12 West 12th Street. The manuscript ones have been microfilmed.

Manuscripts

First Presbyterian Church in the City of New York

Trustee Minutes

1. Memoirs and a Journal of Transactions of the Trustees of the Presbyterian Congregation in the City of New York, 1717–1775.
2. Minutes of Members of the Corporation, May, 1784–May, 1809.
3. 1809–April, 1844.
4. May 11, 1844–December, 1902.

Records of the Session

1. 1765–March 1808. At the end is a brief narrative of the origin and progress of the First Presbyterian Church of New York, 1807.
2. May 3, 1809–October 14, 1862.
3. December 1862–March 12, 1907.
4. April 9, 1907–May 22, 1918.

Register of Baptisms, 1728–1790, 1798–1814.

Register of Deaths, 1786–1804.

Miscellaneous Correspondence.

Madison Square Presbyterian Church

Board of Trustees, December 8, 1853—November 4, 1917.

Church Records: Session

1. March 30, 1853–August 29, 1869.
2. September 30, 1869–September 28, 1882.
3. November 2, 1882–May 16, 1902.
4. October 3, 1902–May 1, 1918.

Board of Deacons, minutes, February 1, 1854–March 1, 1914.

Building Committee–Minutes, 1853.

Mission Book. Minutes of Young Men's Association. 3 vols., 1855–1895.

Mercer Street Presbyterian Church

Session Minutes:

1. October 8, 1835–April 6, 1865.
2. May 12, 1865–July 31, 1870.

   Record of Executive Committee of City Missionary Association Connected with Mercer Street Presbyterian Church, November 25, 1851–April 30, 1870.

University Place Presbyterian Church

Board of Trustee Minutes

1. November 28, 1843–April 30, 1883.
2. May 28, 1883–February 17, 1918.

Session Minutes

1. 1843–1870.
2. July 1870–May 2, 1889.
3. May 23, 1889–September 26, 1906.
4. October, 1906–December, 1918.

Bethlehem Chapel Committee, minutes, April 15, 1870–April 24, 1912.

Memorial Chapel Committee, minutes, 1910–1920.

Miscellaneous correspondence.

First Presbyterian Church in the City of New York-Founded 1716

Old First, University Place and Madison Square Foundation

Minutes of Board of Trustees of the Consolidated Churches

1. February 27, 1918–July 28, 1921.
2. January, 1922–April 17, 1935.
3. May 22, 1935–May 1, 1940.
4. January 23, 1941–November 25, 1945.
5. February, 1946–June, 1947
6. March, 1948–December, 1949.
7. January, 1950–December, 1952.
8. 1953.
9. January, 1954–January, 1956.
10. February 17, 1956–November 22, 1960.
11. January 18, 1961–October 15, 1963.
12. January 21, 1964–June 5, 1973.

Minutes of the Session of the Consolidated Churches

1. May 31, 1918–June 1, 1924.
2. September 25, 1924–July 31, 1932.
3. September 22, 1932–August 13, 1942.
4. September, 1942–June 8, 1949.
5. September, 1949–February 2, 1958.
6. March 18, 1958–December 31, 1964.
7. January 20, 1965–March 26, 1972.

Minutes of the Board of Deacons of the Consolidated Churches, 1918–1948.

Miscellaneous Correspondence including file of Fosdick Papers.

Bicentennial Scrapbook.

Printed Records

Madison Square Presbyterian Church

Manual for Use of Members of the Madison Square Presbyterian Church, 1883.

Year Book, Ladies Association, 1887.

Year Books of Madison Square Presbyterian Church, 1893–1916.

University Place Presbyterian Church

Services Commemorative of the Fiftieth Anniversary of the University Place Presbyterian Church, November 24–28, 1895.

Year Books of the Presbyterian Church on University Place; 1893–1919.

First Presbyterian Church in the City of New York—Founded 1716, Old First, University Place, and Madison Square Foundation.

Alexander Memorial Chapel. Services of Dedication, 1938.

Bethlehem Memorial Presbyterian Church. Church Directory and Year Book, by Gaetano Lisi.

Dry Dock Mission, Emmanuel Chapel and Emmanuel Presbyterian Church. One Hundredth Anniversary, 1952.

Presbyterian Home for Aged Women in the City of New York: First Hundred Years, 1866–1966.

Services in Celebration of the Two Hundredth Anniversary of the Founding of the Old First Presbyterian Church in the City of New York, December, 1916.

The Church Programs, 1918–

The Church Tower, 1923–

The Church Year Books, 1919–1947.

The First Presbyterian Church of New York and Dr. Fosdick, authorized by the session, December 11, 1924.

GOVERNMENT DOCUMENTS.

Corwin, Edward, ed. *Ecclesiastical Records of the State of New York.* 7 vols., Albany, New York, 1901–5.

New York City. *Minutes of the Common Council of New York, 1675–1770.* 8 vols., New York, 1905.

New York City. *Minutes of the Common Council of the City of New York, 1784–1831.* 19 vols., New York, 1832.

O'Callaghan, Edmund Bailey. ed. *The Documentary History of the State of New York.* 4 vols., Albany, New York, 1849.

SECONDARY WORKS

Abbott, Wilbur C. *New York in the American Revolution.* New York: Charles Scribner's Sons, 1929.

Adams, James Truslow. *Provincial Society, 1690–1763*. New York: Macmillan Co., 1927.

Adams, John. *Diary and Autobiography of John Adams*, edited by L. H. Butterfield. New York: Atheneum, 1964. Vol. II.

Ahlstrom, Sydney E. *A Religious History of the American People*. New Haven, Conn., Yale University Press, 1972.

Alexander, S. D. *The Presbytery of New York, 1738–1888*. New York: Anson, D. F. Randolph and Co., 1887.

Bancroft, George. *History of the United States from the Discovery of the Continent*. New York: D. Appleton and Co., 1888.

Banks, James Lenox. *Genealogical Notes concerning the Banks and Allied Families*. New York: privately printed, 1938.

Barck, Oscar Theodore. *New York City during the War for Independence*. Port Washington, Long Island: Ira J. Friedman, 1931.

Becker, Carl Lotus. *The History of Political Parties in the Province of New York, 1760–1776*. Madison, Wisconsin: University of Wisconsin Press, 1960.

Bonomi, Patricia. *A Factious People: Politics and Society in Colonial New York*. New York: Columbia University Press, 1971.

Booth, Mary L. *History of the City of New York*. 2 vols., New York: W. D. C. Clark, 1867.

Bourne, William Oland. *History of the Public School Society of the City of New York*. New York: George P. Putnam and Sons, 1879.

Bridenbaugh, Carl. *Mitre and Sceptre. TransAtlantic Faiths: Ideas, Personalities and Politics, 1680–1775*. New York: Oxford University Press, 1962.

Briggs, Charles Augustus. *American Presbyterianism*. New York: Charles Scribner's Sons, 1885.

Brown, Henry Collins. *Fifth Avenue Old and New*. New York: Fifth Avenue Association, 1924.

Brown, Henry Collins. *The Story of Old New York*. New York: E. P. Dutton & Co., 1934.

Burnett, Edmund Cody. *The Continental Congress*. New York: Macmillan Co., 1941.

Calvin, John. *Institutes of the Christian Religion*, translated by Henry Beveridge. 2 vols., Grand Rapids: Wm. B. Eardmans Publishing Co., 1966.

Champagne, Roger J. *Alexander McDougall and the American Revolution in New York*. Schenectady, New York: Union College Press, 1975.

Cubberley, E. P. *Public Education in the United States*. Boston: Houghton, Mifflin Co., 1919.

Cutler, William Parker and Julia Perkins Cutler. *Life Journal and Correspondence of Rev. Manasseh Cutler. LL.D.* 2 vols., Cincinnati: Robert Clarke and Co., 1888.

Dangerfield, George. *Chancellor Robert R. Livingston of New York, 1746–1815*. New York: Harcourt, Brace and Co., 1960.

Dawson, Henry B. *The Sons of Liberty in New York*. New York Historical Society, 1859.

Dillon, Dorothy. *The New York Triumvirate. A Study of the Legal and Political Careers of William Livingston, John Morin Scott, William Smith, Jr*. New York: Columbia University Press, 1949.

Disosway, Gabriel. *The Earliest Churches of New York and its Vicinity*. New York: James G. Gregory, 1864.

Dunkak, Brother Harry M. *John Morin Scott and Whig Politics in New York, 1732–1769*. Ph.D. thesis, St. John's University, 1968.

Edwards, George W. and Arthur E. Peterson. *New York as an Eighteenth Century Municipality, 1731–1776*. New York: Longmans Green, 1917.

Flick, Alexander C., ed. *History of the State of New York*. 10 vols., New York: New York Historical Society, 1933–1937.

Fosdick, Harry Emerson. *The Living of These Days: an Autobiography*. New York: Harper and Brothers, 1956.

Francis, John. *Old New York.* New York: W. J. Widdleton, 1865.

Furniss, Norman K. *The Fundamentalist Controversy, 1918–1931.* New Haven: Yale University Press, 1954.

Gardner, Charles W. *The Doctor and the Devil or The Midnight Adventures of Dr. Parkhurst.* New York: Gardner and Co., 1894.

Gillett, E. H. *History of the Presbyterian Church in the United States of America.* 2 vols., Philadelphia: Presbyterian Board of Publication. Revised edition, 1873.

Greene, Evarts Boutell. *The Revolutionary Generation, 1763–1790.* New York: The Macmillan Company, 1943.

Greenleaf, Jonathan. *A History of the Churches of all Denominations in the City of New York from the First Settlement to the year 1846.* New York: E. French, 1846.

Hall, Edward Hagaman. "The First Presbyterian Church of New York," *22d Annual Report* of the American Scenic and Historic Preservations Society, 1917. Albany: J. B. Lyon, 1917.

Hamlin, Paul Mahlon. *Legal Education in Colonial New York.* New York: New York University Press, 1939.

Hardie, James. *Description of the City of New York.* New York: Samuel Marks, 1827.

Harrington, Virginia D. *The New York Merchant on the Eve of the Revolution.* New York: Columbia University Press, 1935.

Heitman, Francis. *Historical Register of Officers of the Continental Army during the War of the Revolution.* Baltimore: Genealogical Publishing Co., 1967.

Hodge, Charles. *The Constitutional History of the Presbyterian Church in the United States of America.* 2 vols., Philadelphia: William S. Martien, 1840.

Hone, Philip. *The Diary of Philip Hone, 1828–1851.* New York: Dodd, Mead and Co., 1910.

Hudson, Winthrop. *Religion in America.* New York: Charles Scribner's Sons, 1965.

Irving, Washington. *The Life and Letters of Washington Irving,* edited by Pierre M. Irving. Philadelphia: J.B. Lippincott and Co., 1871.

Jones, E. Alfred. *The Old Silver of American Churches.* Letchworth, England: National Society of Colonial Dames of America at the Arden Press, MDCCCCXIII.

Jones, Thomas. *History of New York during the Revolutionary War and the Leading Events in the other Colonies at that Period,* edited by Edward Floyd de Lancey. 2 vols., New York: New York Historical Society, 1879.

Keep, Austin Baxter. *History of the New York Society Library.* New York: The De Vinne Press, 1908.

Kerr, Hugh Thomson, ed., *A Compend of the Institutes of Christian Religion by John Calvin.* Philadelphia: Presbyterian Board, 1939.

Knapp, Shepherd. *A History of the Brick Presbyterian Church in the City of New York.* New York: Brick Presbyterian Church, 1909.

Koke, Richard J. *Accomplice in Treason. Joshua Hett Smith and the Arnold Conspiracy.* New York Historical Society, 1973.

Kouwenhoven, John A. *Partners in Banking, 1818–1968.* New York: Doubleday Co., 1968.

Krout, John Allen. *The Completion of Independence, 1790–1830.* New York: Macmillan, 1944.

Lamb, Martha J. *History of the City of New York: its Origin, Rise and Progress.* 3 vols., New York.

Leith, John H. *Assembly at Westminister.* Richmond, Va.: John Knox Press, 1973.

Livingston, Edwin Brockholst. *The Livingstons of Livingston Manor.* New York: Knickerbocker Press, 1910.

Loetscher, Lefferts A. *A Brief History of the Presbyterians.* Philadelphia: The Westminster Press, 1958.

Lyman, Susan Elizabeth. *The Story of New York.* Revised edition. New York: Crown Publishers, 1975.

Makemie, Francis. "A Good Conversation," *Collections of the New York Historical Society, 1870*.

Makemie, Francis. *A Narrative of a New and Unusual American Imprisonment*. New York: H.H. Gaine, 1755.

Maurice, Arthur Bartlett. *Fifth Avenue*. New York: Dodd, Mead, and Co., 1918.

Mercantile Library Association. *New York City during the American Revolution*. New York: The Association, 1861.

Miller, Kenneth and Ethel Prince Miller. *The People are the City. 150 Years of Social and Religious Concern in New York City*. New York: Macmillan, 1962.

Miller, Samuel. *Life of Samuel Miller*. 2 vols., Philadelphia: Claxton, Remsen and Haffelfinger, 1869.

Miller, Samuel. *Memoirs of the Rev. John Rodgers, D.D.* New York: Whiting and Watson, 1813.

Miller, Samuel. *Sketch of the Early History of the First Presbyterian Church, 1796.* Reprint, 1937. Brooklyn: F. Weidner Printing and Publishing Co.

Mohl, Raymond. *Poverty in New York, 1783–1825*. New York: Oxford University Press, 1971.

Morris, Lloyd. *Incredible New York*. New York: Random House, 1951.

Morrison, David Baillie. *Two Hundredth Anniversary, 1756–1956, of Saint Andrew's Society of the State of New York*. Philadelphia: Clark Printing House, 1956.

Myers, Gustavus. *The History of Tammany Hall*. New York: Boni and Liveright, 1917.

National Cyclopaedia of American Biography. New York: White, 1892–1971.

Nicoll, William Leonard. *Genealogy of the Nicoll Family*. New York: B. Taylor, 1886.

Norris, Charles. *Makers of New York*. Philadelphia: L. R. Hamersley and Co., 1895.

Old Buildings in New York City with some Notes regarding their Origin and Occupants. New York: Brentano's, 1907.

Parkhurst, Charles H. D.D. *A Brief History of the Madison Square Presbyterian Church and its Activities*. New York: Privately printed, 1906.

Parkhurst, Charles H. *My Forty Years in New York*. New York: Macmillan Co., 1923.

Parkhurst, Charles H. *Our Fight with Tammany*. New York: Charles S. Scribner's Sons, 1895.

Pemberton, E. *A Sermon Preached at the Presbyterian Church in the City of New York on Occasion of the Death of John Nicoll, M.D.* New York: James Parker, 1743.

Pomerantz, Sidney I. *New York. An American City, 1783–1803*. Second edition. New York: Ira J. Friedman, 1965.

Roosevelt, Theodore. *An Autobiography*. New York: Macmillan Co., 1914.

Roosevelt, Theodore. *Letters of Theodore Roosevelt*, edited by Elting Morison et al. 8 vols., Cambridge, Mass.: Harvard University Press, 1951–1954.

Rosenberg, Carroll Smith. *Religion and the Rise of the American City. The New York City Mission Movement*. Ithaca: Cornell University Press, 1971.

Rosenwaike, Ira. *Population History of New York City*. Syracuse: University Press, 1972.

Savage, Theodore Fiske. *The Presbyterian Church in New York City*. New York: Presbytery of New York, 1949.

Schlenther, Boyd S. *The Life and Writings of Francis Makemie*. Philadelphia: Presbyterian Historical Society, 1971.

Sedgwick, Theodore, Jr. *A Memoir of the Life of William Livingston*. New York: J. & J. Harper, 1833.

Singleton, Esther. *Social New York Under the Georges, 1714–1776*. New York: D. Appleton, 1902.

Smith, Thomas E. *The City of New York in the Year of Washington's Inauguration, 1789*. New York: Anson D. F. Randolph & Co., 1889.

Smith, William. *Historical Memoirs from 16 March 1763 to 9 July 1776 of William Smith*, edited by William H.W. Sabine. New York: Colburn and Tegg, 1956.

Smith, William. *The History of the late Province of New York from its Discovery to the Appointment of Governor Colden in 1762,* edited by Michael Kammen. 2 vols., Cambridge, Mass., The Belknap Press of Harvard, 1972.

Steffens, Lincoln. *The Autobiography of Lincoln Steffens.* 2 vols., New York: Harcourt Brace and Co., 1931.

Stephens, Captain R. M. *The Burning Bush.* Bexhill-on-Sea: F. J. Parsons, 1967.

Stevens, Henry. *Recollections of Mr. James Lenox of New York and the Formation of his Library.* London: Henry Stevens, 1886.

Still, Bayrd. *Mirror of Gotham. New York as Seen by Contemporaries from Dutch Days to the Present.* New York: New York University Press, 1956.

Still, Bayrd. *Urban America.* Boston: Little, Brown, & Co. 1974.

Stoddard, Lothrop. *Master of Manhattan. The Life of Richard Crocker.* New York: Longmans, Green and Co., 1931.

Stokes, Isaac Newton Phelps, ed., *Iconography of Manhattan Island.* 8 vols., New York: Robert H. Dodd, 1916–1928.

Strong, George Templeton. *The Diary of George Templeton Strong,* ed. by Allan Nevins. 4 vols., New York: Macmillan Co., 1952.

Sweet, William Warren. *The Story of Religion in America.* New York: Harper and Brothers, 1950.

Todd, Charles Burr. *The Story of the City of New York.* New York: G. P. Putnam's Sons, 1888.

Ulmann, Albert. *A Landmark History of New York.* New York: D. Appleton, 1903.

Upton, L.F.S. *The Loyal Whig. William Smith of New York and Quebec.* Toronto: University of Toronto Press, 1969.

Valentine, David. *History of the City of New York.* New York: G. P. Putnam and Co., 1953.

Van Deusen, Glyndon G. *Thurlow Weed, Wizard of the Lobby.* Boston: Little, Brown and Co., 1947.

Van Doren, Carl. *Secret History of the American Revolution.* New York: The Viking Press, 1941.

Villard, Oswald Garrison, "The Early History of Wall Street, 1653–1789," in *Historical New York.* 2 vols., New York: G. P. Putnam's Sons, 1899.

Watts, George B. *The Waldenses in the New World.* Durham, No. Ca.: Duke University Press, 1941.

Weis, Frederick Lewis. *The Colonial Clergy of the Middle Colonies: New York, New Jersey and Pennsylvania, 1628–1776.* Proceedings of the American Antiquarian Society, vol. 66 (October 17, 1956).

Werner, M. R. *It Happened in New York.* New York: Coward-McCann, 1957.

Wertenbaker, Thomas Jefferson. *Father Knickerbocker Rebels.* New York: Charles Scribner's Sons, 1948.

Wilson, James Grant. *Memorial History of the City of New York.* 4 vols., New York: History Company, 1892.

Winslow, Ola E. *Jonathan Edwards, 1703–1758.* New York: Macmillan Co., 1940.

PERIODICALS

Alexander, George, "History of the University Place Presbyterian Church," in *The Church Tower,* II, January-May, 1925.

Baird, Charles W. "Civil Status of the Presbyterians in New York," *Magazine of American History,* III, no. 10 (Oct., 1879), 593–628.

Bullivant, Benjamin. "A Glance at New York in 1697," in *The New York Historical Society Quarterly,* XL (January, 1956), 55–73.

Delafield, Maturin, "William Smith," *Magazine of American History,* April-June, 1881.

Duffield, Howard, "Annals of the Old First Church," in *The Church Tower,* I, January-July, 1924.

Felt, Jeremy P. "Vice Reform as a Political Technique: The Committee of Fifteen in New York, 1900–1901," in *New York History,* LIV, no. 1 (Jan. 1973), 24–51.

"Gilbert Livingston," in *New York Genealogical and Biographical Record,* vol. 84, no. 1–3 (July, 1953).

Gemmill, Benjamin. "The Judicial Decision of the General Assembly in 1925," *Princeton Theological Review,* July, 1925.

Handy, Robert T. "John Rodgers, 1727–1811. A Life of Usefulness on Earth." in *Journal of the Presbyterian Historical Society,* XXXIV (June, 1956).

Hines, Albert B. "Getting the Boy," in *The Church Tower,* I, Jan. 1924.

Klein, Milton M. "Rise of the New York Bar. Legal Career of William Livingston," in *William and Mary Quarterly,* 3d series, XV (July, 1958), 334–59.

Klett, Guy, "Made in Philadelphia: Two Constitutions," in *Presbyterian Life,* March 31, 1956.

Lagemann, John Kord. "Don't Waste your Time in Church" by John Mellin, in *Ladies Home Journal,* 1952.

Livermore, Charles H. "The Whigs of Colonial New York," in *American Historical Review,* I, no. 2 (Jan. 1896), 238–51.

McCook, H.C. "An Early Document Concerning the First Presbyterian Congregation of New York," in *Journal of the Presbyterian Historical Society,* I, no. 3 (Mar. 1902), 236–45.

Macnab, John B. "Bethlehem Chapel: Presbyterians and the Italian Americans in New York City," in *Journal of Presbyterian History,* v. 55, no. 2 (summer, 1977), 145–160.

Macnab, John B. "Fosdick at First Church," in *Journal of Presbyterian History,* v. 52, no. 1, (spring, 1974), 59–72.

Olmstead, Charles H. "The Old Communion Silver," in *The Church Tower,* I (1923), 25–26.

Osgood, Herbert L. "The Society of Dissenters. Founded in New York in 1769," in *American Historical Review,* VI (1901) 498–507.

Parkhurst, Charles H. "Historical Sketch of the Madison Square Presbyterian Church," *The Church Tower,* I (Sept., Oct., 1924).

"Presbyterians and the American Revolution: A Documentary Account," in *Journal of Presbyterian History,* vol. 52, no. 4 (winter, 1974).

Schlenther, Boyd S. ed., "Presbyterian Church of N.Y. v. John Nicoll, M.D." in *Journal of Presbyterian History,* 42, no. 3 (Sept. 1964), 198–214, no. 4 (December, 1964), 272–285.

Scoville, Gordon Trumbull, "America's Spiritual Revolution," in *Presbyterian Life,* March 31, 1956, 14–22.

"Sessional Records of Booth Bay, Maine, 1767–78," in *Journal of the Department of History,* Presbyterian Historical Society, XVI, no. 6 (June, 1935), 243–8.

Dictionary of American Biography, edited by Allen Johnson and Dumas Malone. 10 vols., New York: Charles Scribner's Sons, 1927–1936.

Cushman, R. E., "Henry Brockholst Livingston," XI:312.
Day, Richard E., "David Jamison," V:603–4.
Faulkner, H. W., "Anson Greene Phelps," XIV:525–6.
Haskell, Daniel C., "Alexander McDougall," XII:21–22.
Kent, Frank R., "James Brown," III:126–7.
Krout, John A., "Peter Van Brugh Livingston," XI:315–6.
Krout, John A., "Philip Livingston," XI:316–8.
Krout, John A., "William Livingston," XI:325–7.
Lydenberg, Henry Miller, "James Lenox," VI:172.
Morris, Richard B., "John Morin Scott," XVI:495–6.
Morris, Richard B., "William Smith, 1697–1769," XVII:352–3.
Morris, Richard B., "William Smith, 1728–1793," XVII:357–8.
Muzzey, David S., "Charles Butler," II:360.
Persons, Frederick Torel, "William Adams," I:101–2.
Rockwell, William Walker, "George Lewis Prentiss," VIII:189–90.
Rowe, Robert R., "James Boorman," I:443.
Shaw, William Bristow, "Daniel Willis James," IX:573–4.
Starr, Elwood, "John Rodgers," XVI: 75.

Index